THE SUPER DUPER GIGANTIC BOOKMARKS

COLORING BOOK

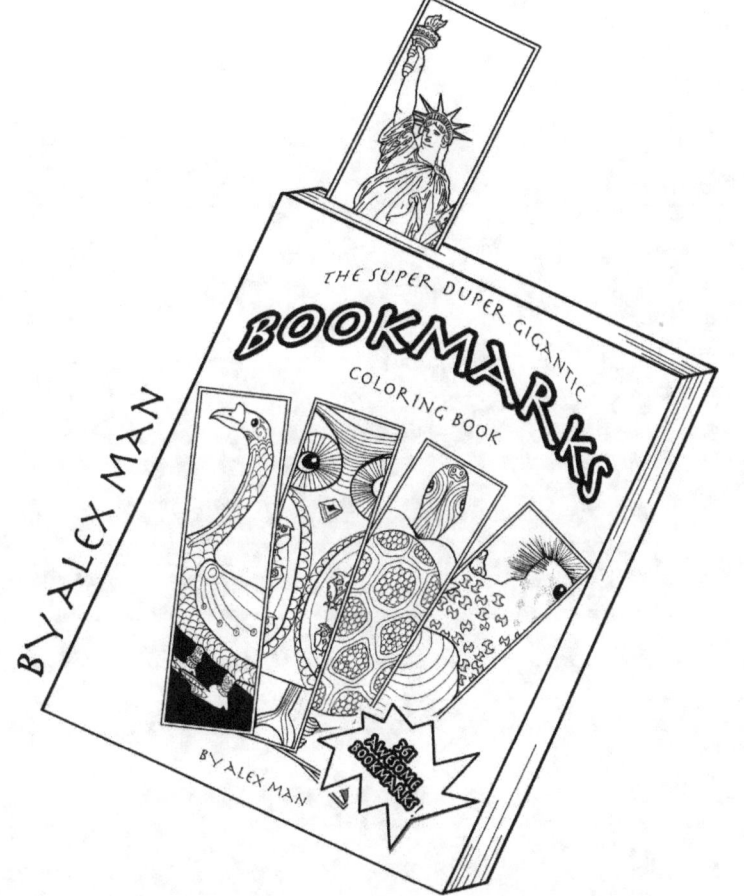

INSTRUCTIONS:
COLOR AND CUT THE BOOKMARKS.

TIP:
FOR THE BOOKMARKS TO LAST,
LAMINATE OR PASTE THEM ONTO A CARDBOARD.
ENJOY READING!

TABLE OF CONTENTS:

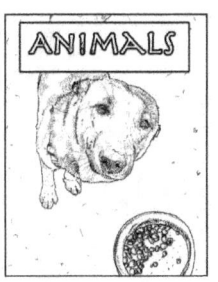

ANIMALS - 56 - BOOKMARKS

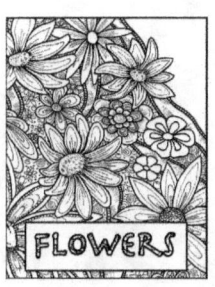

FLOWERS - 92 - BOOKMARKS

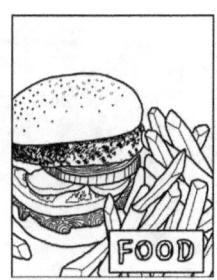

FOOD - 32 - BOOKMARKS

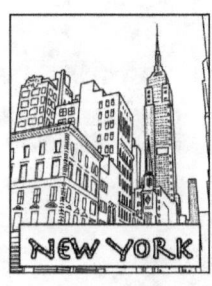

NEW YORK - 60 - BOOKMARKS

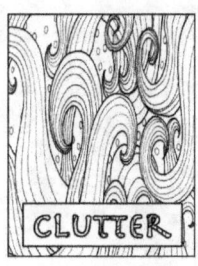

CLUTTER - 40 - BOOKMARKS

CHRISTMAS - 20 - BOOKMARKS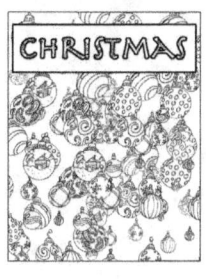

HALLOWEEN - 24 - BOOKMARKS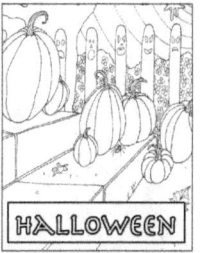

VALENTINE'S DAY - 12 - BOOKMARKS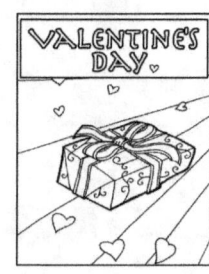

PASSOVER - 8 - BOOKMARKS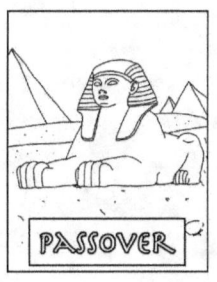

HANUKKAH - 8 - BOOKMARKS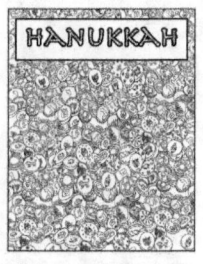

UNICORN - 9 - BOOKMARKS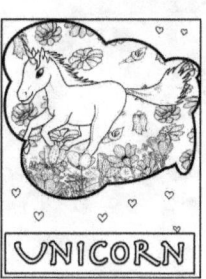

ANIMALS

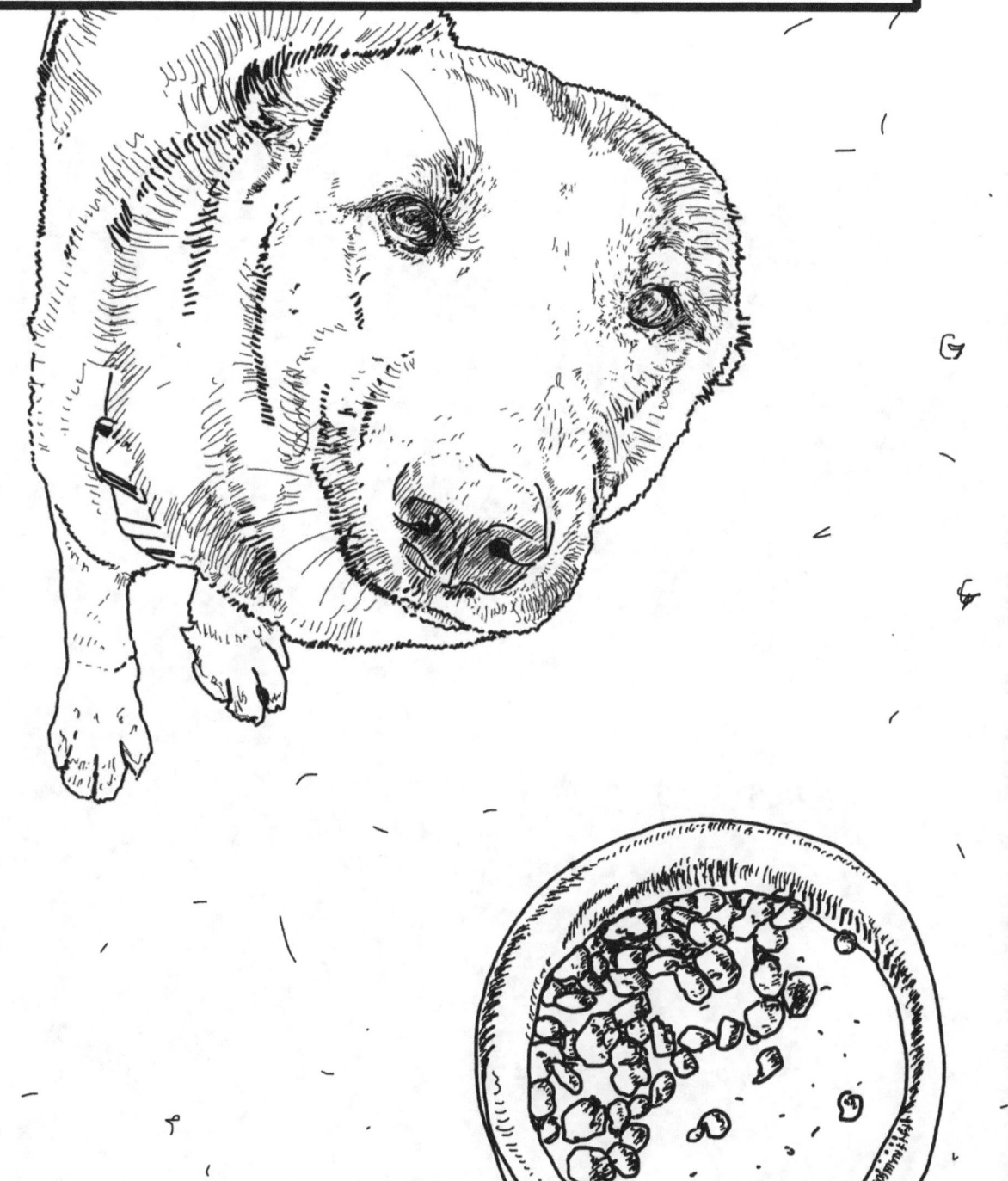

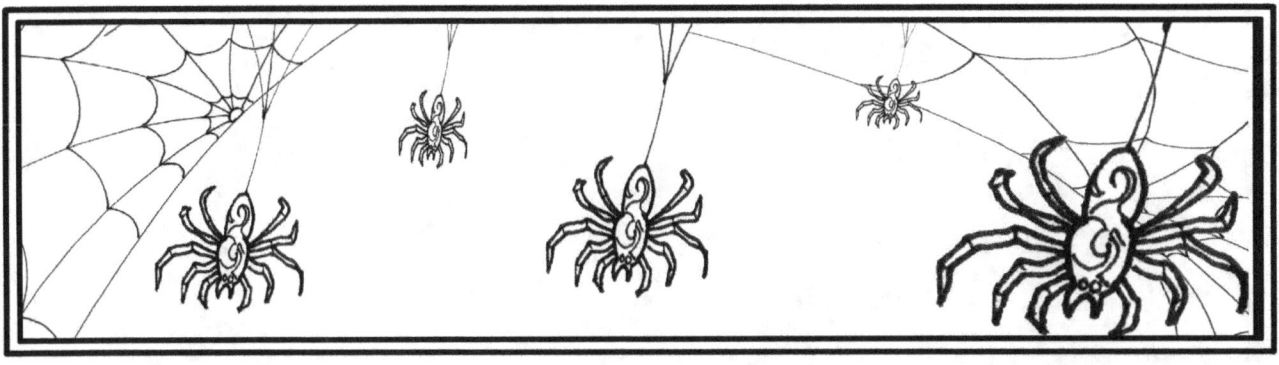

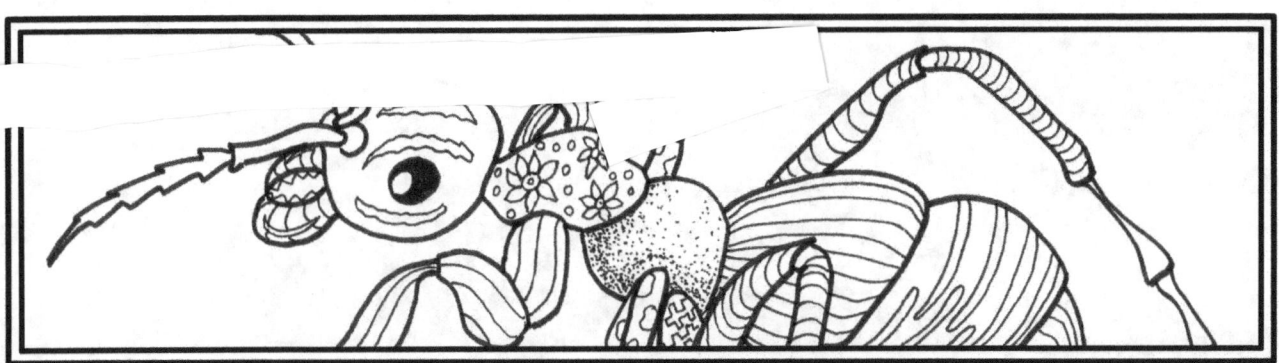

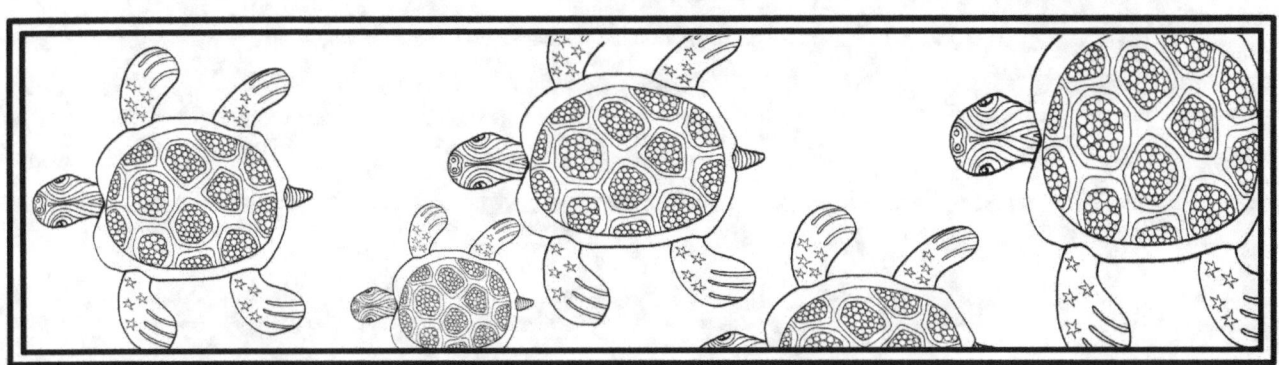

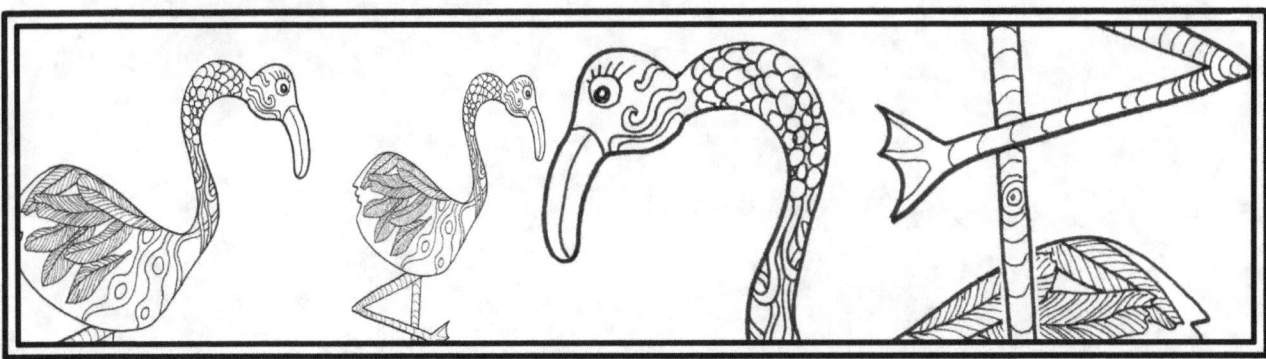

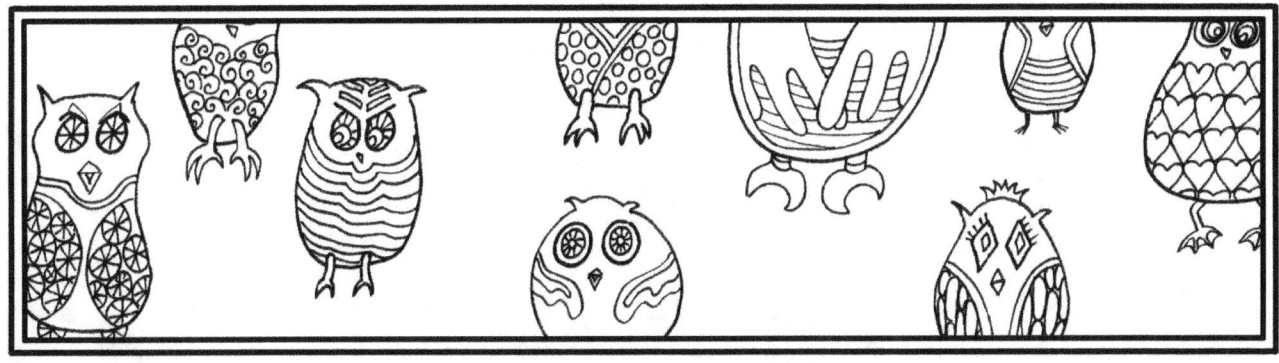
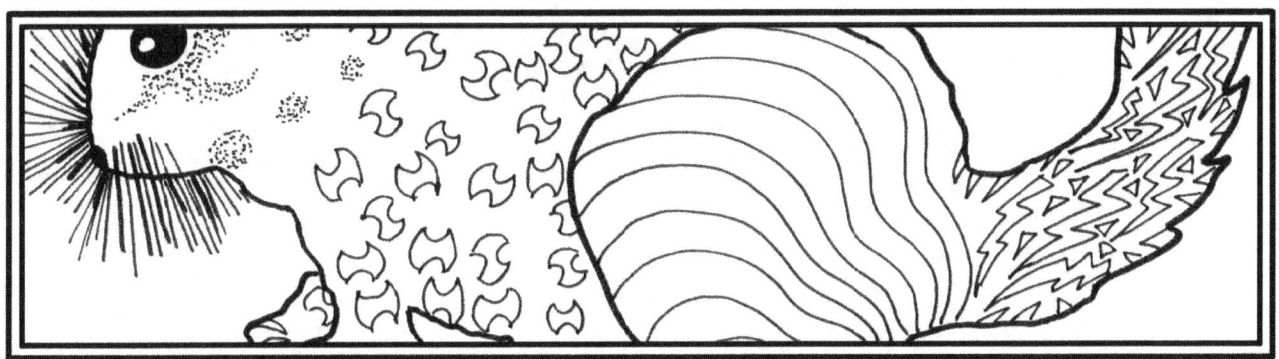
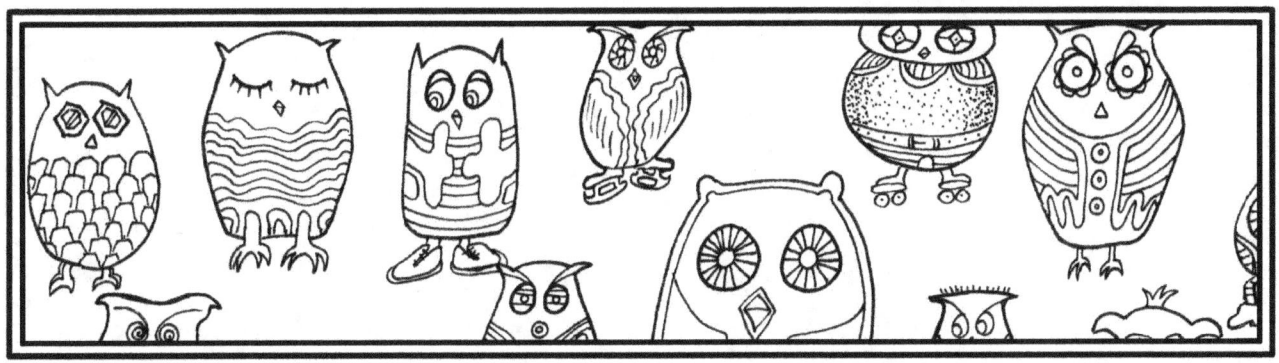
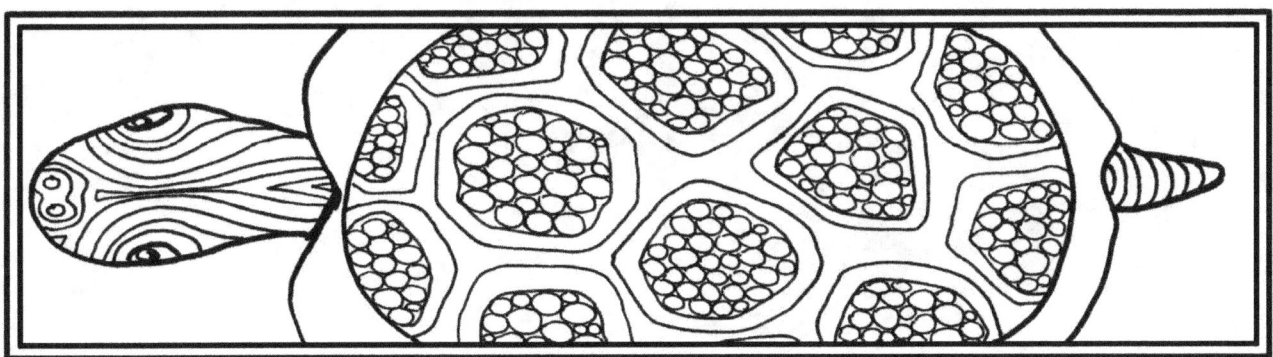

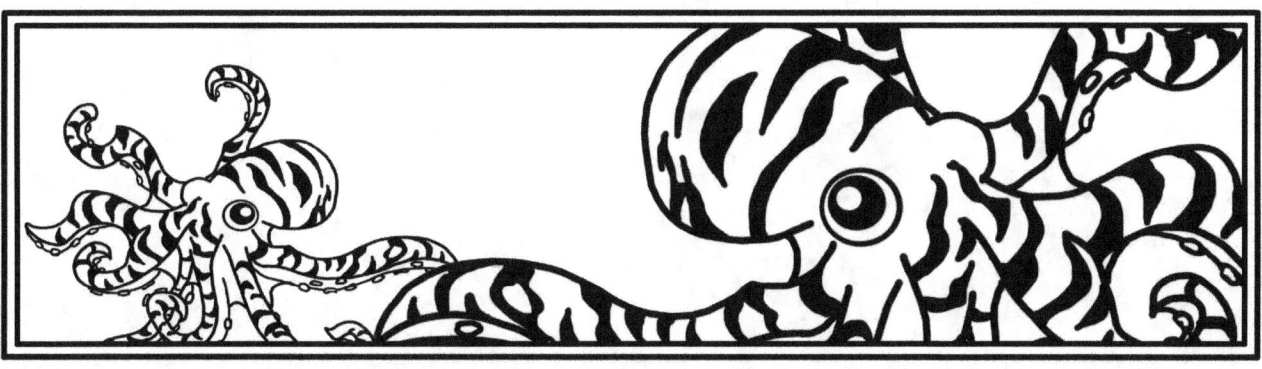

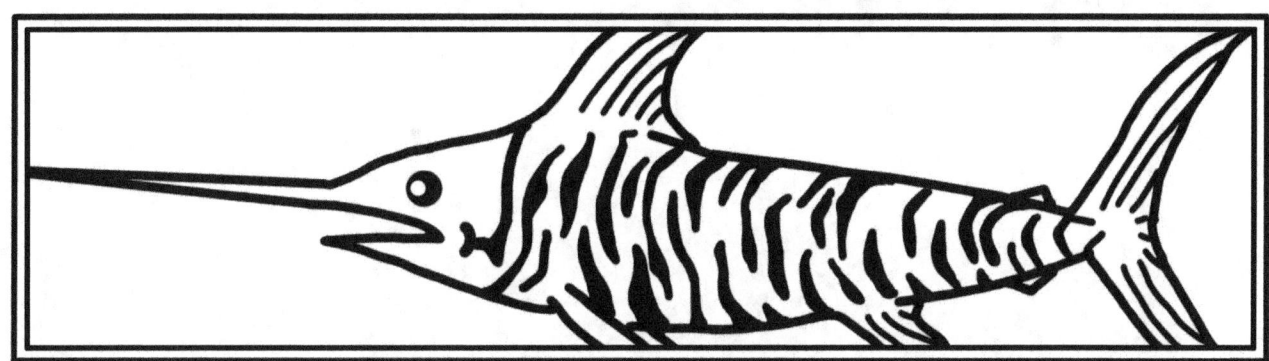

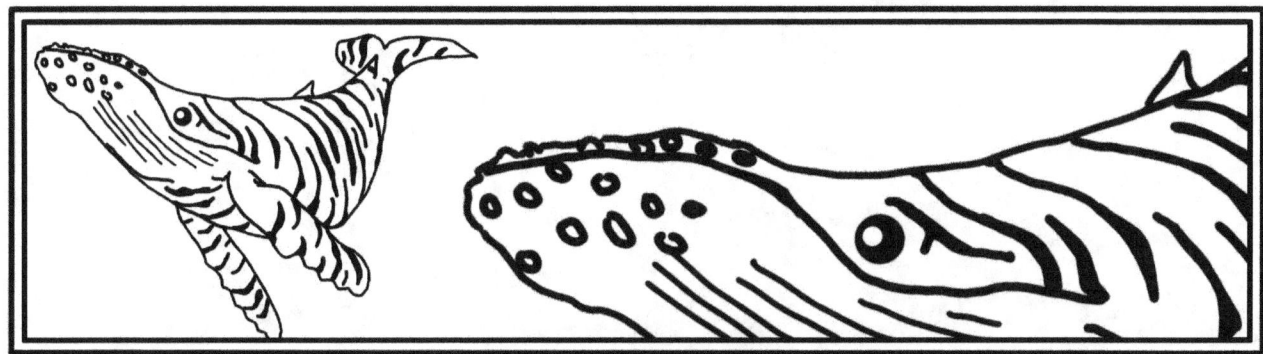

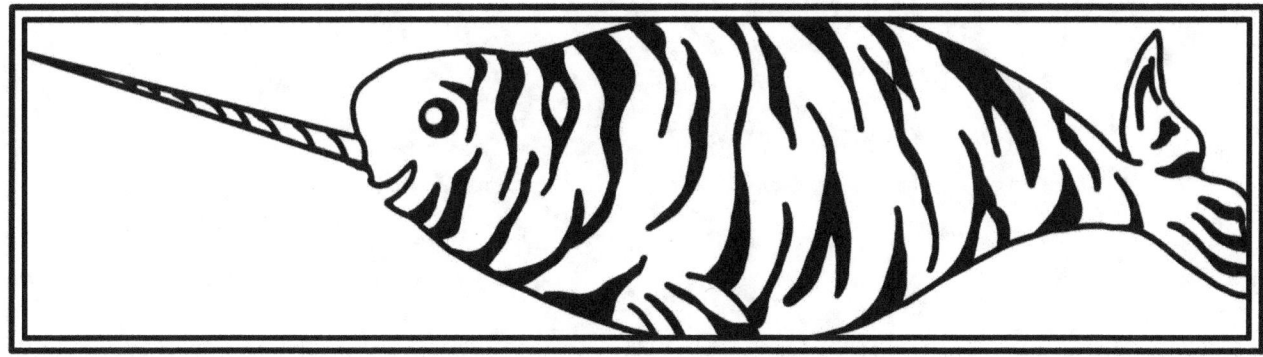

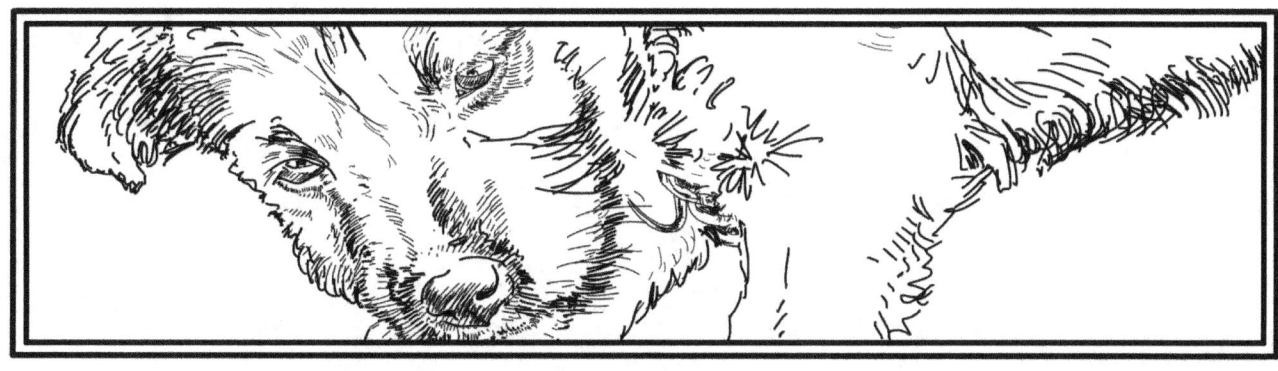

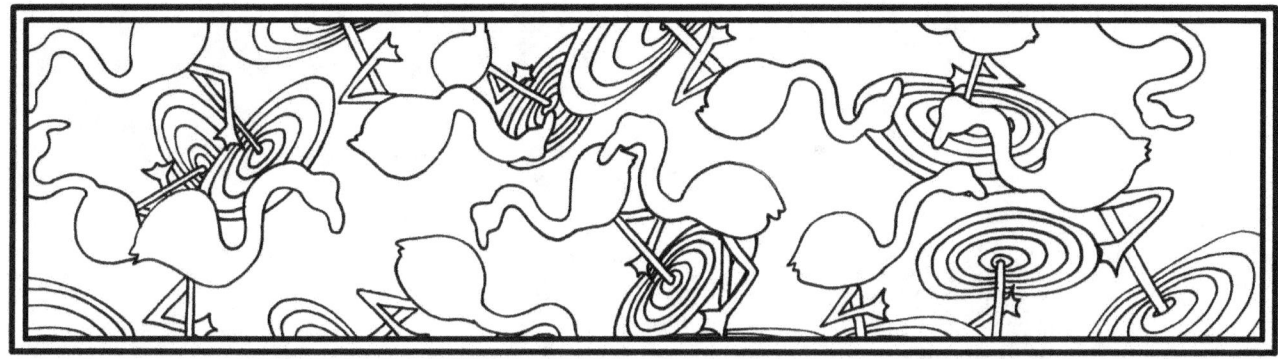

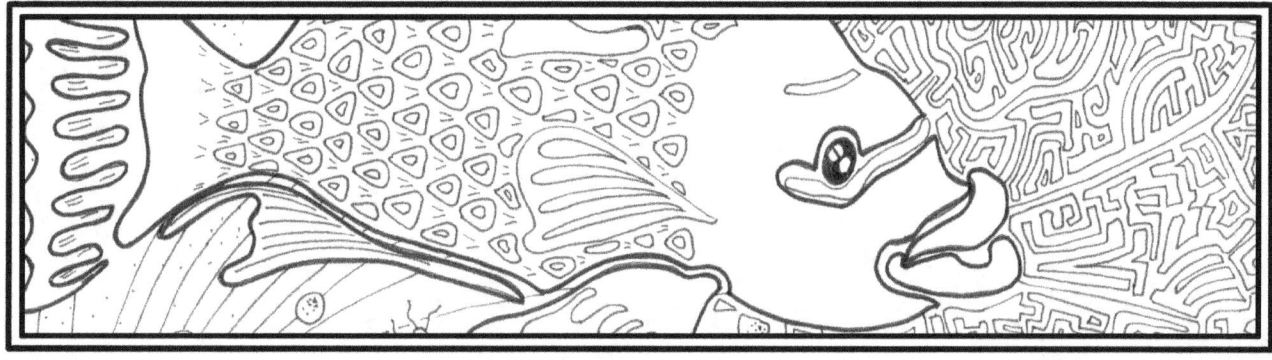

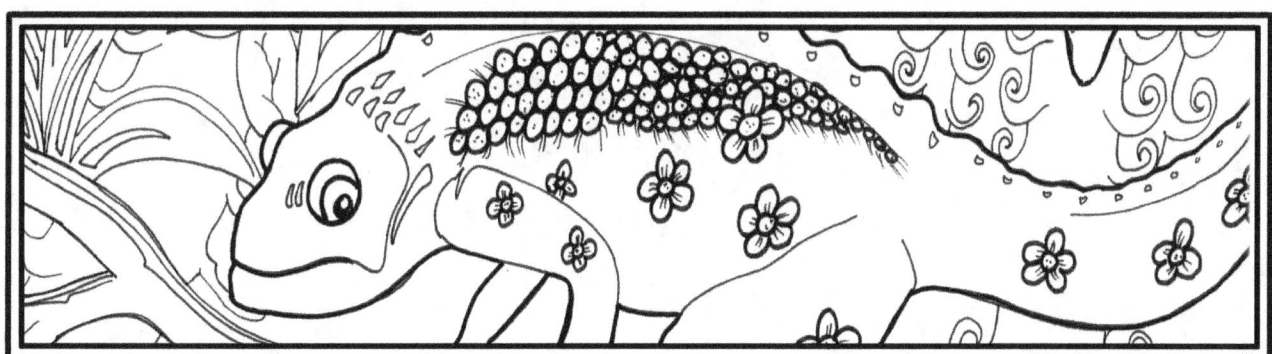

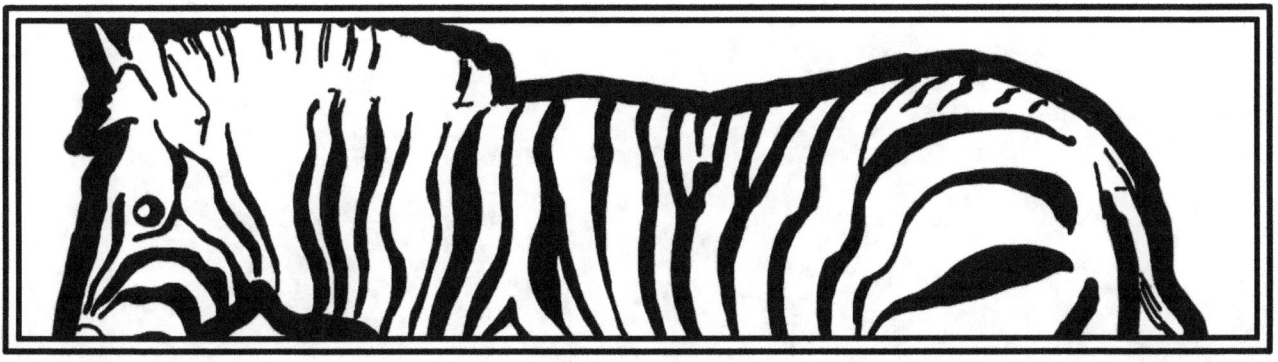
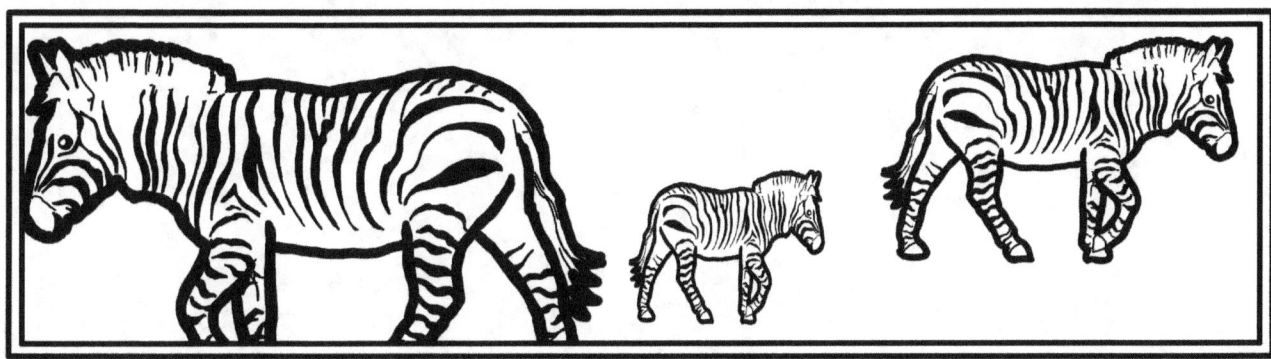
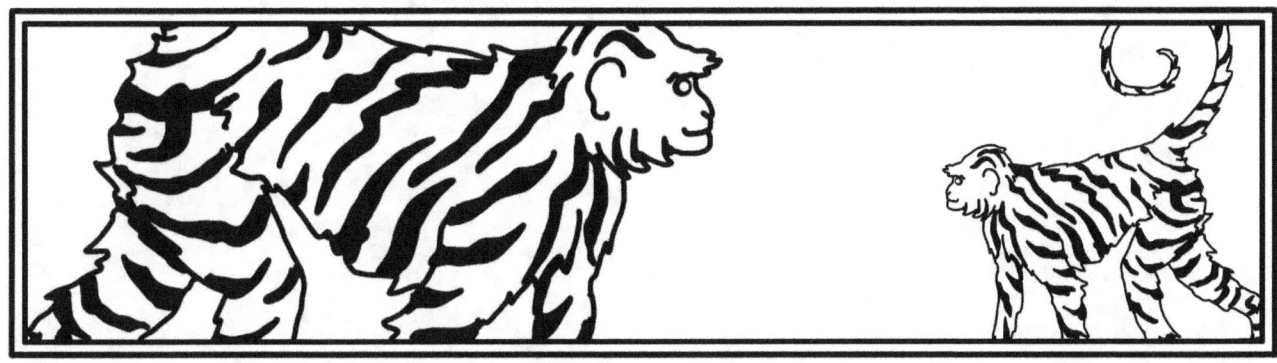
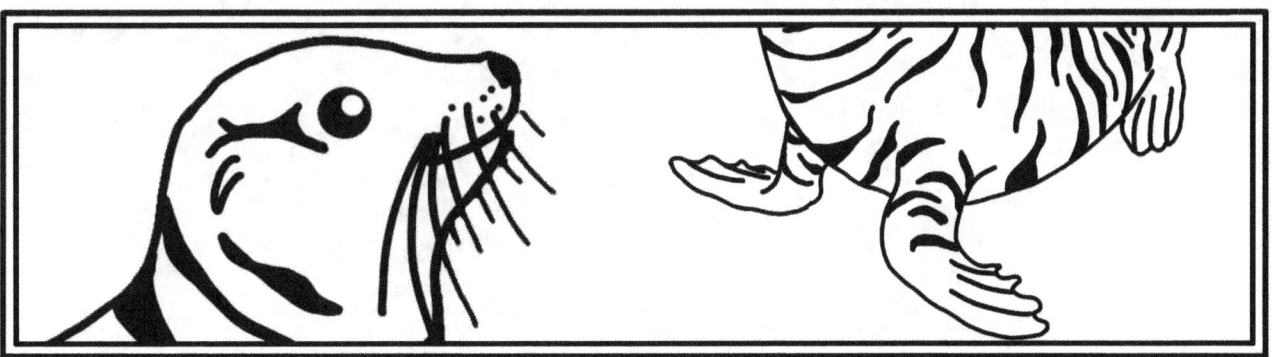

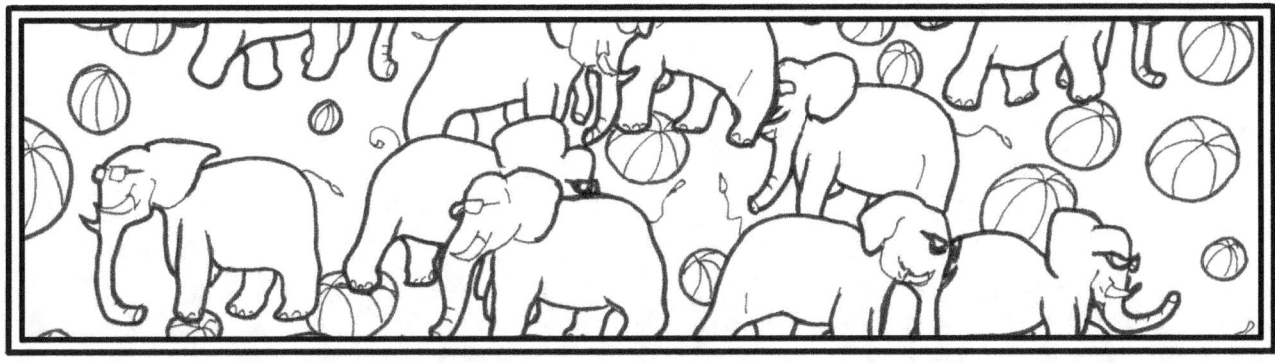

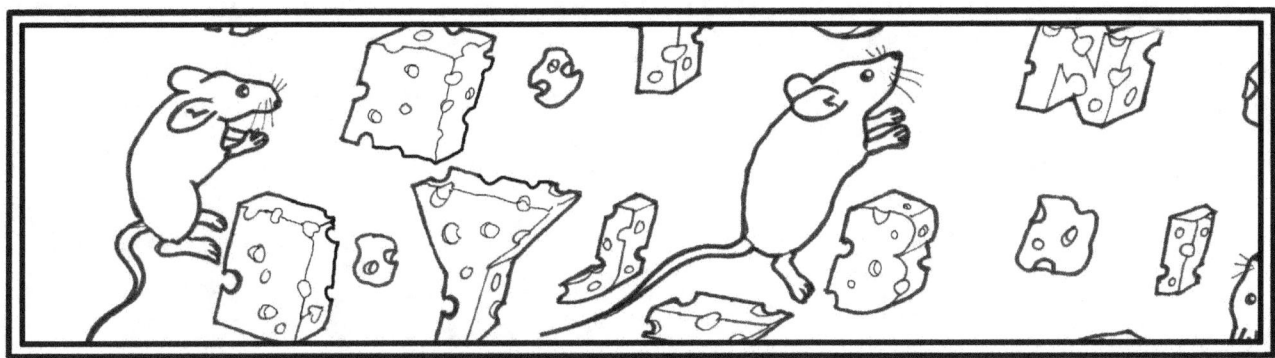

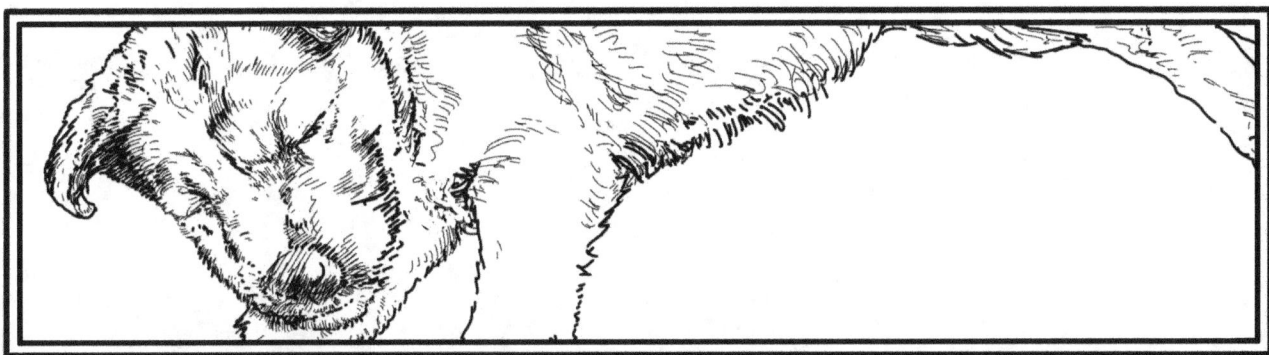

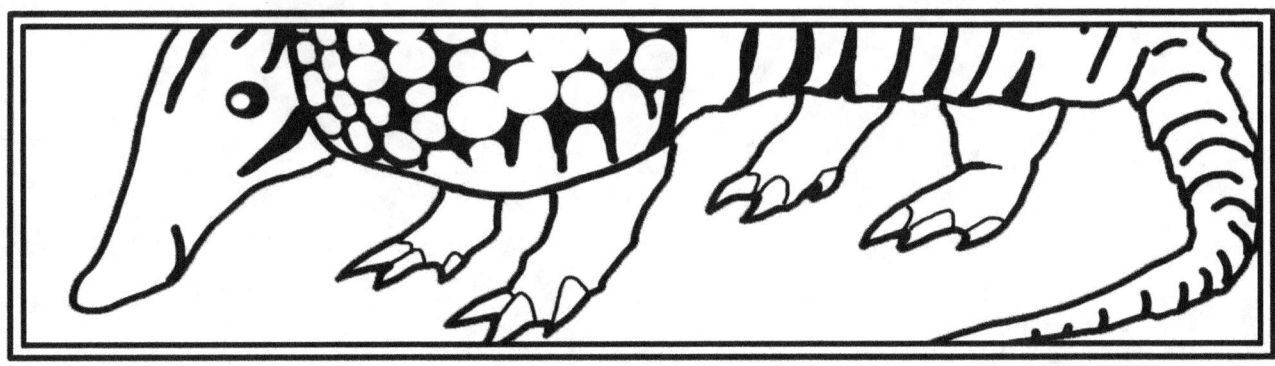

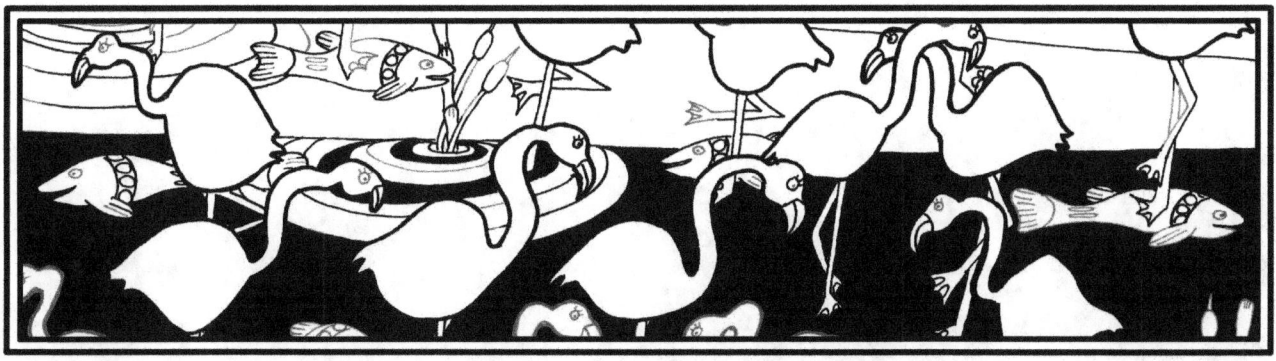
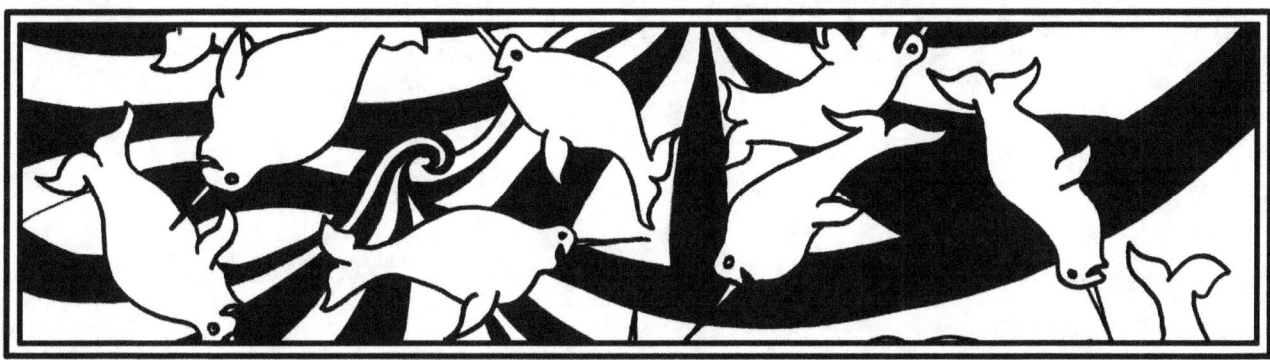
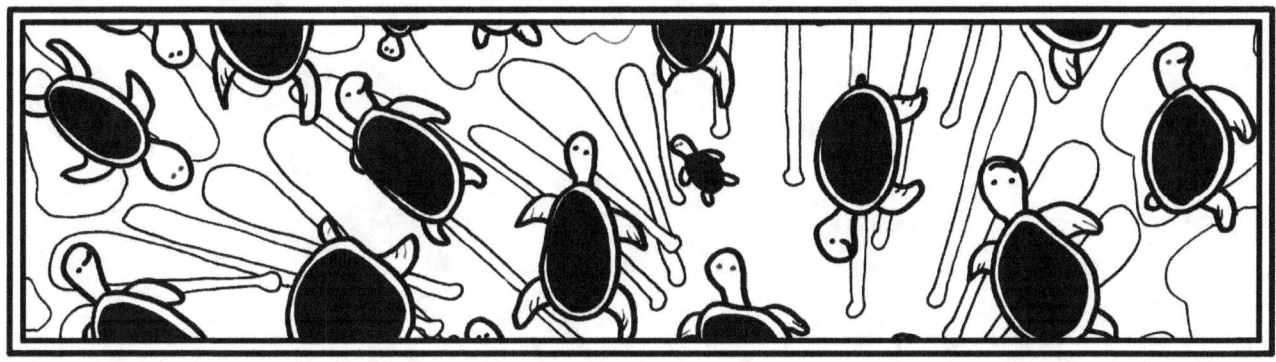
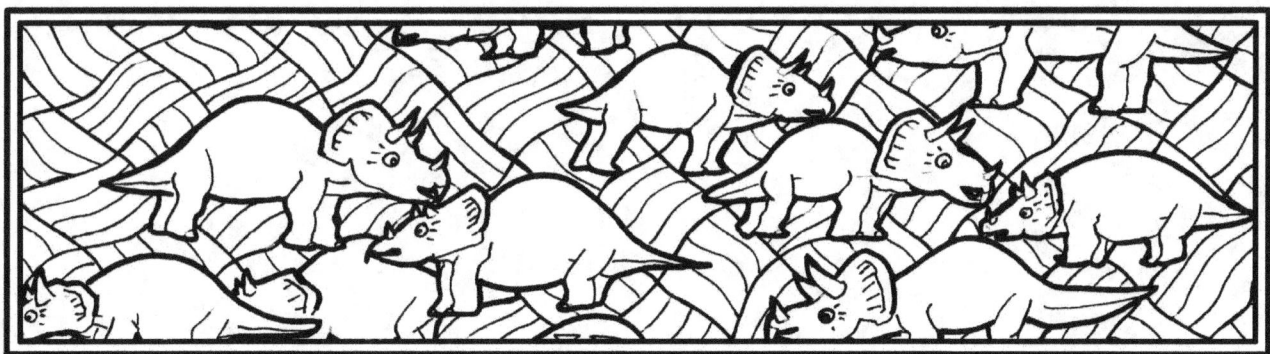

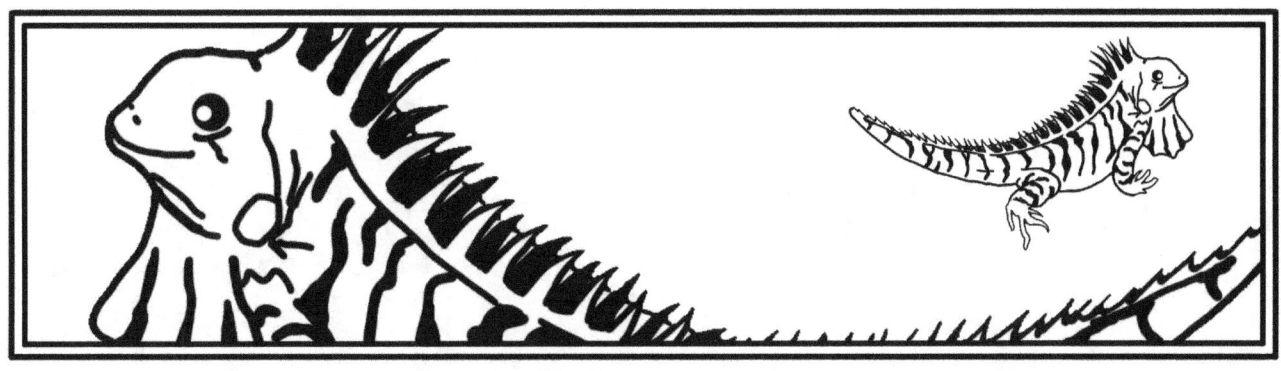
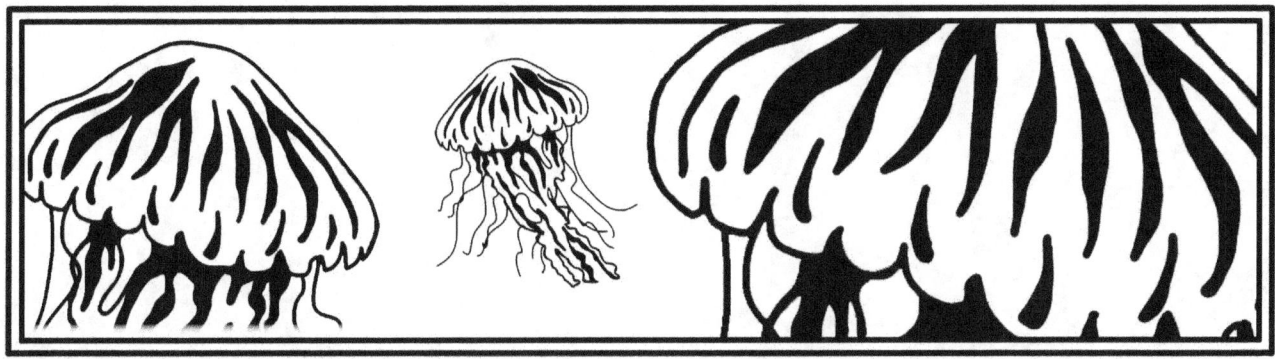
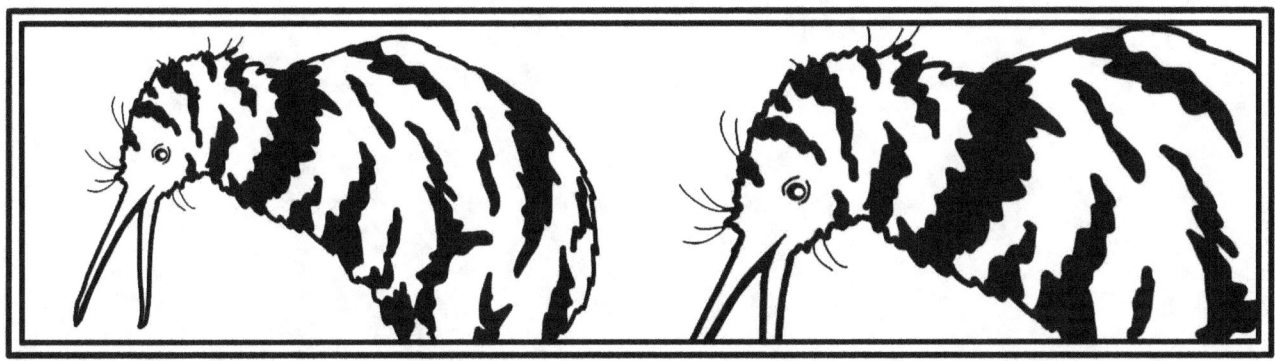
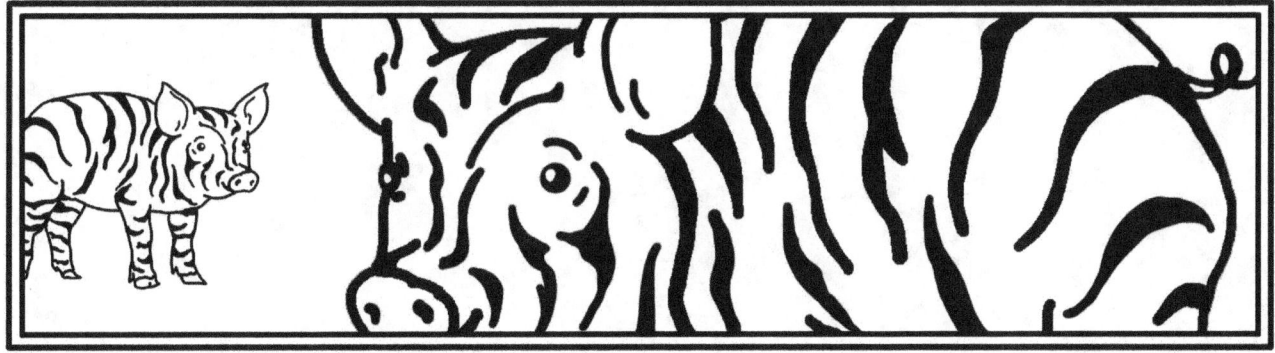

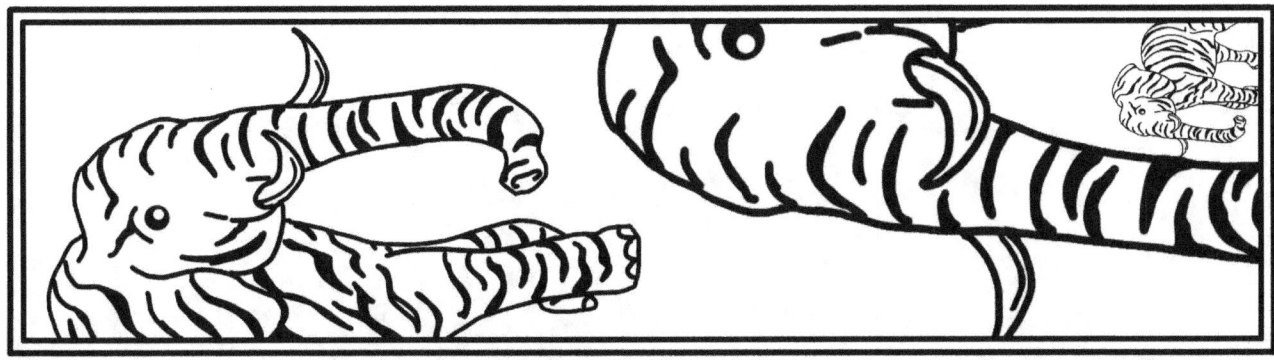

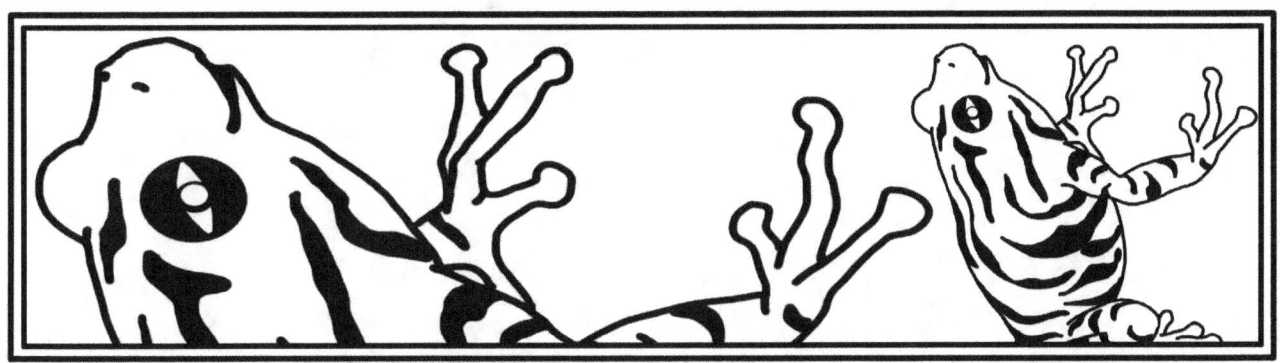

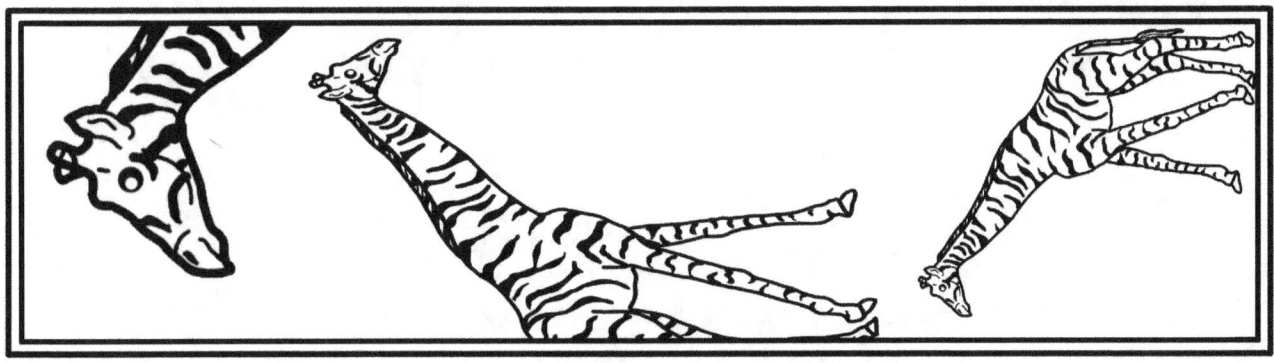

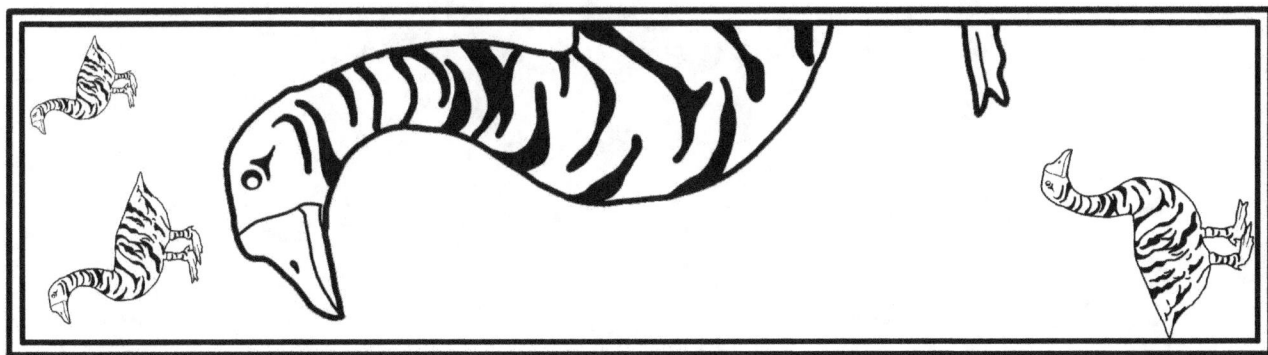

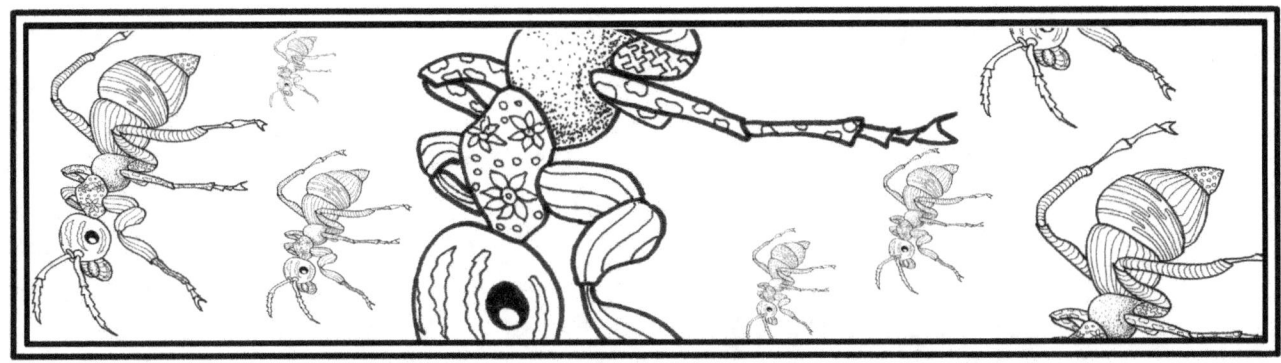

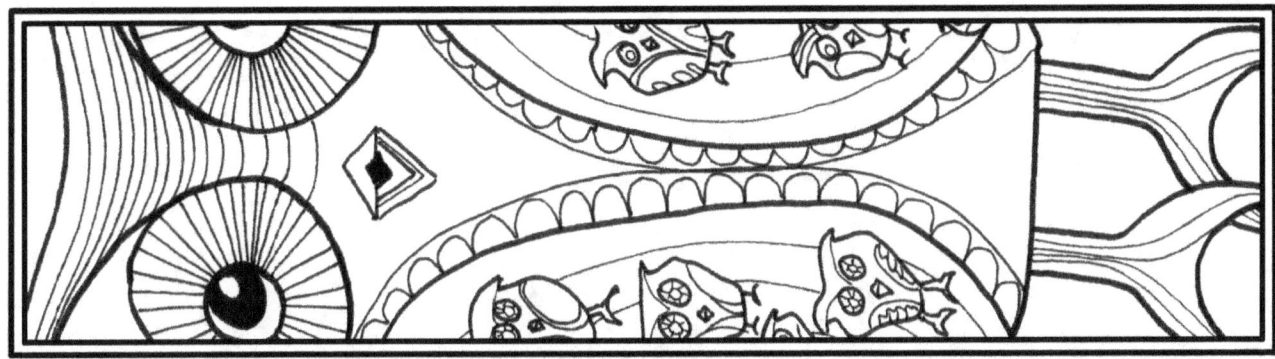

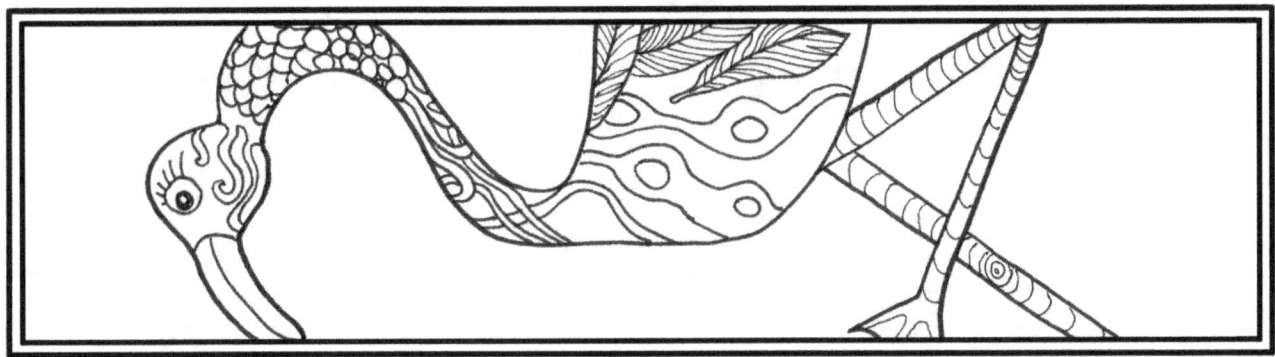

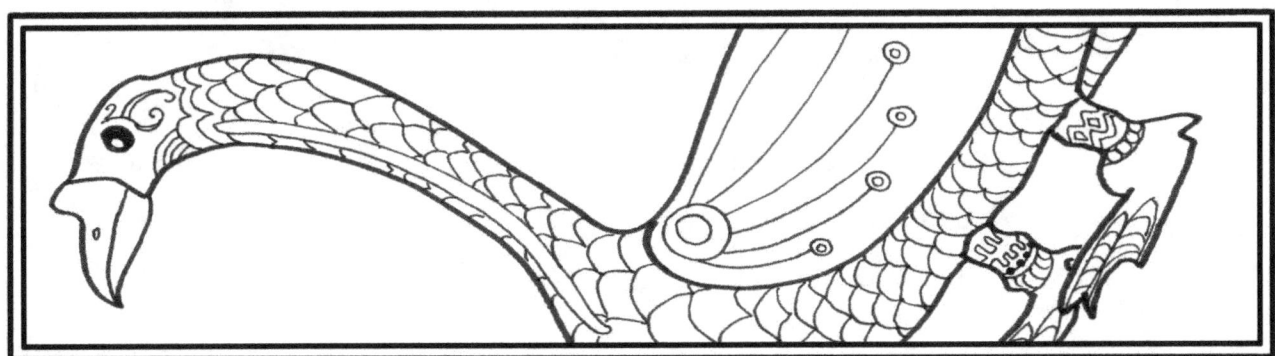

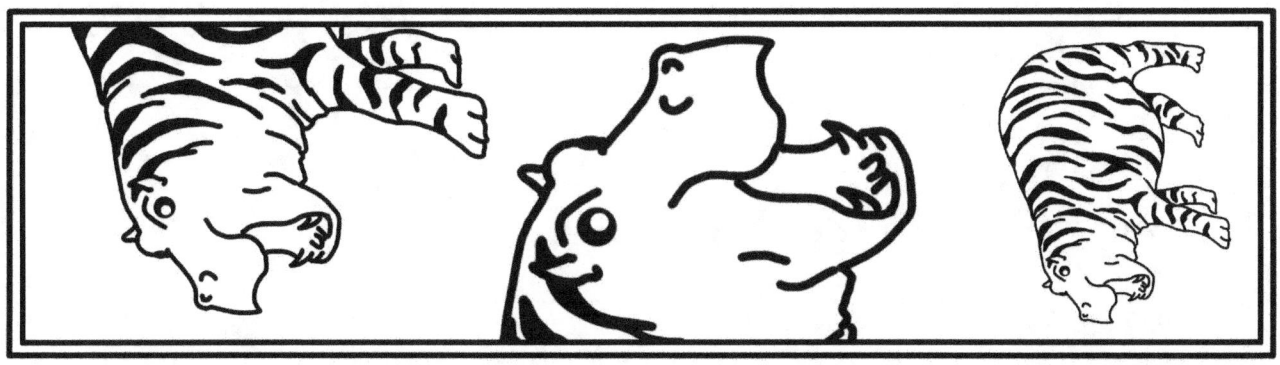

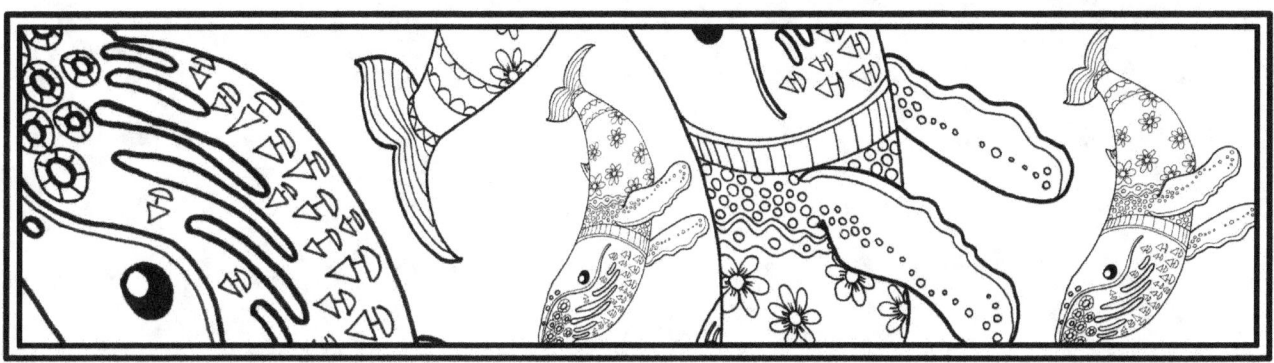

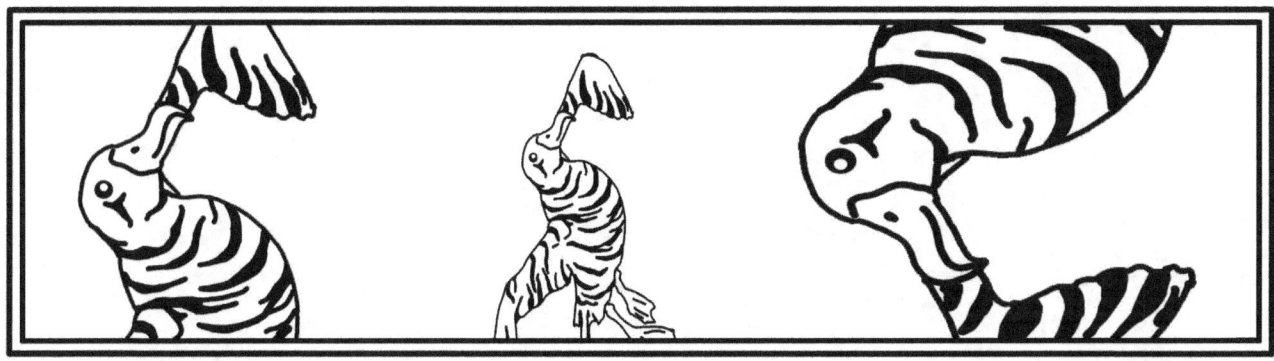

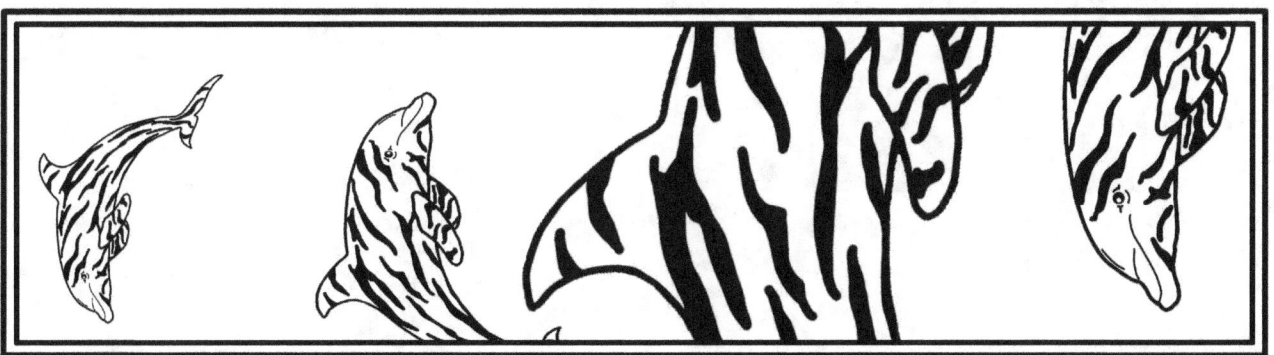

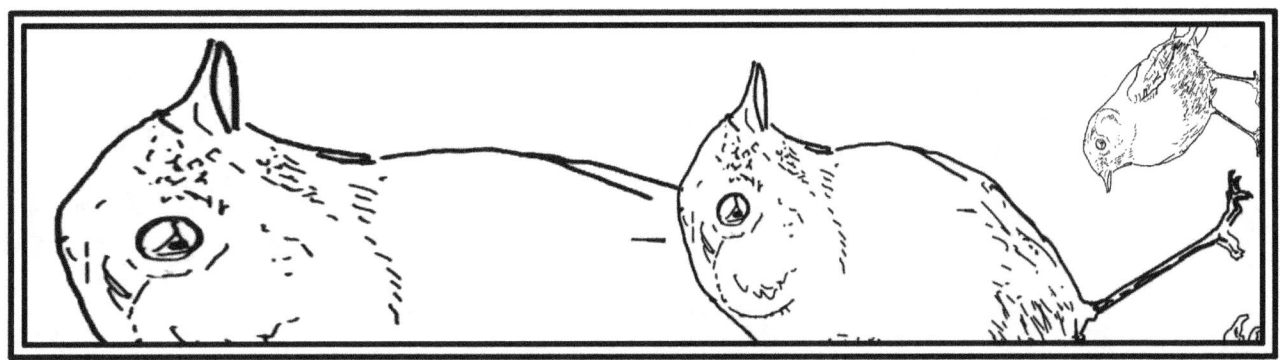
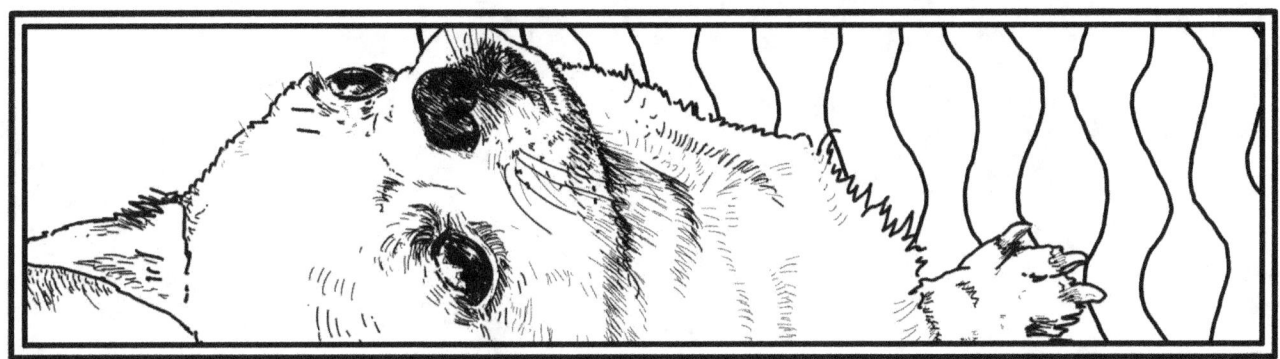
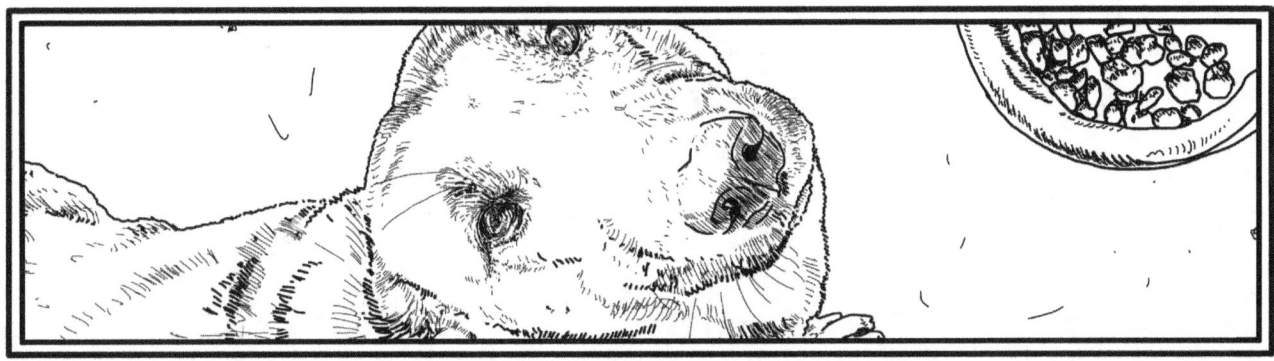
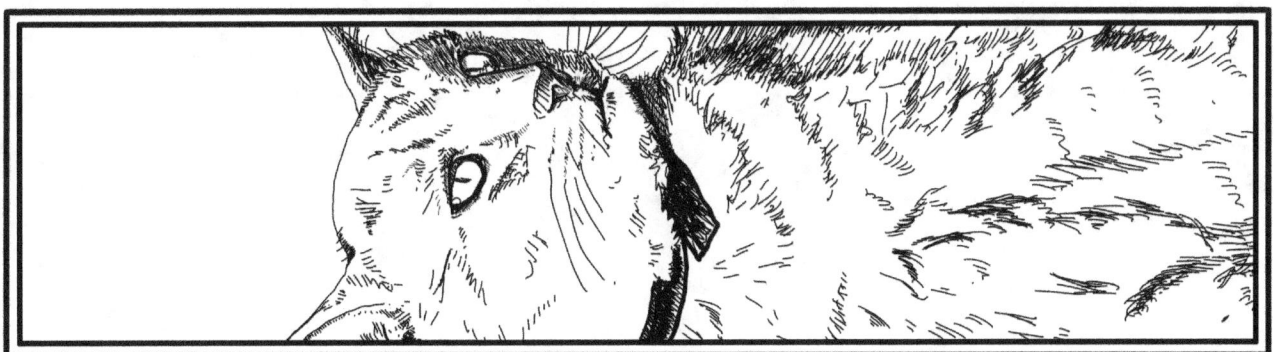

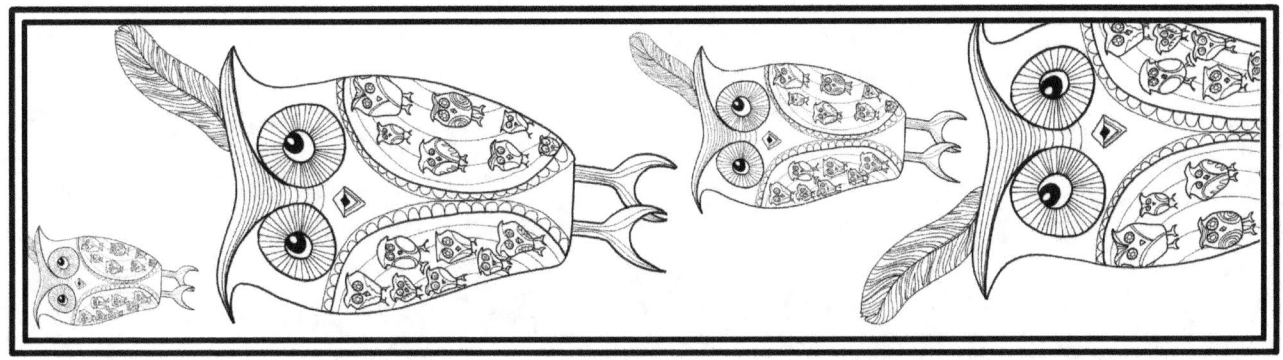
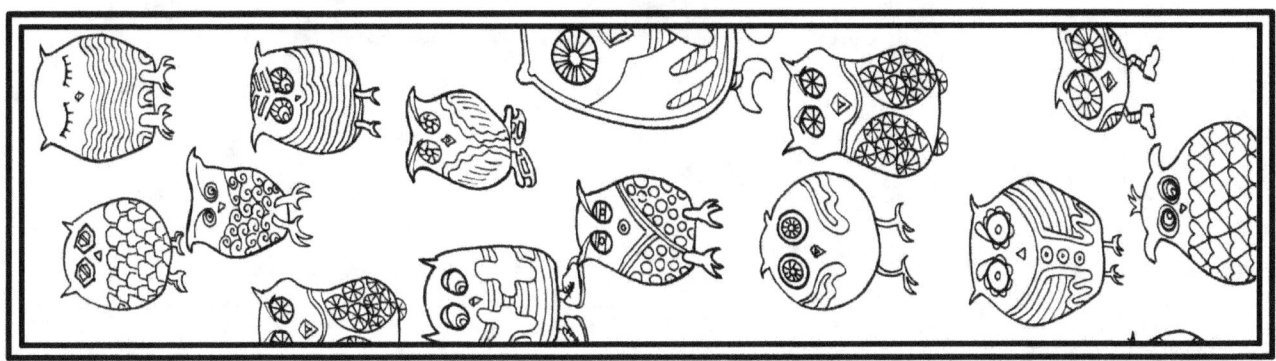
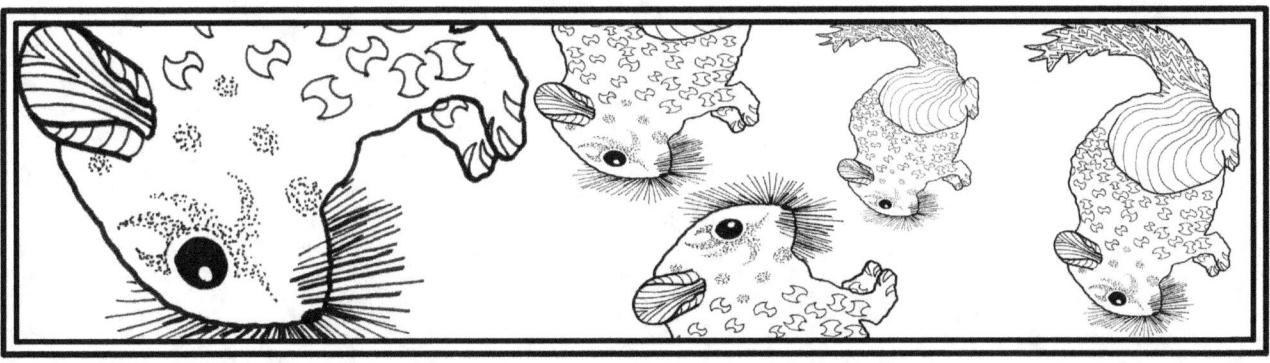
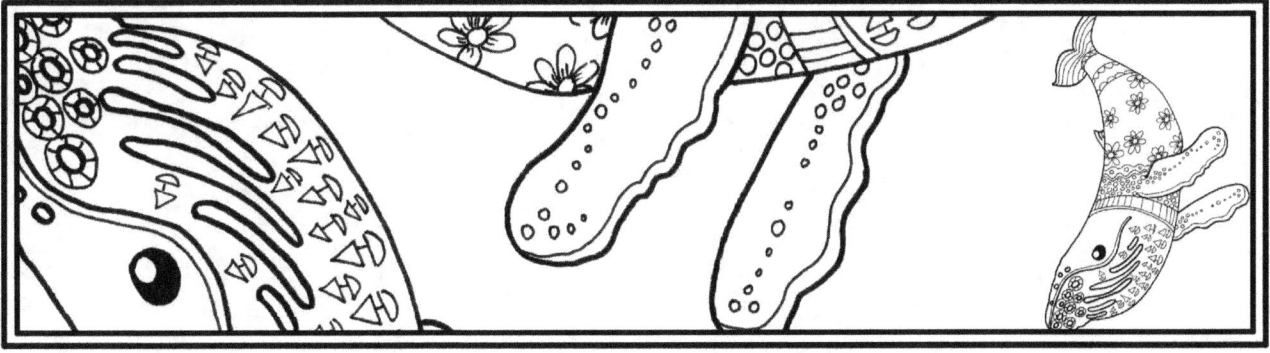

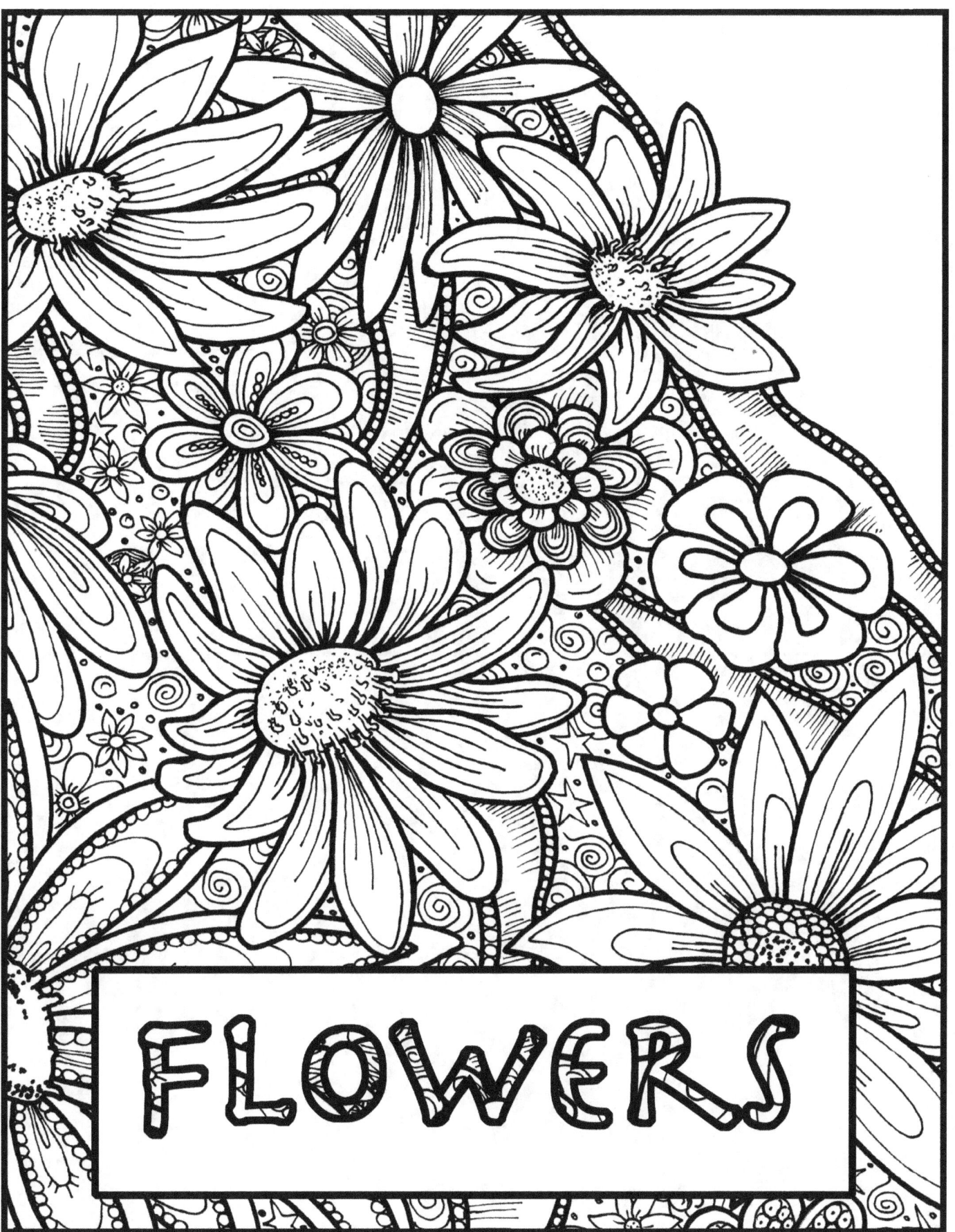

FLOWERS

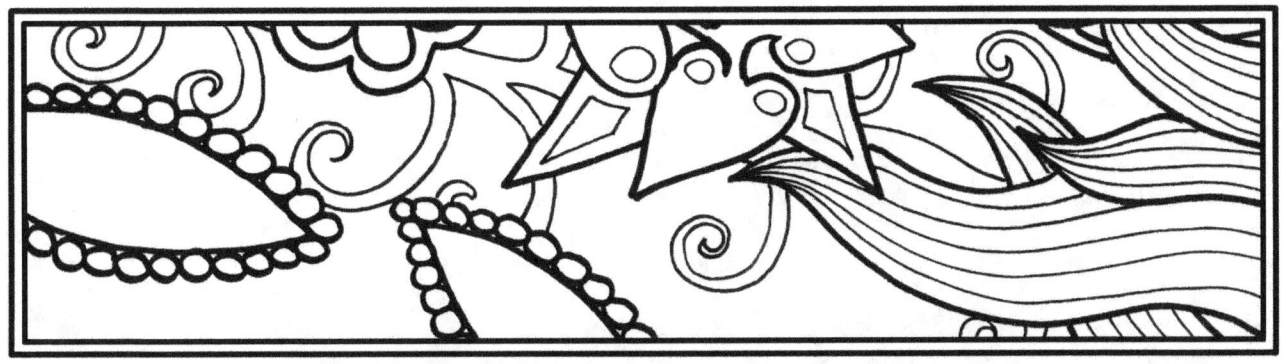

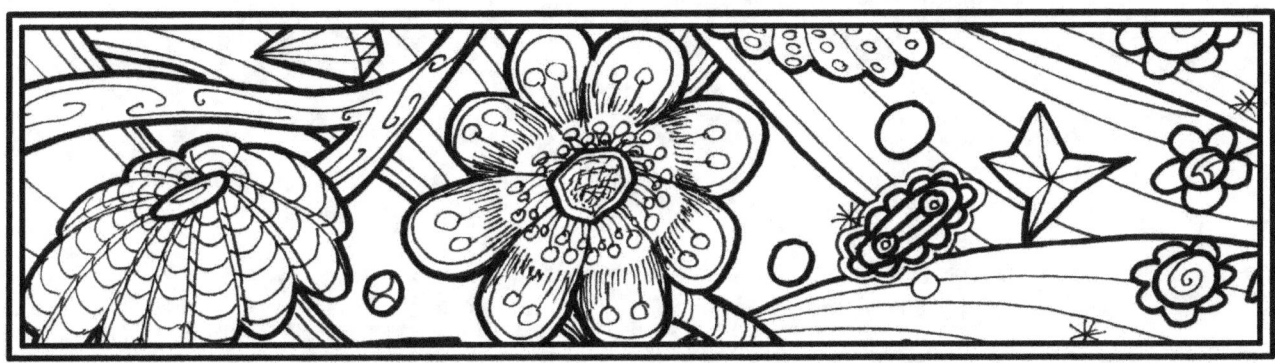

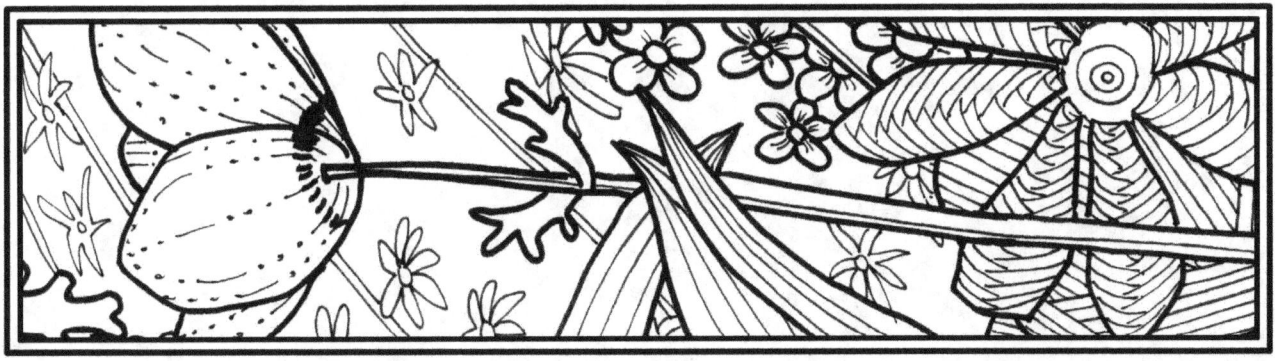

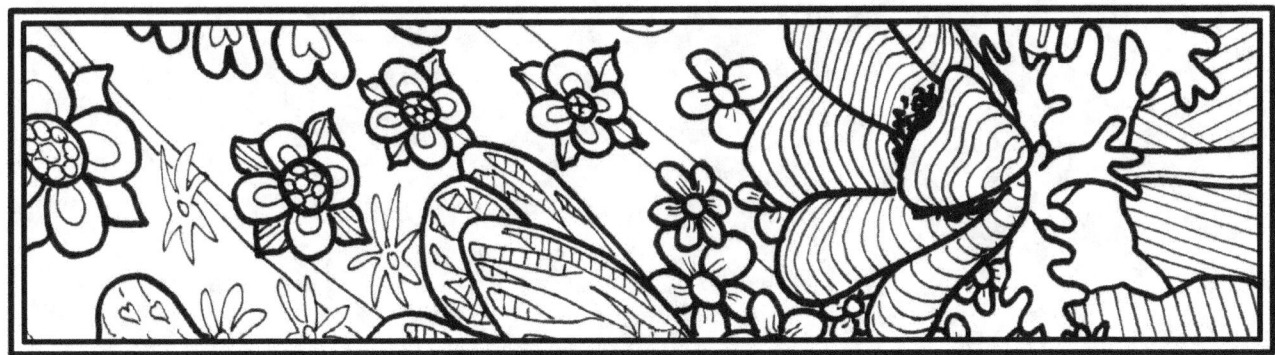

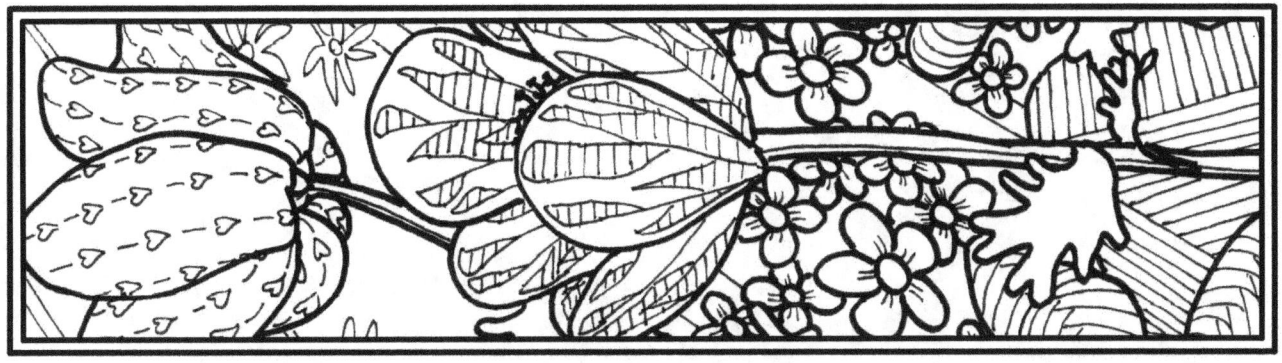

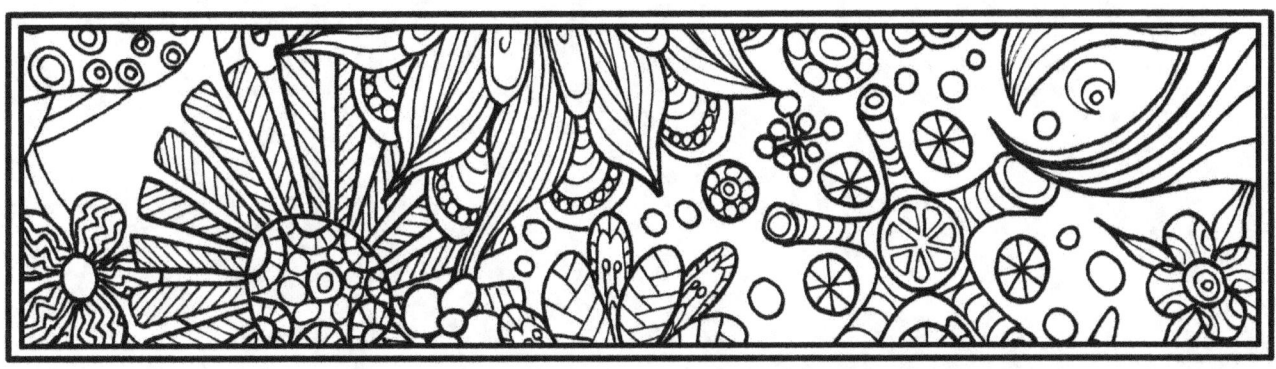
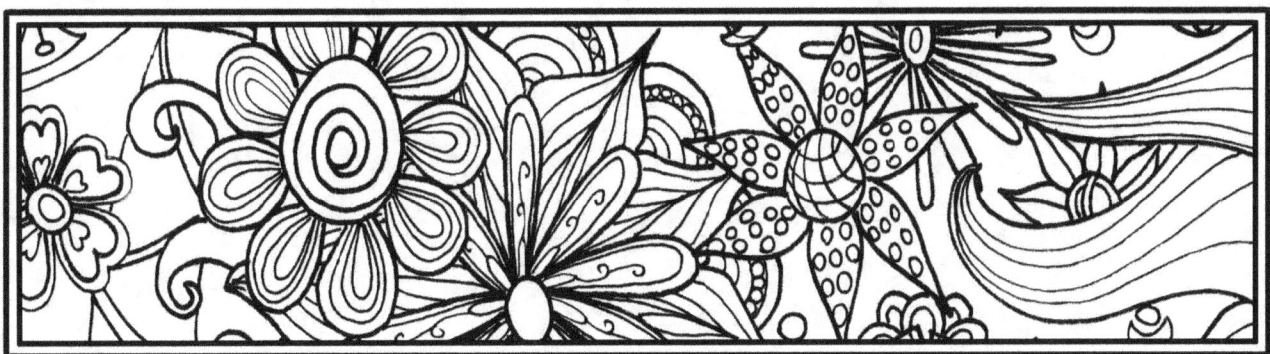

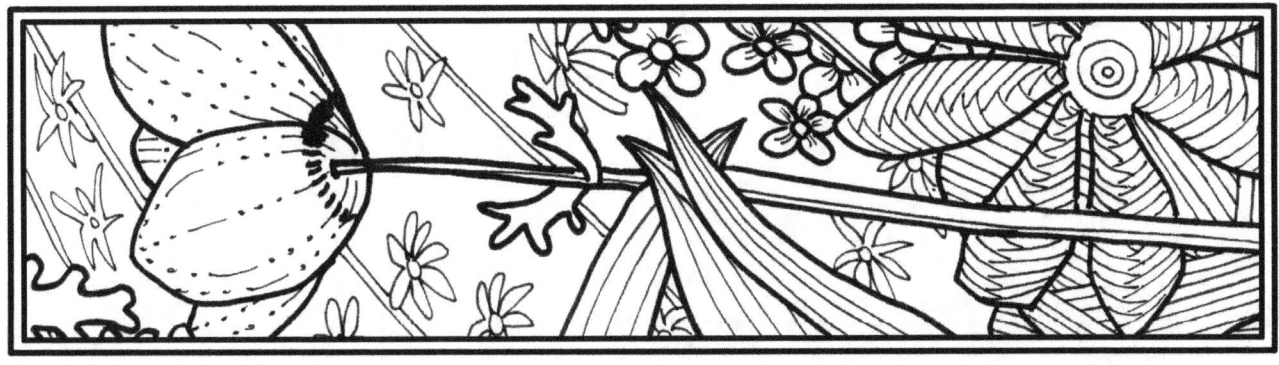
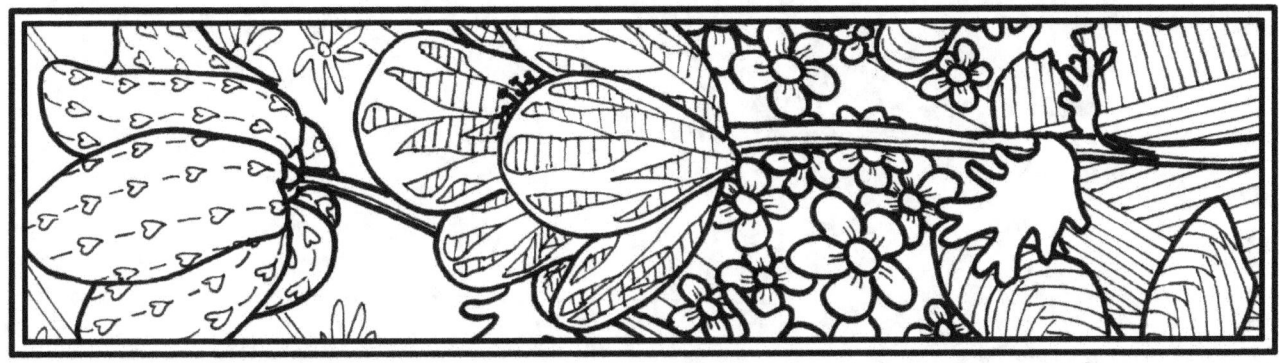
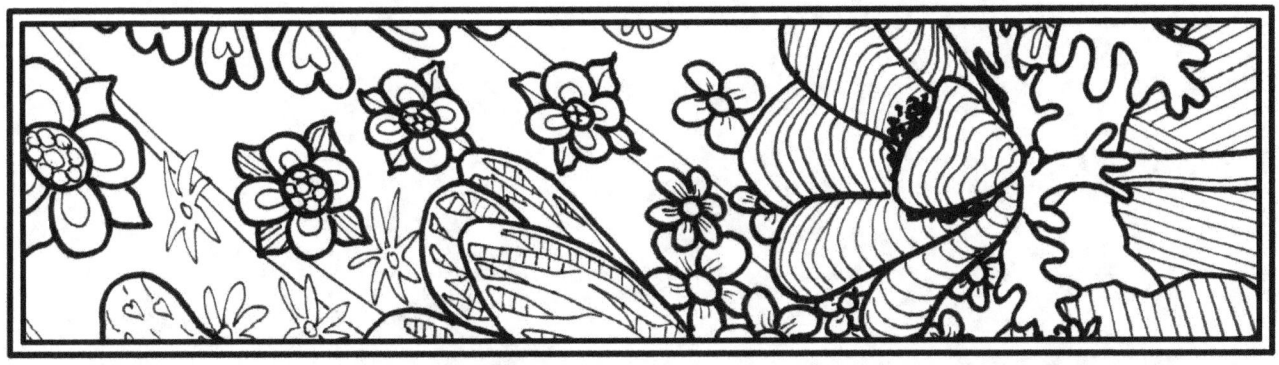
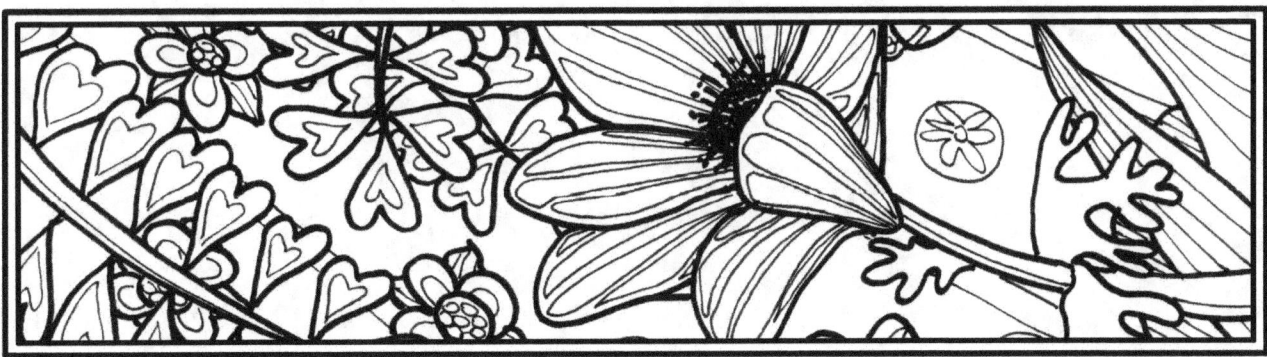

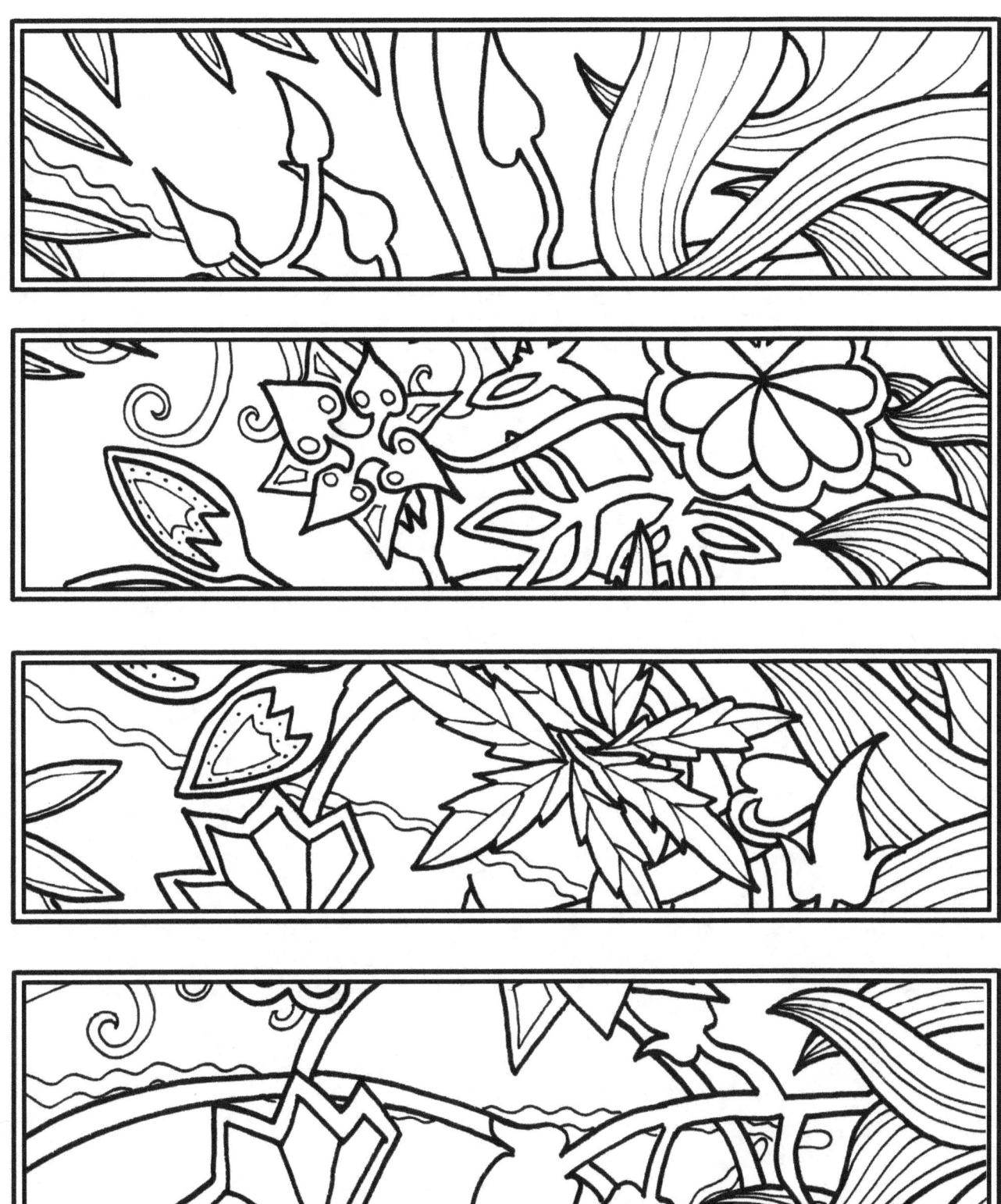

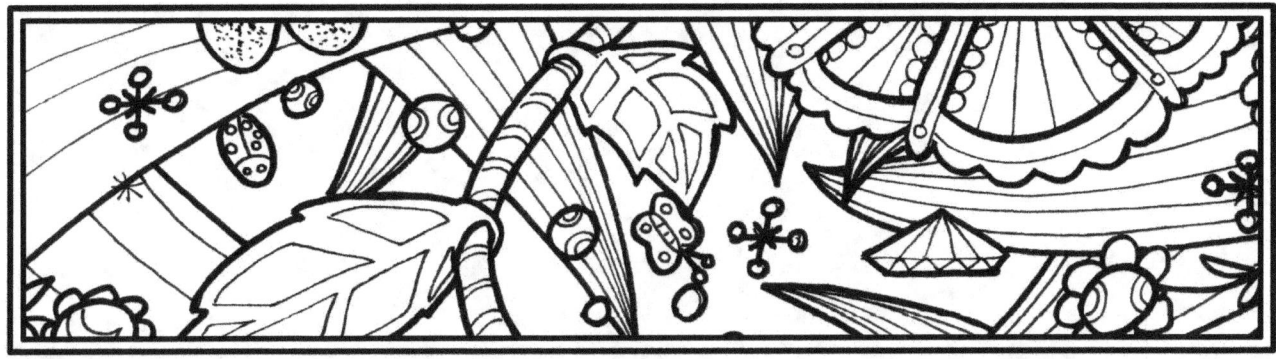
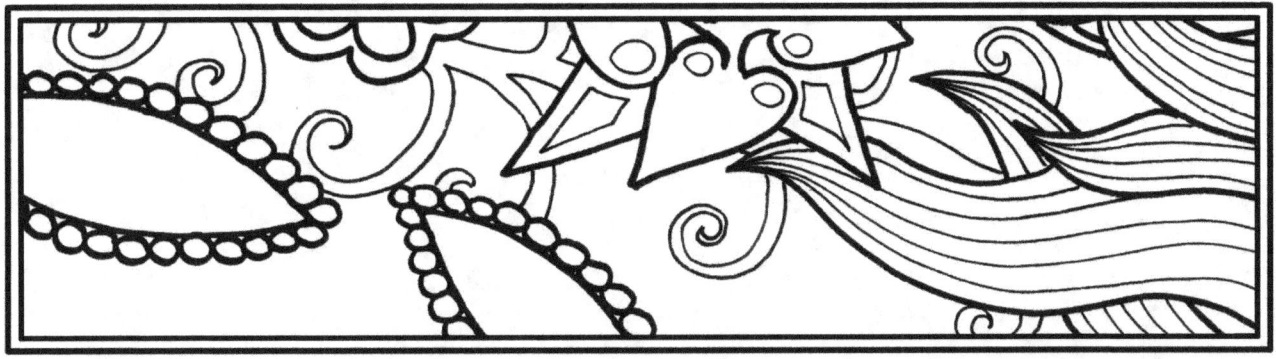
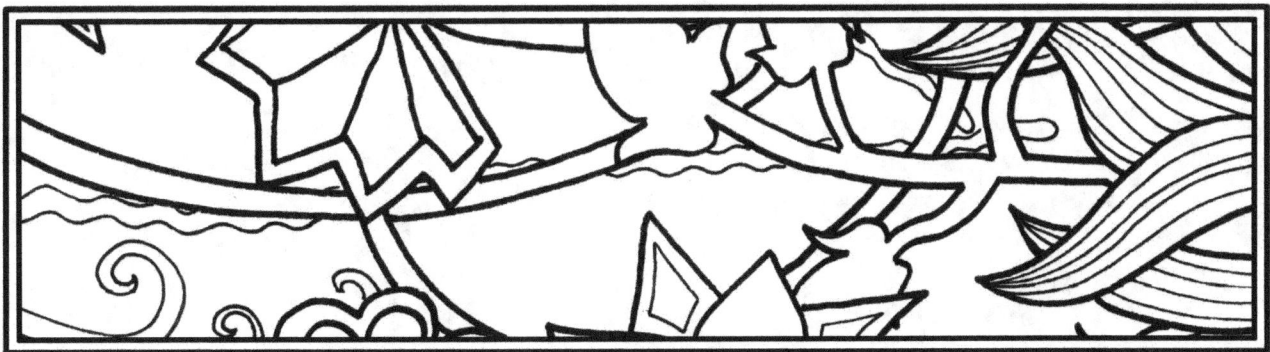

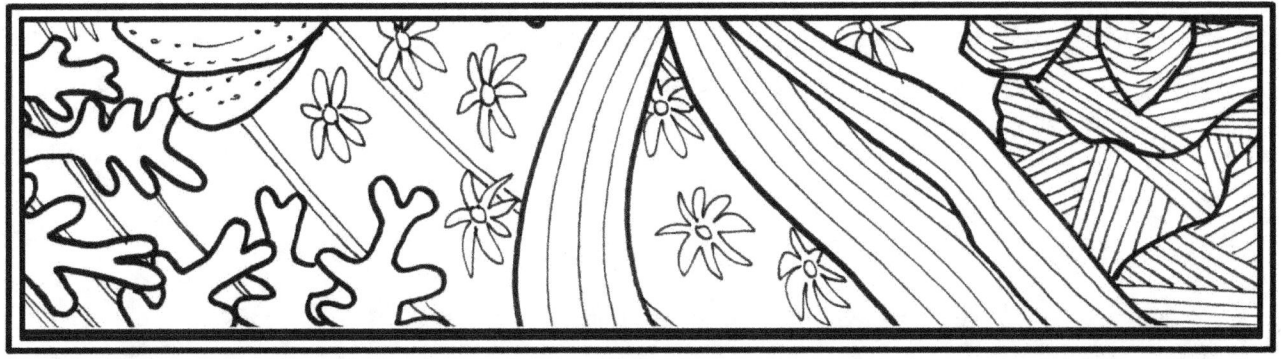

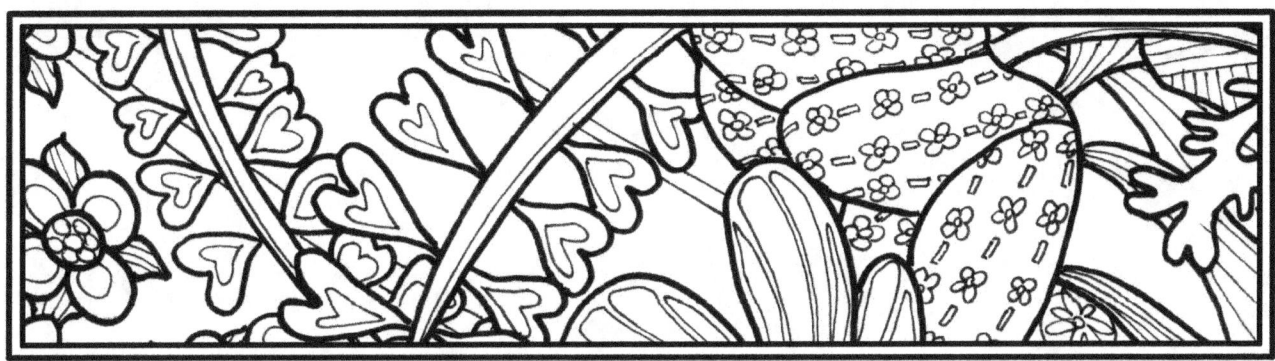

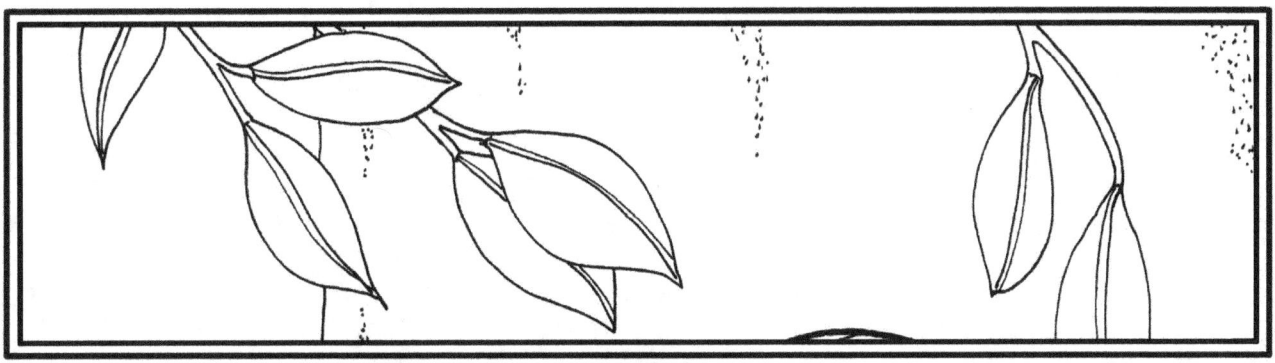

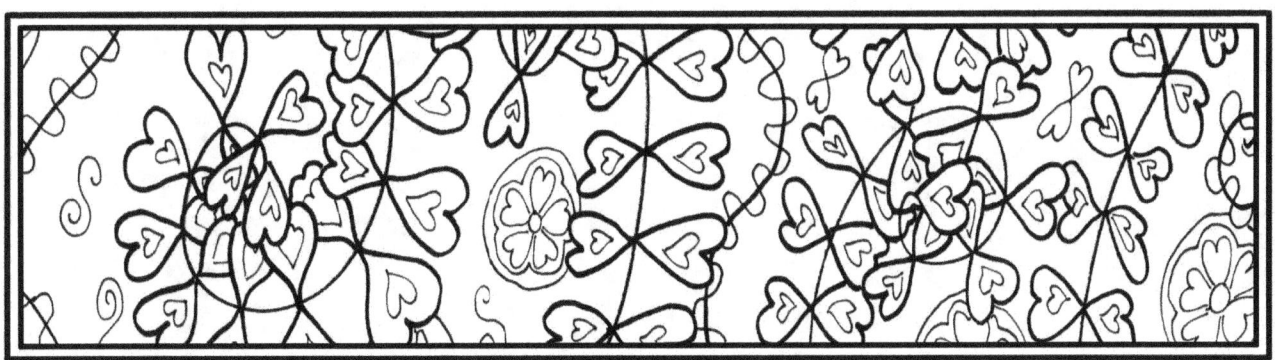

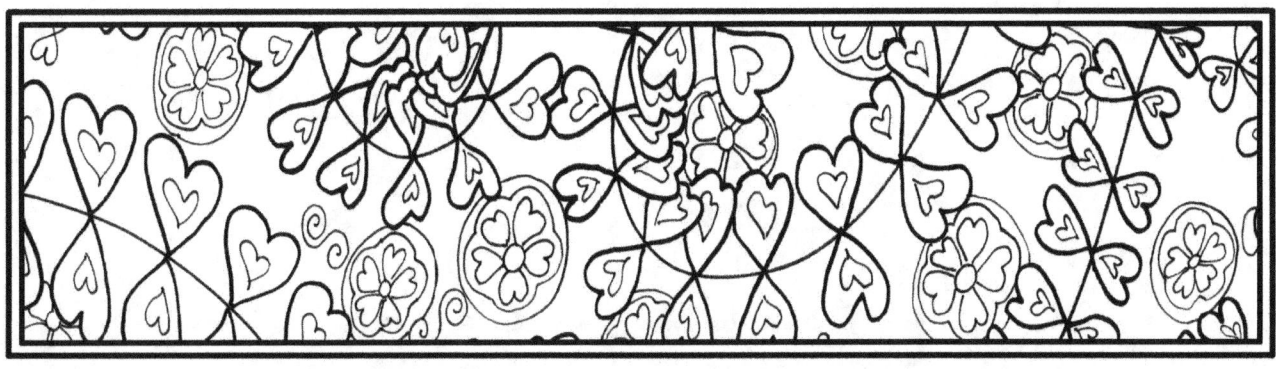

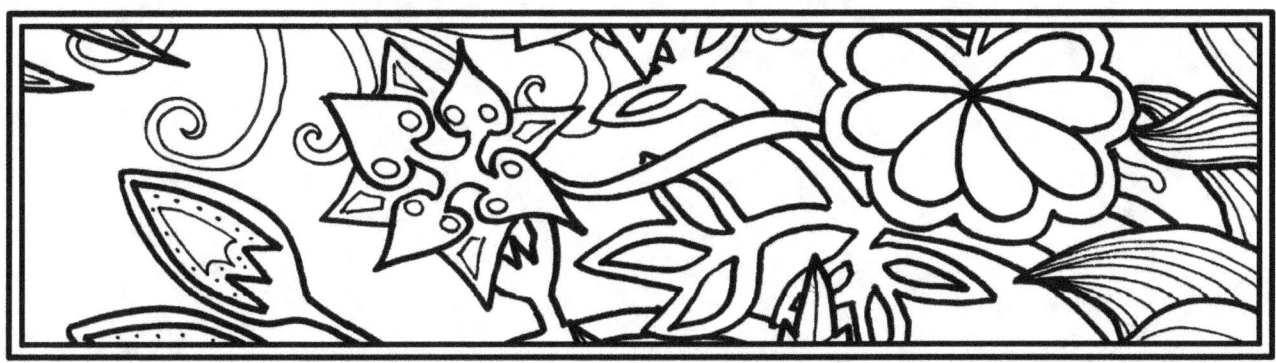

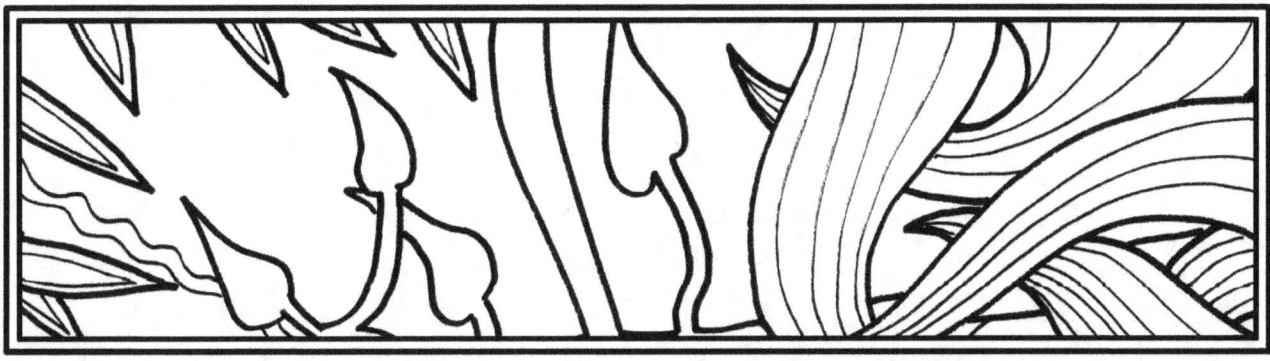

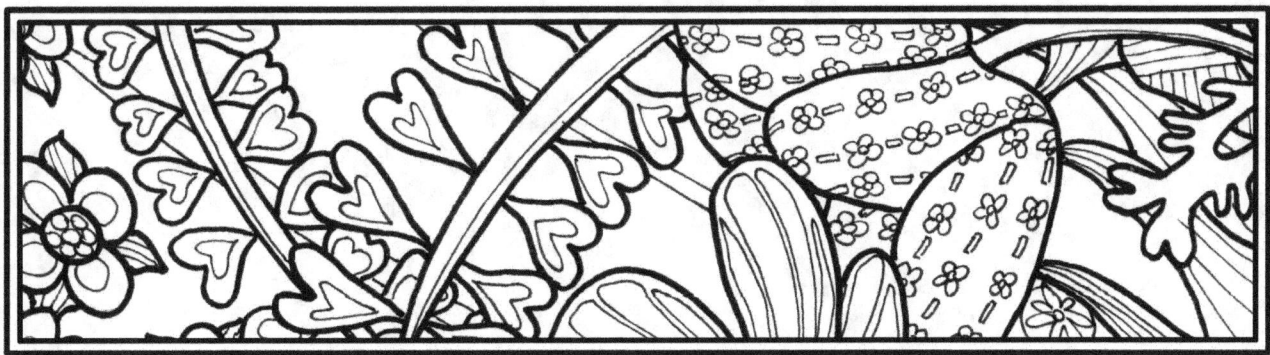

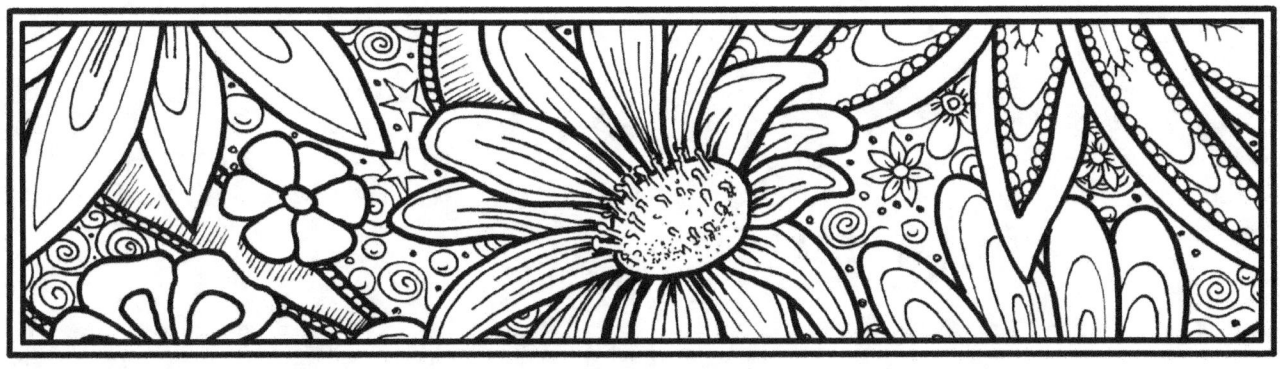

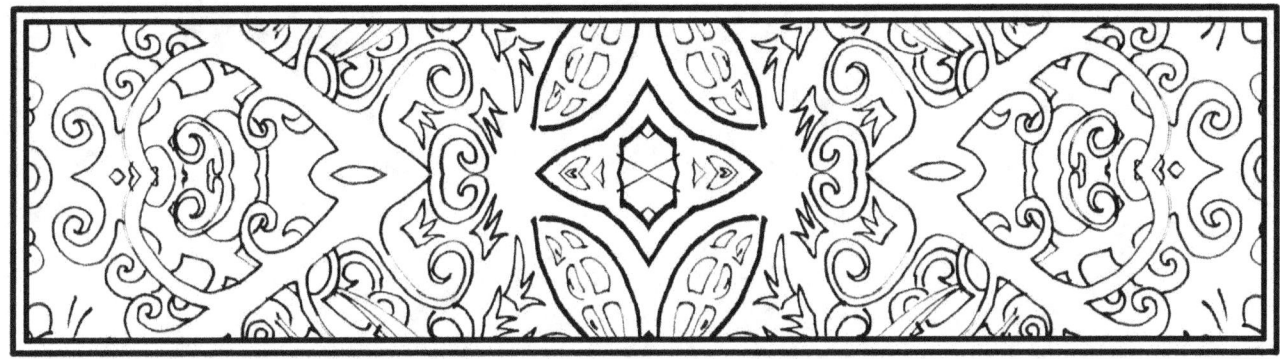

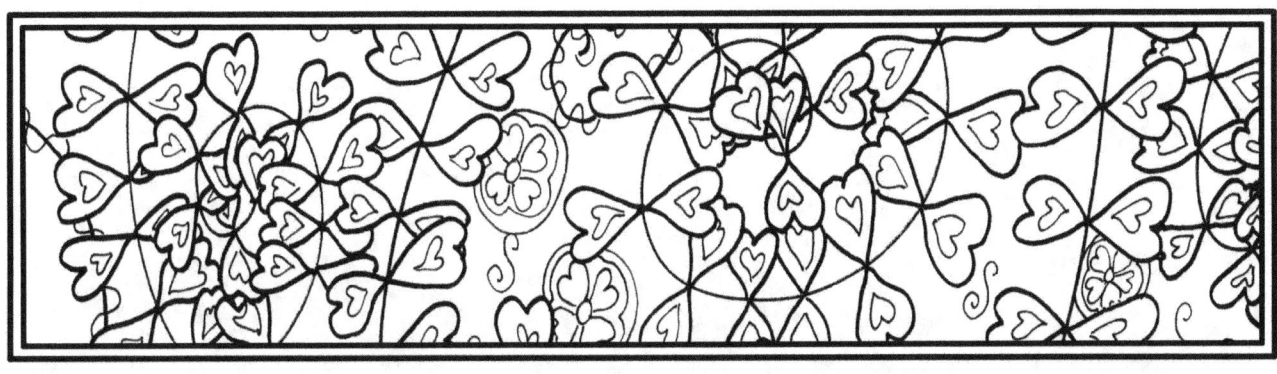

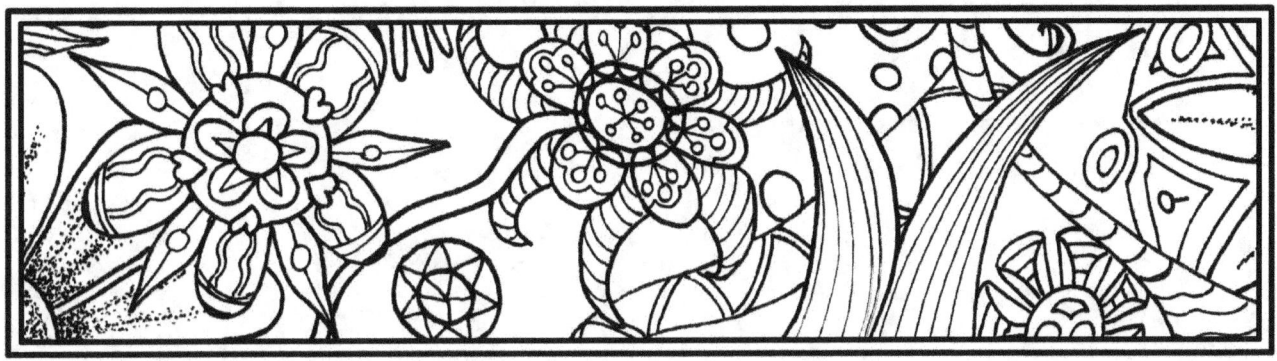

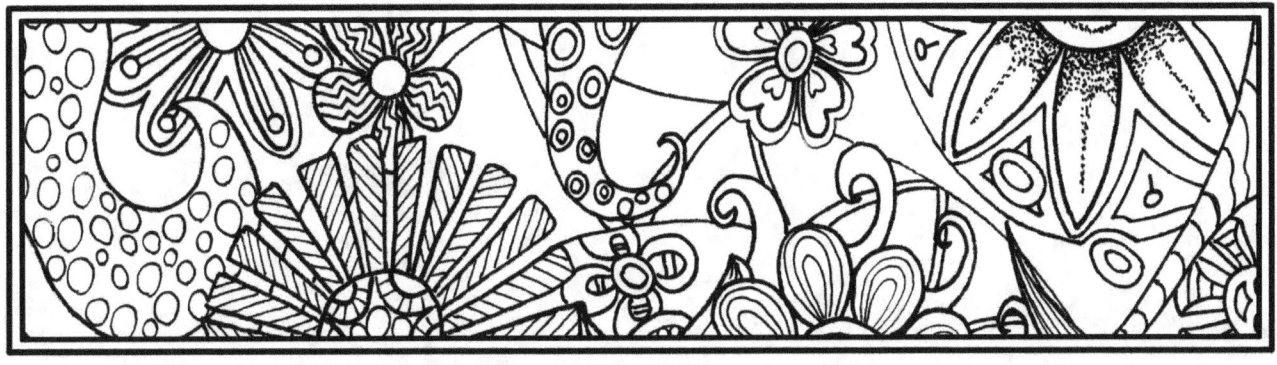

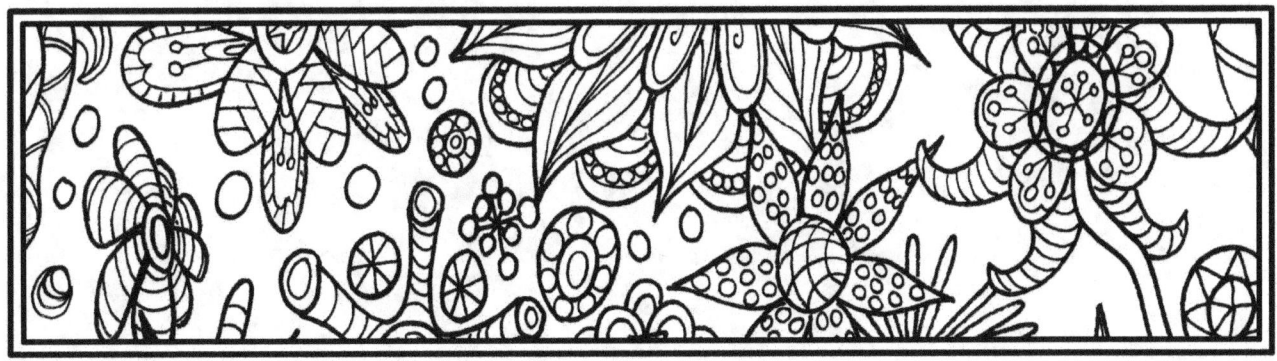

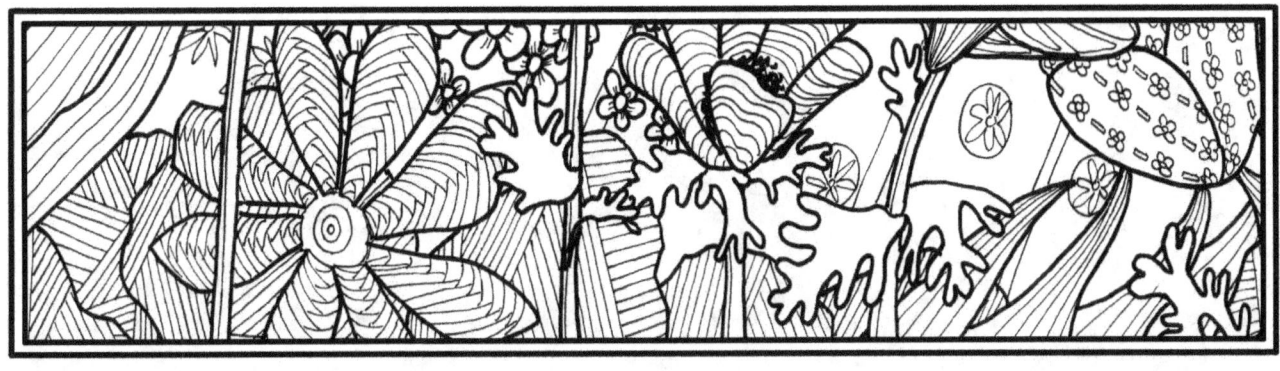

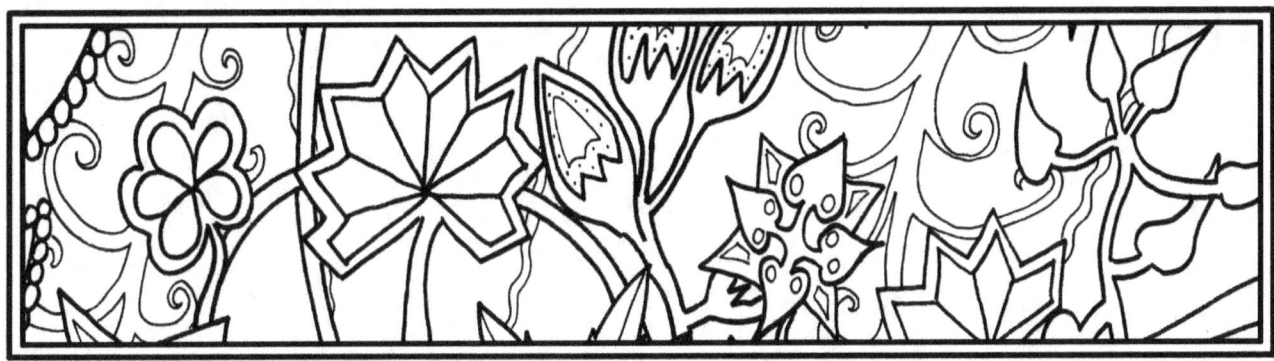

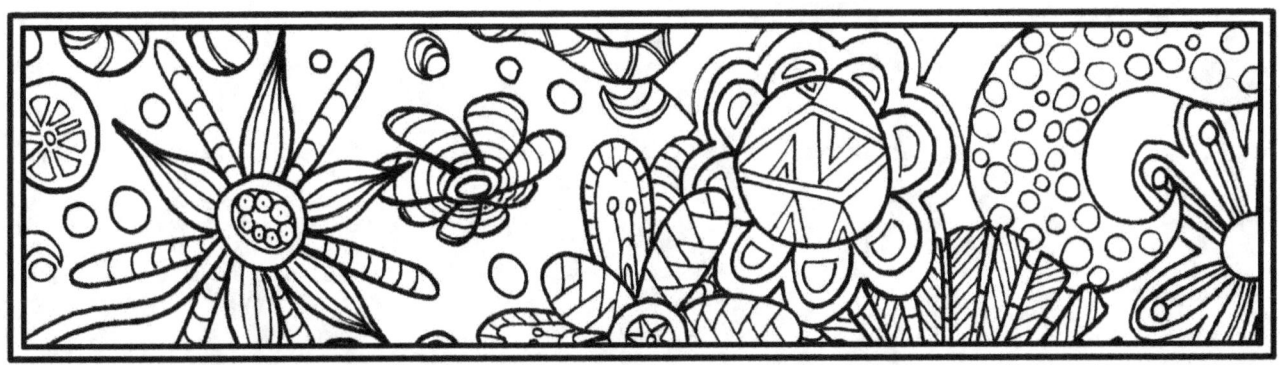

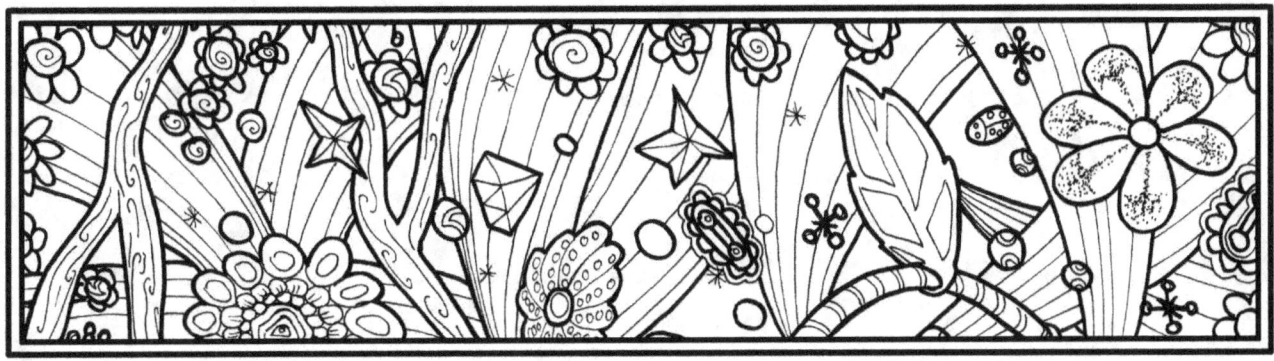

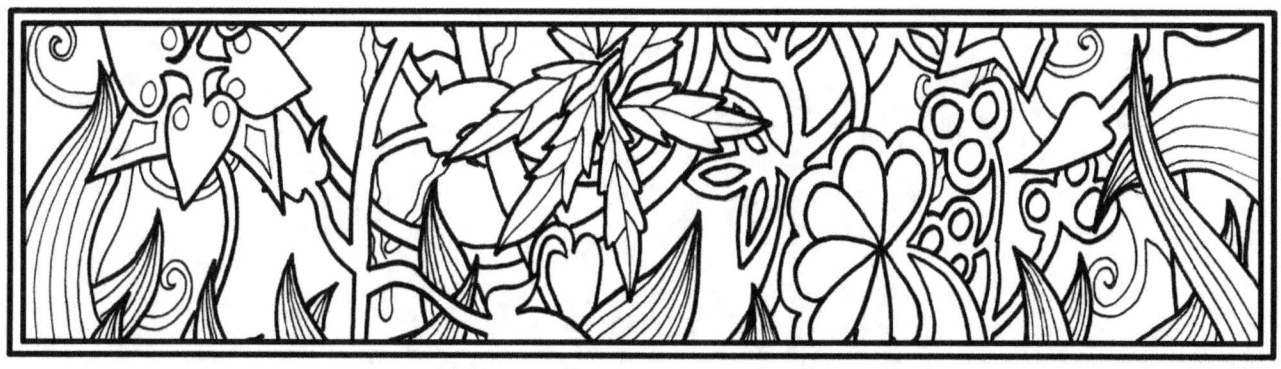

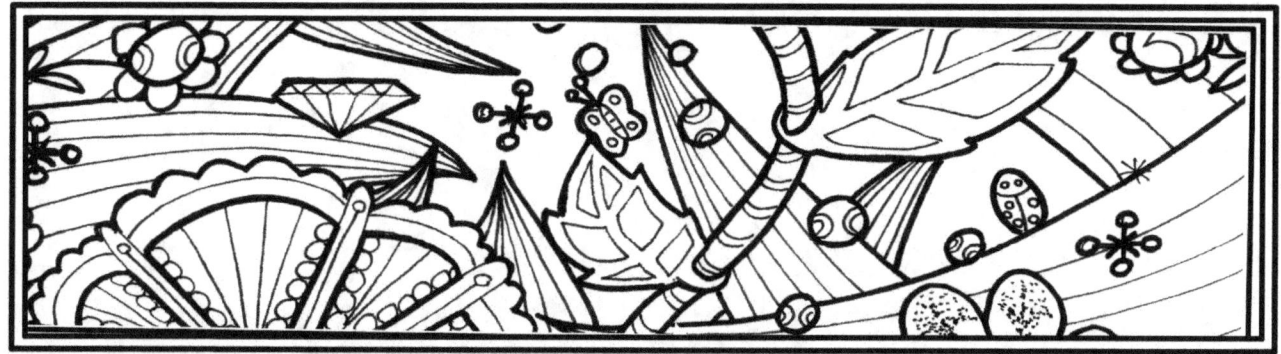

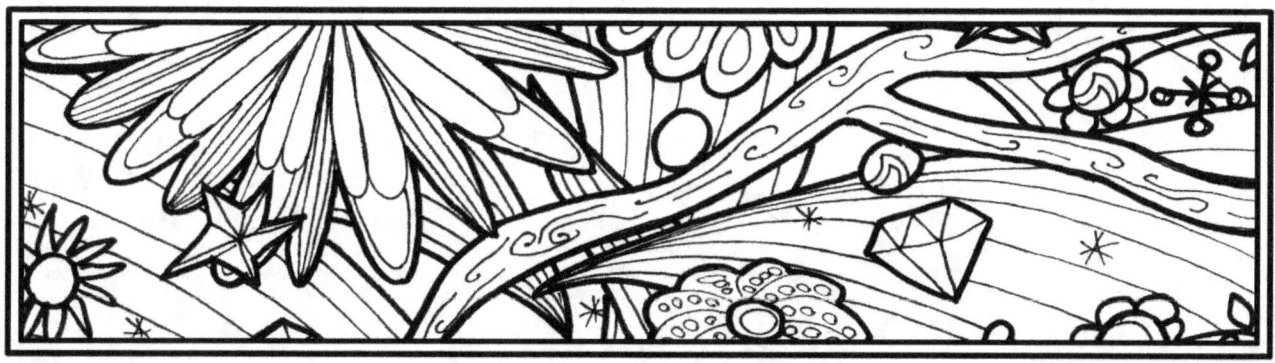

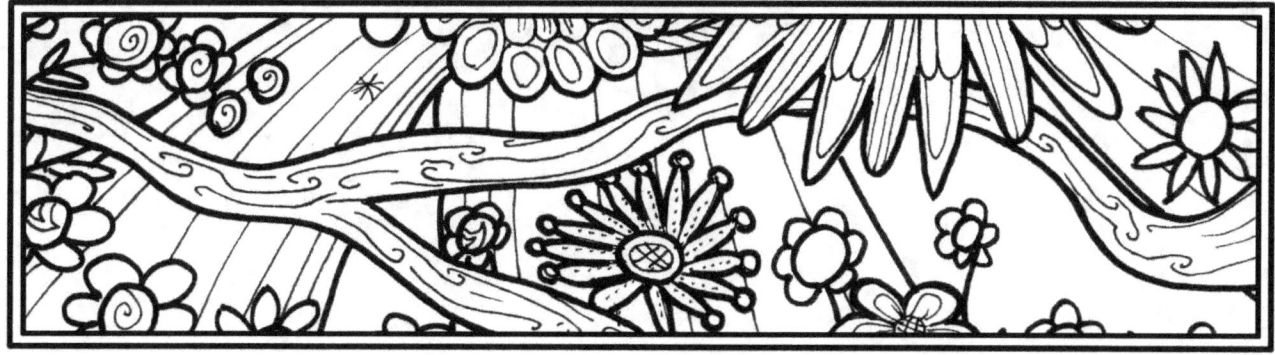

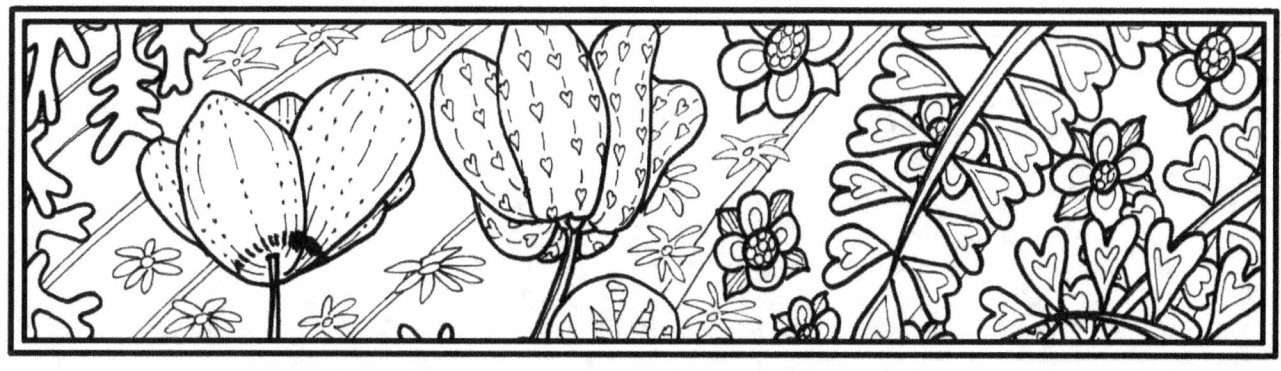

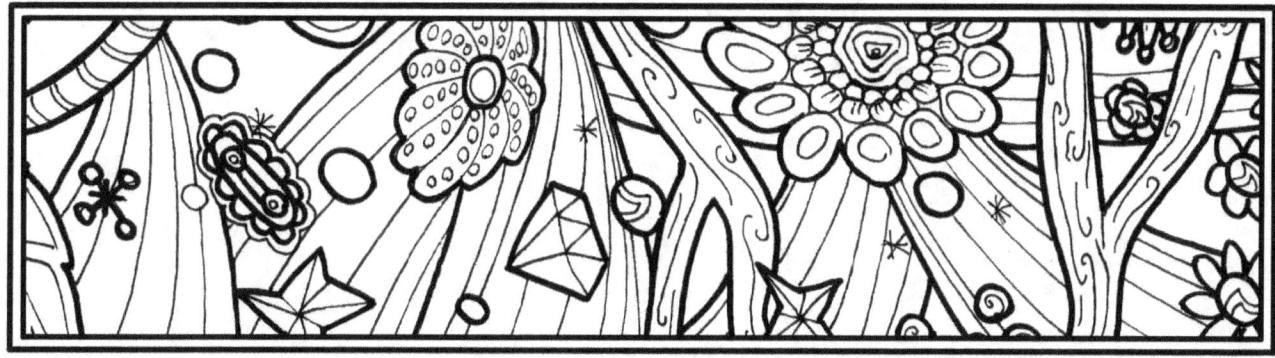

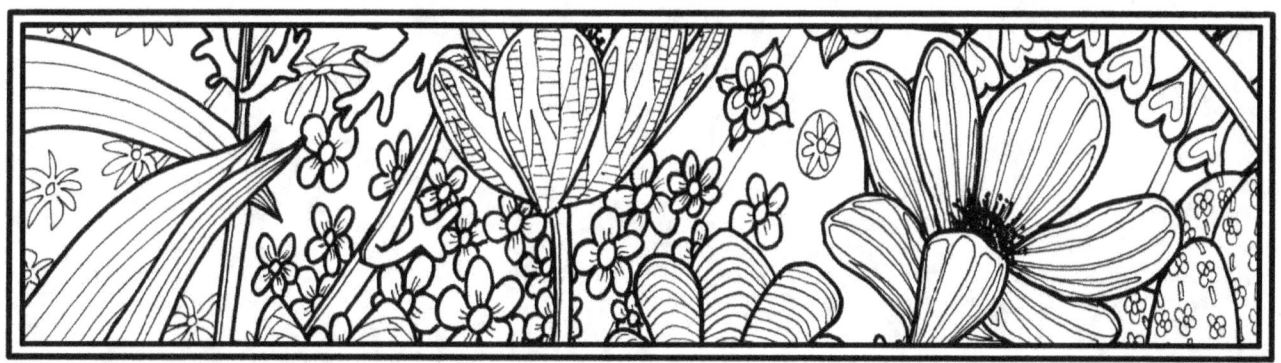

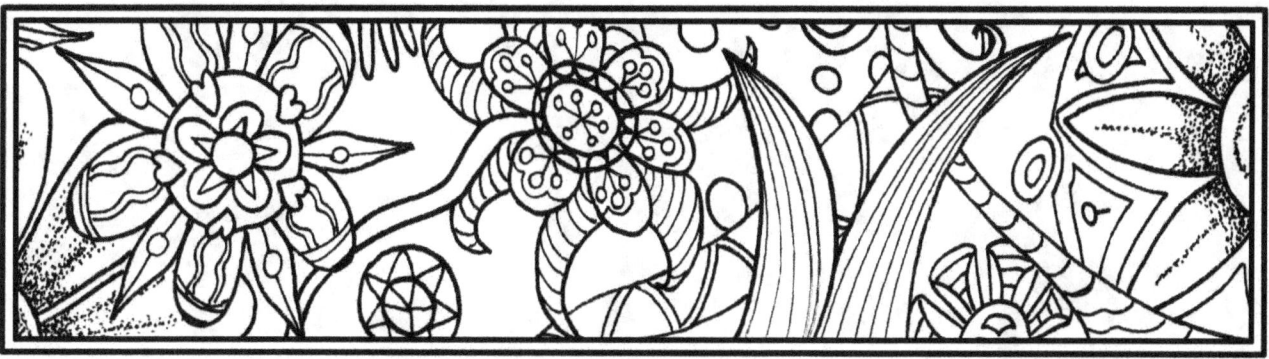

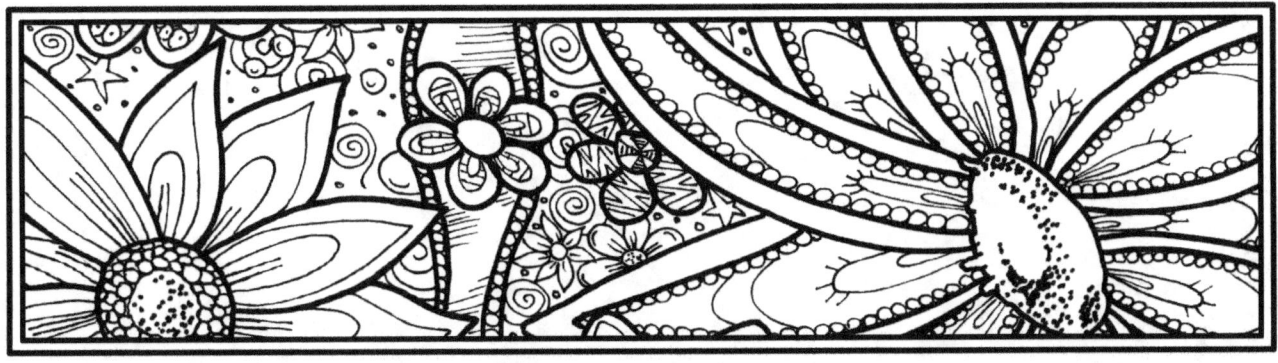
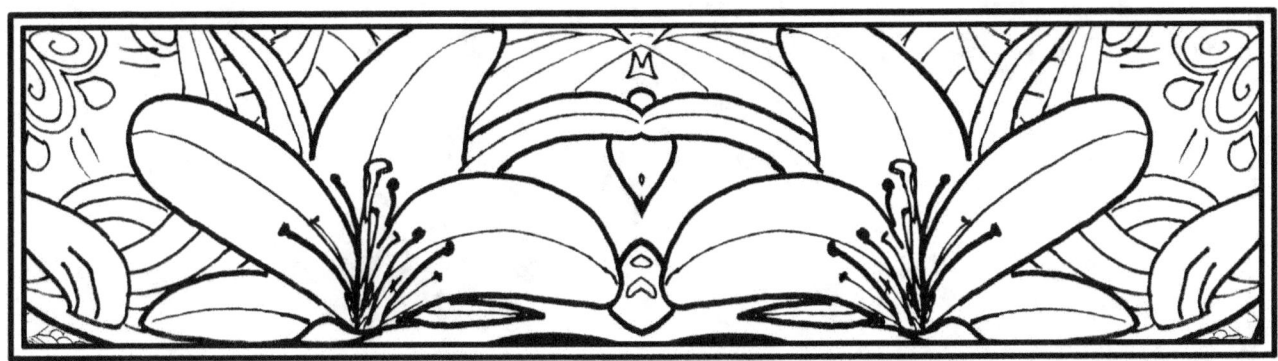
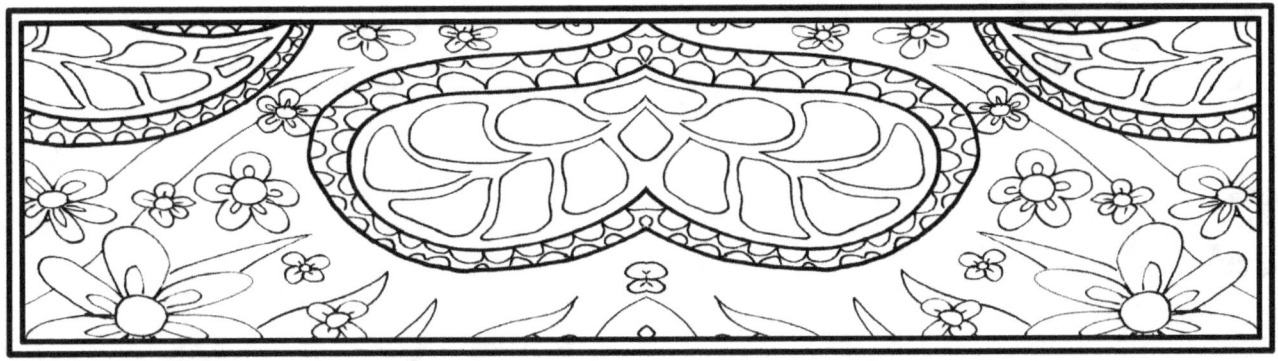
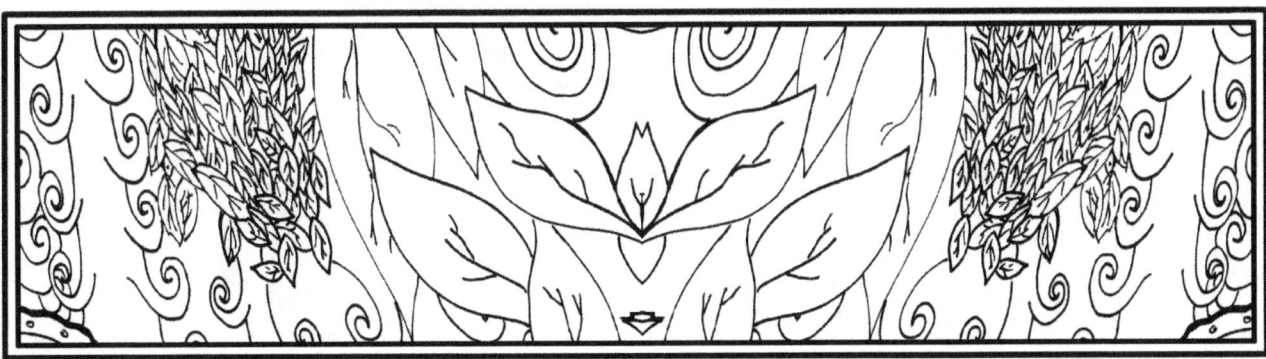

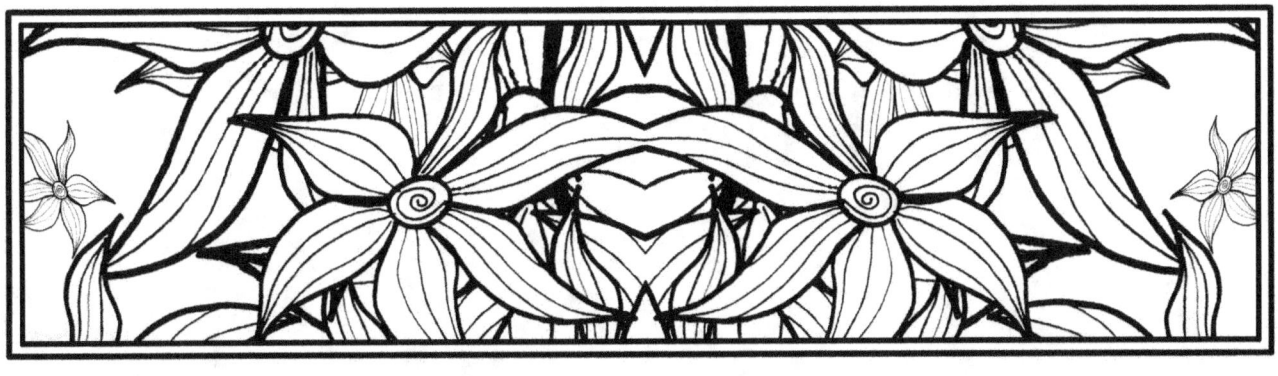

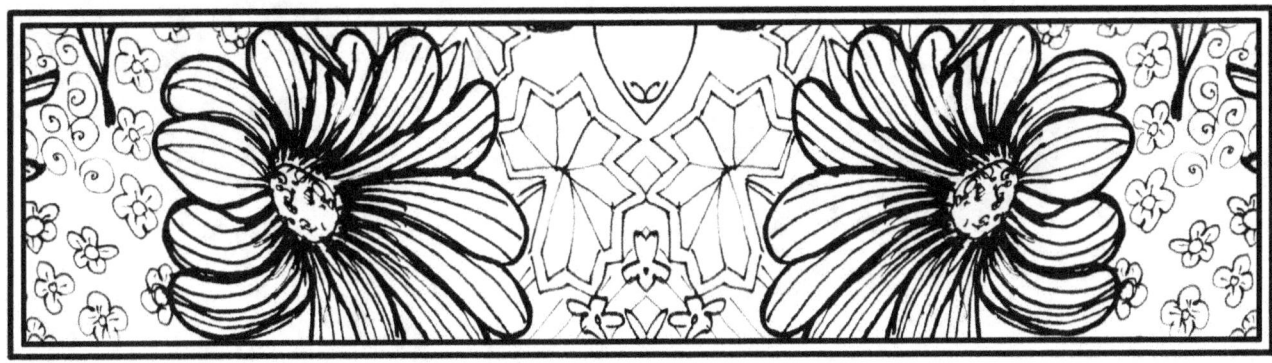

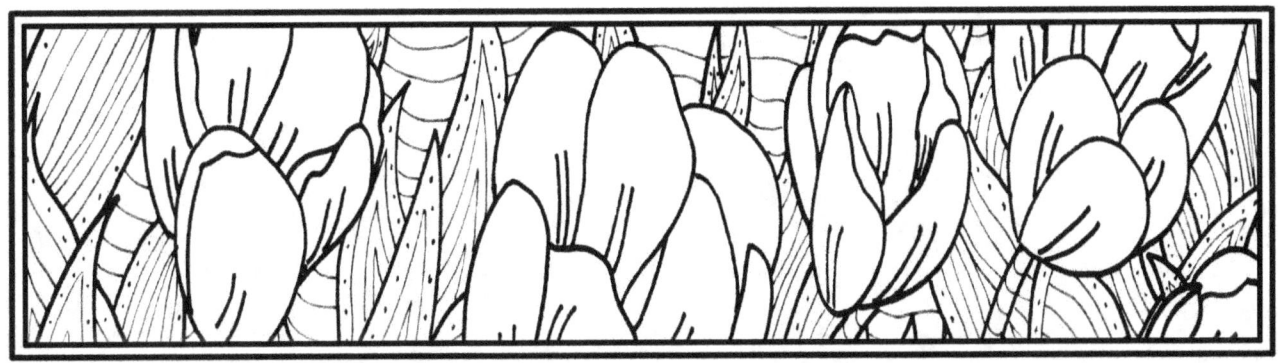

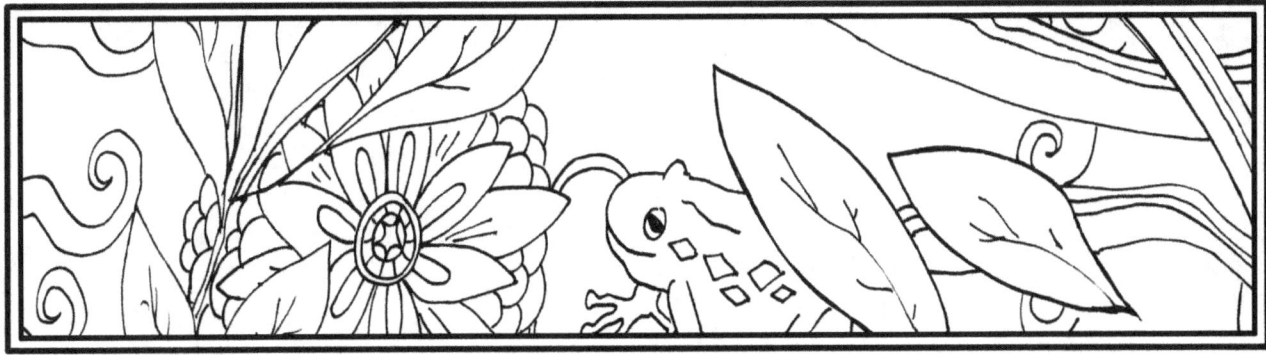

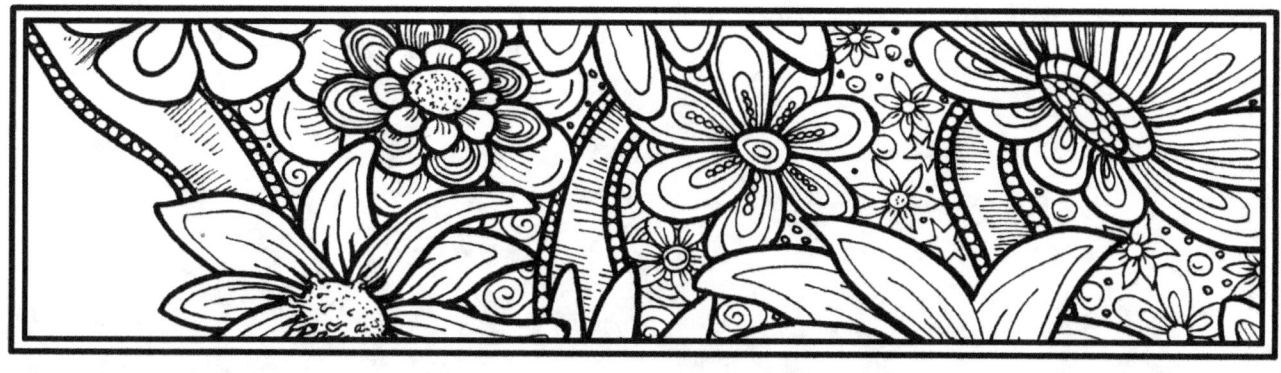

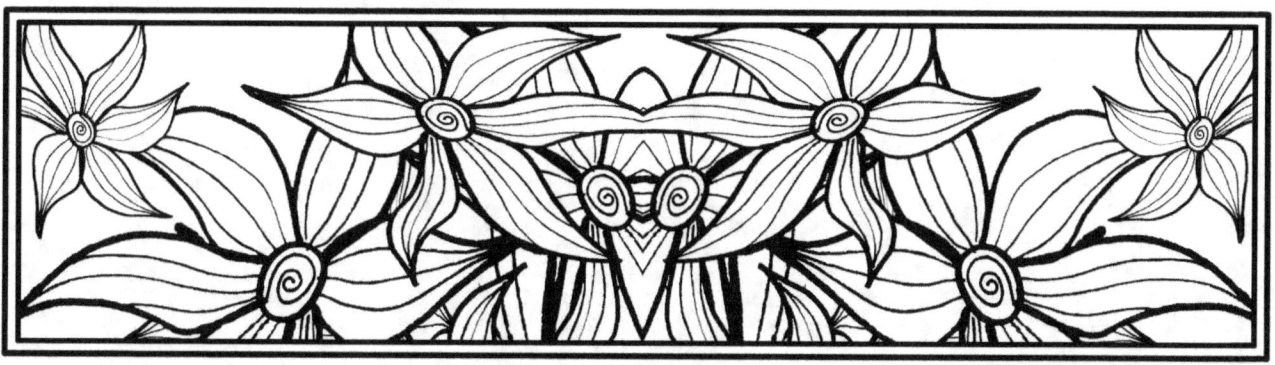

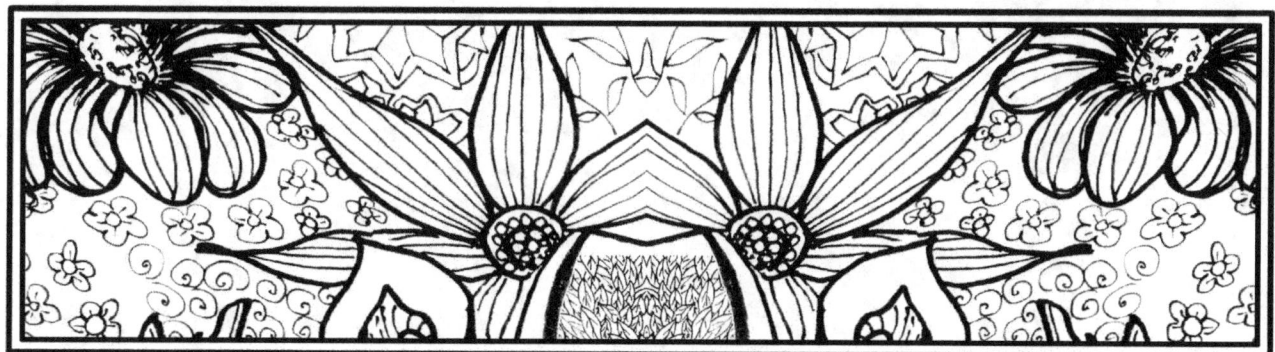

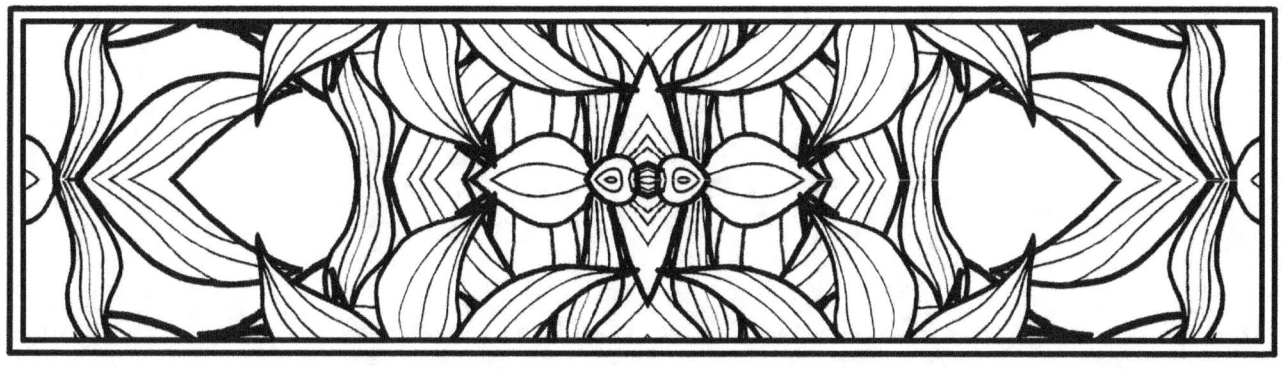

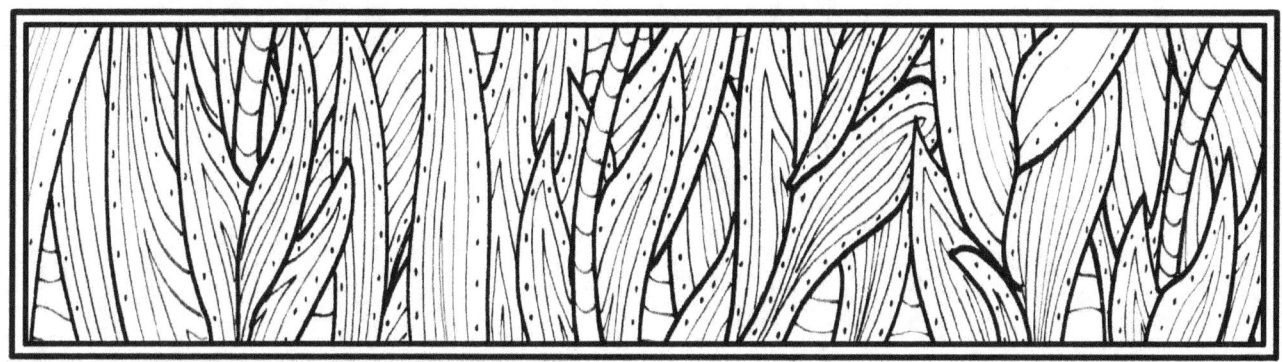

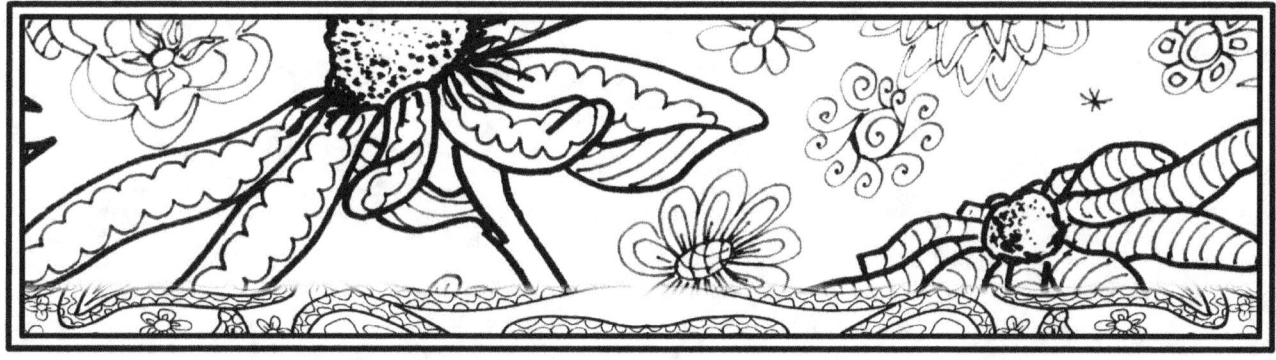

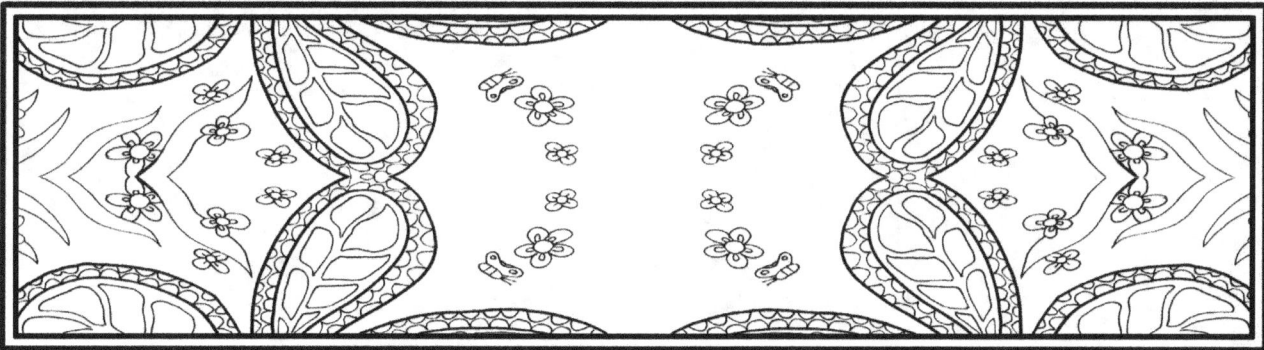

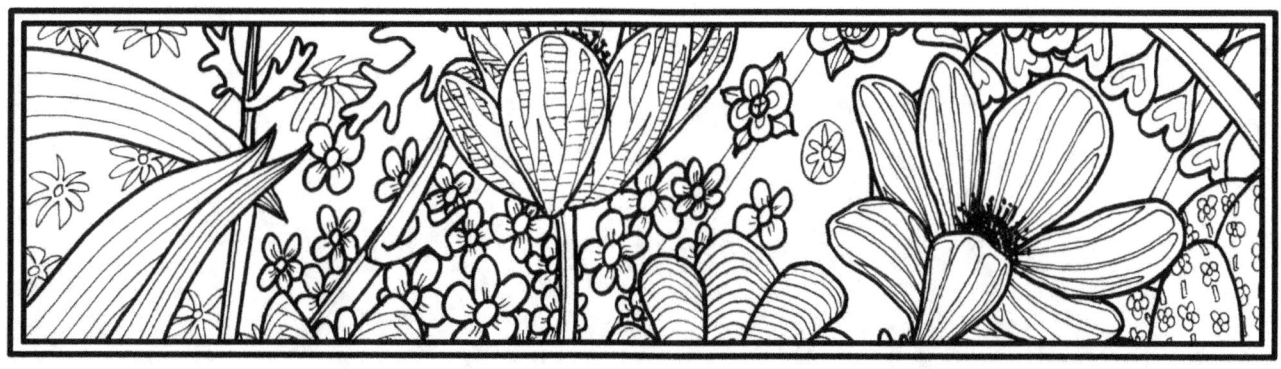
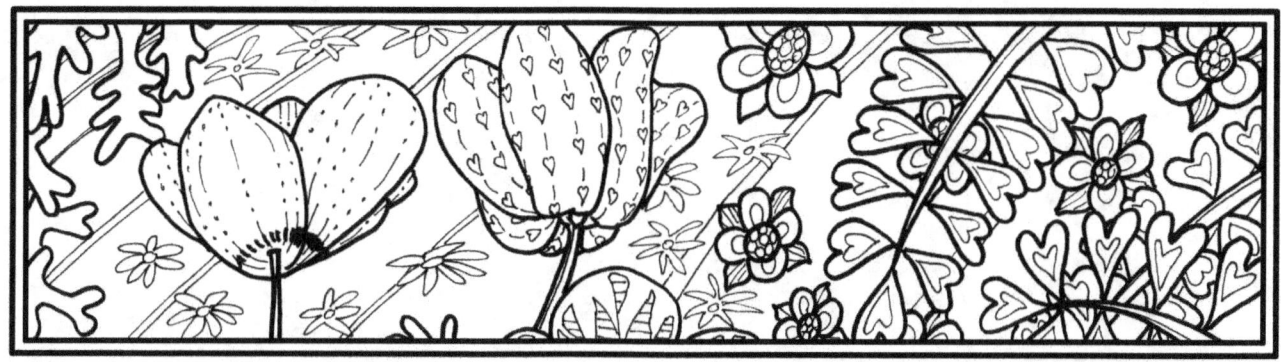
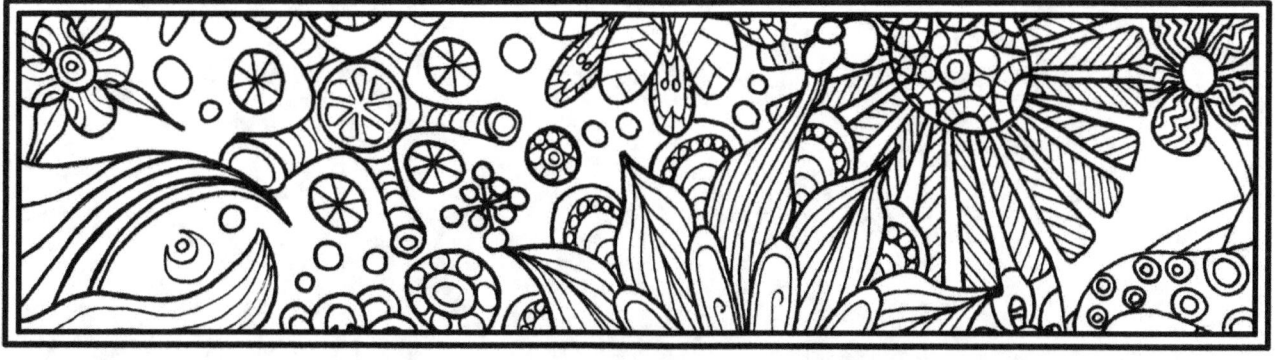
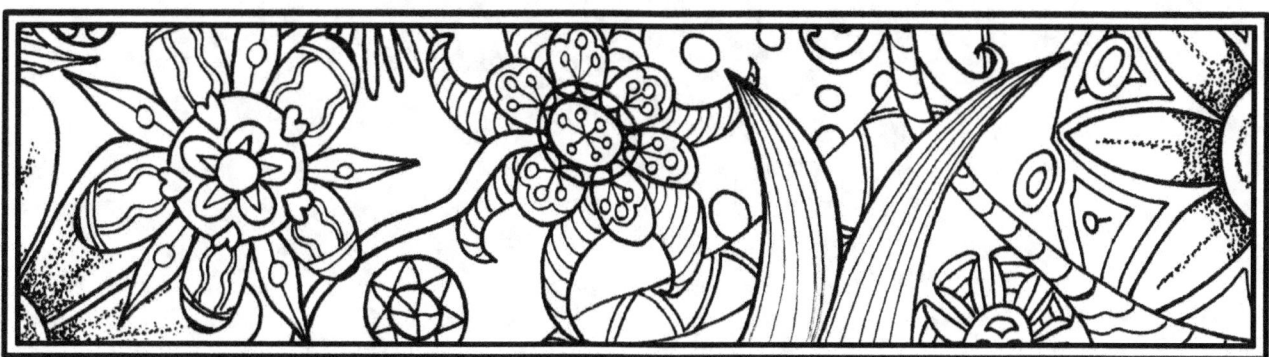

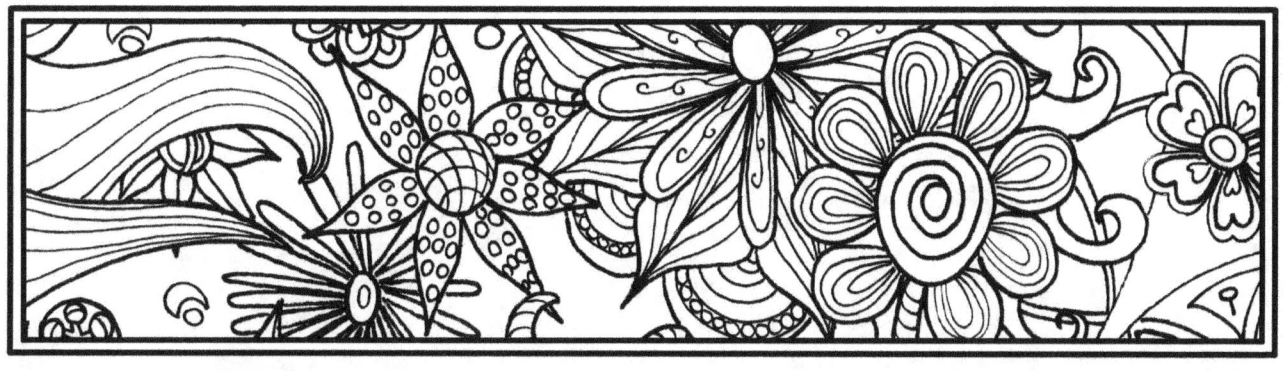

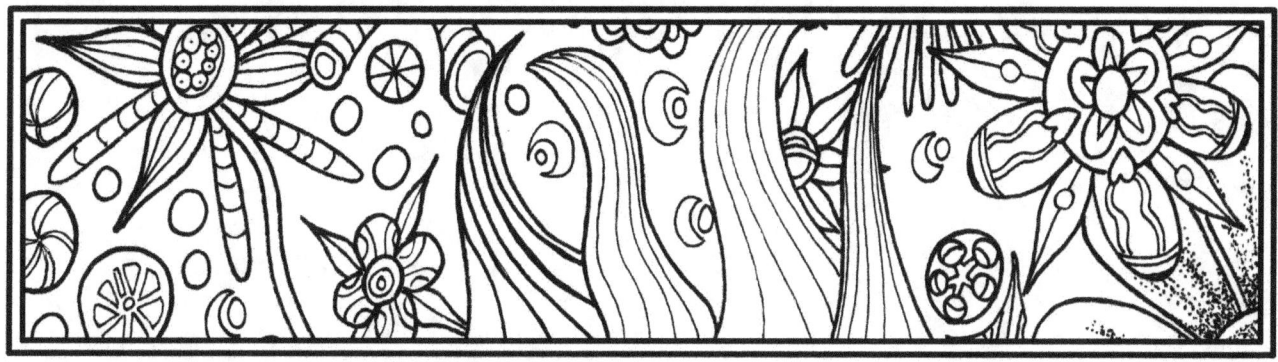

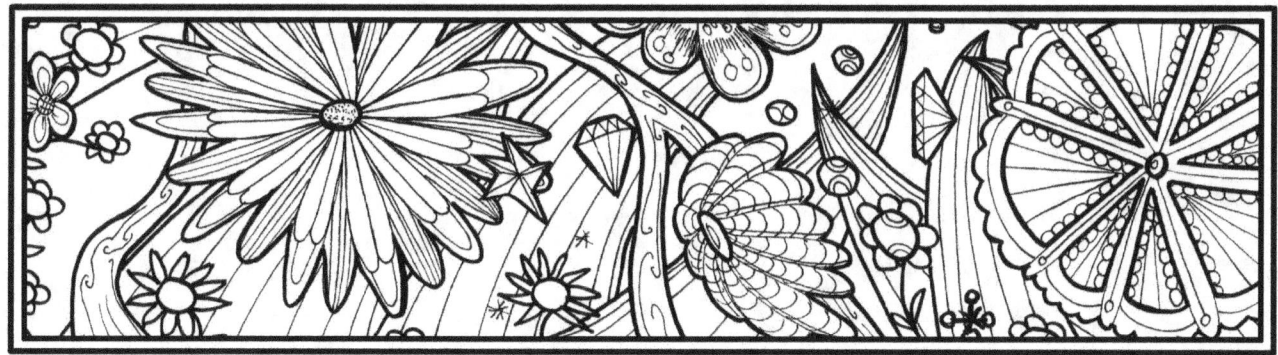

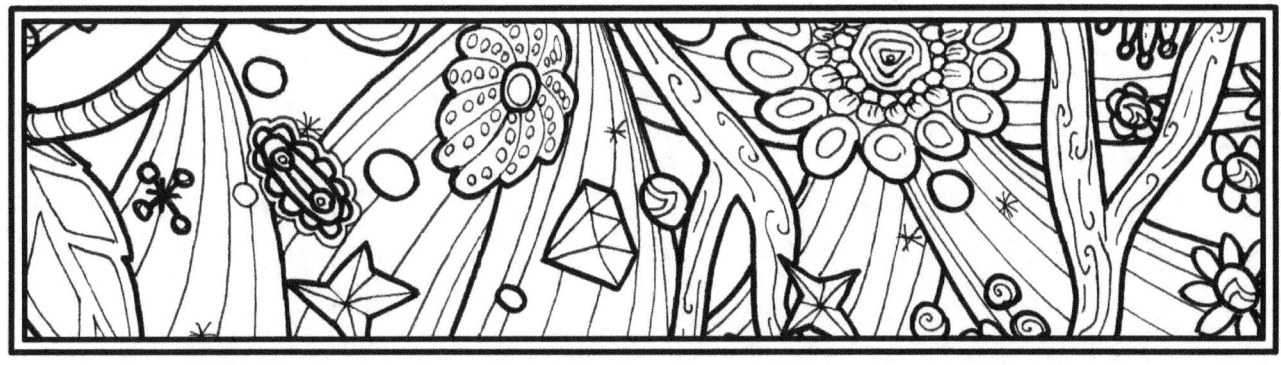

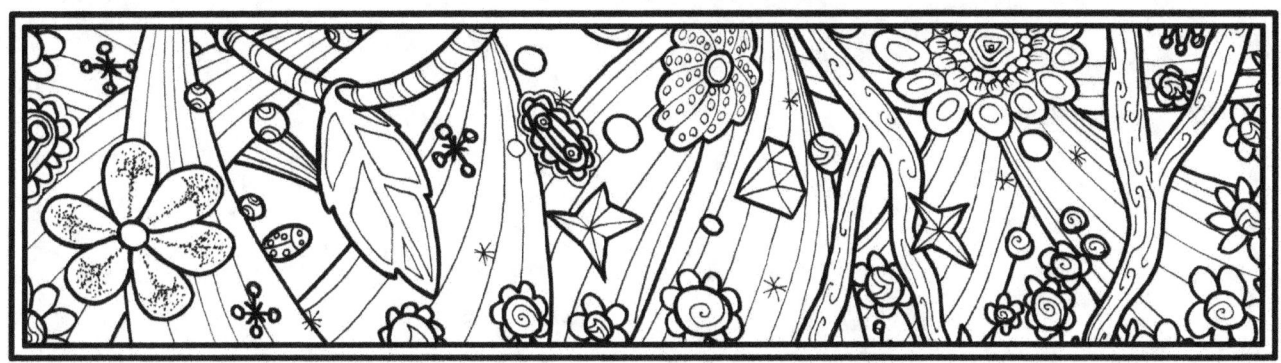

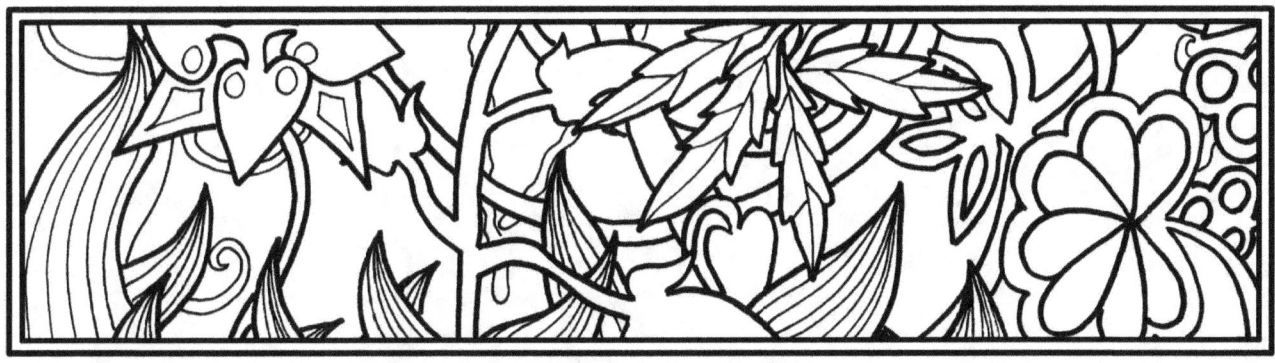

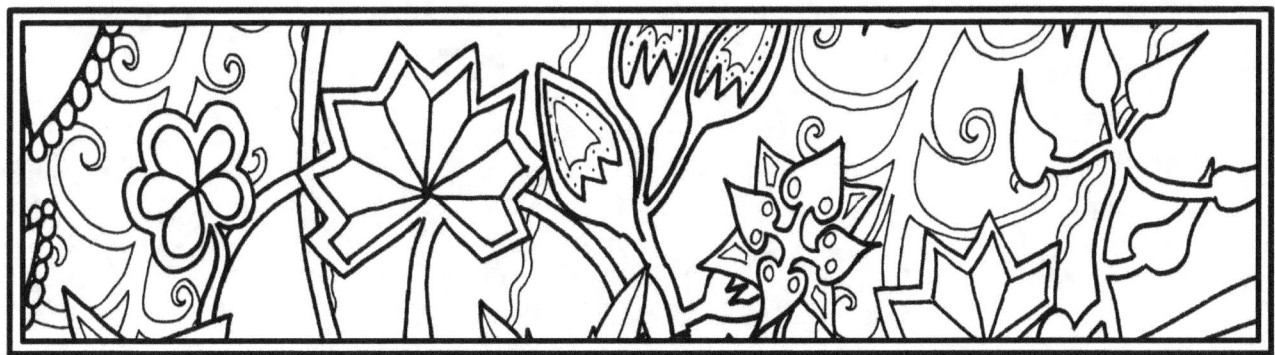

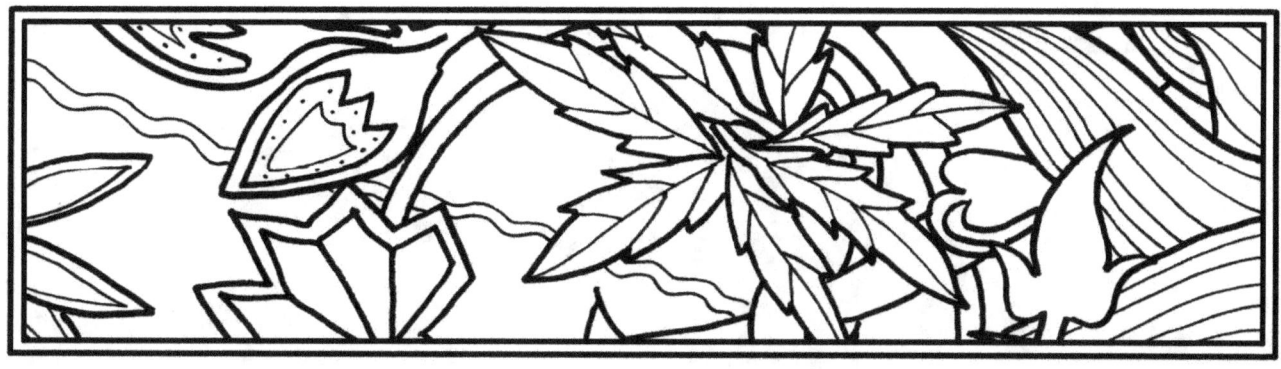

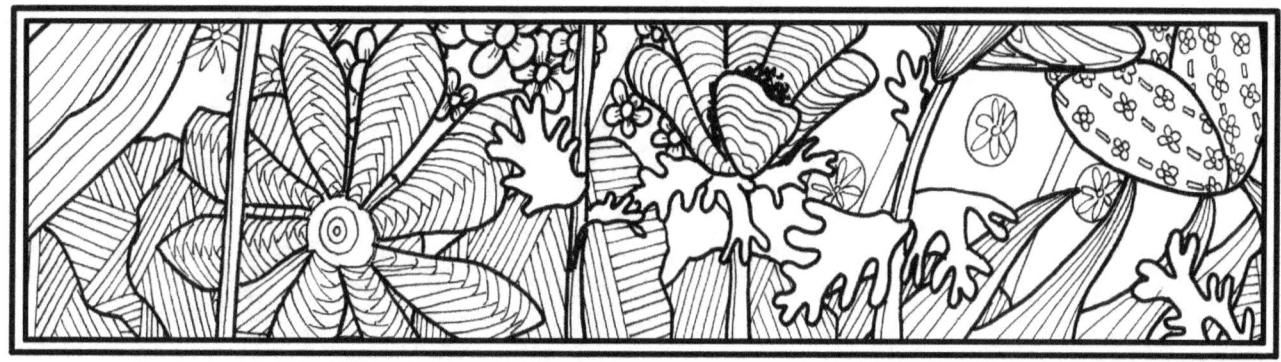

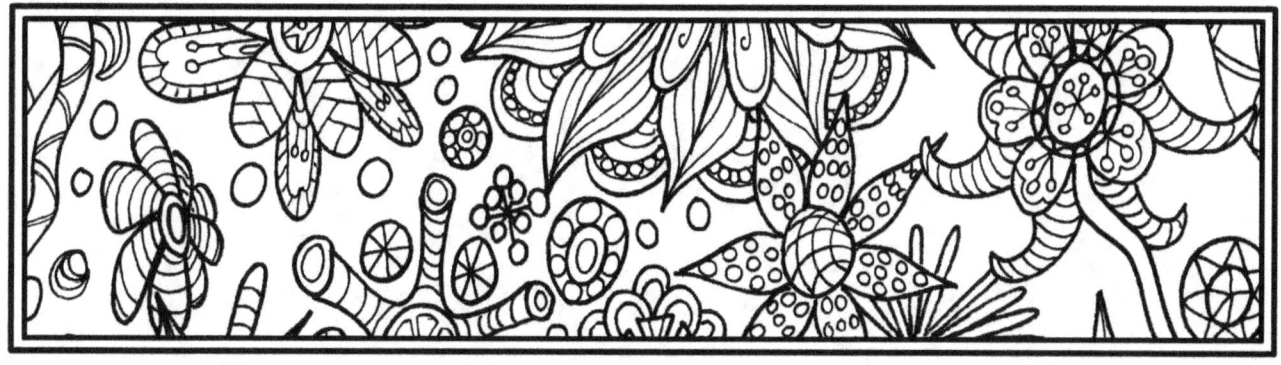

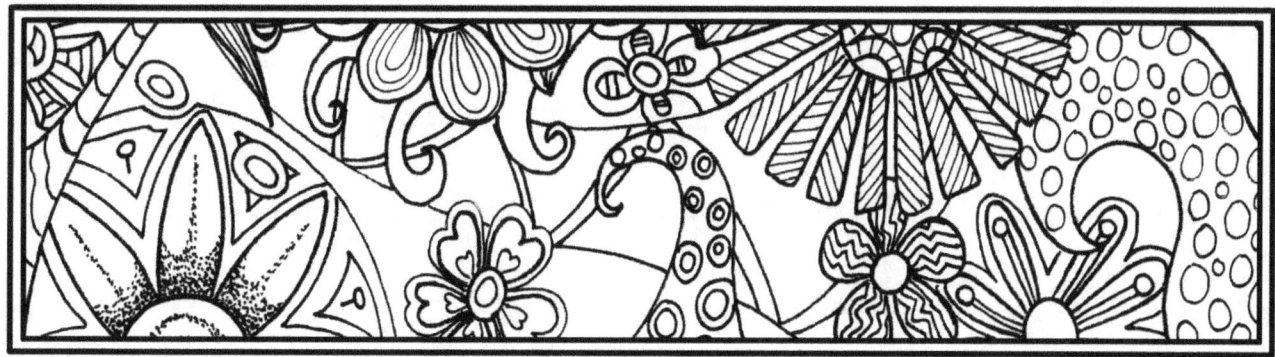

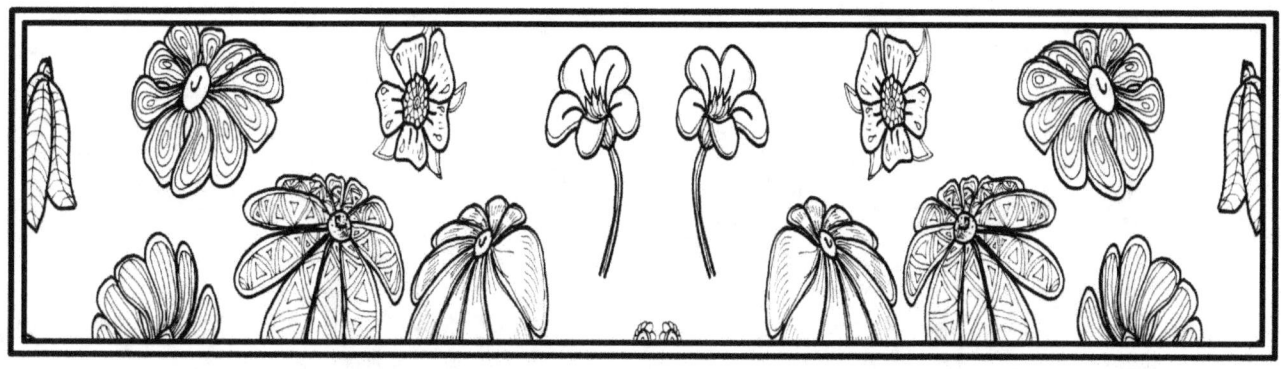

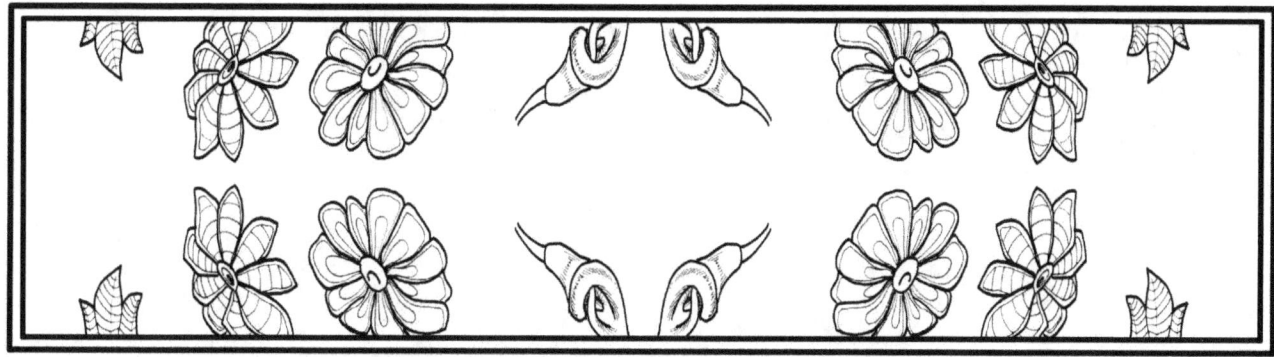

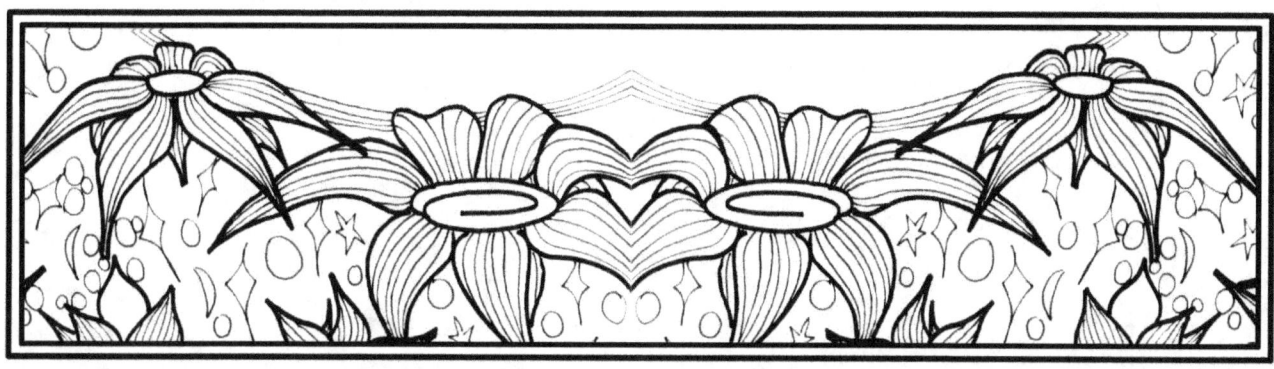

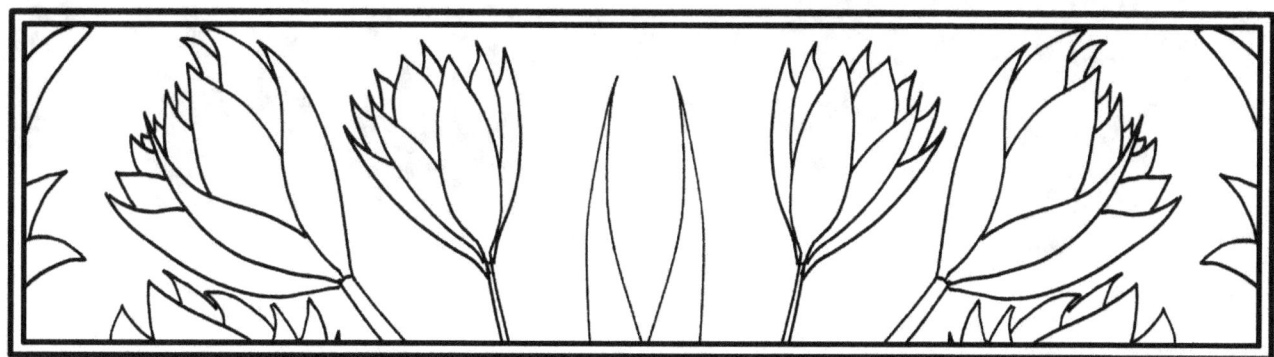

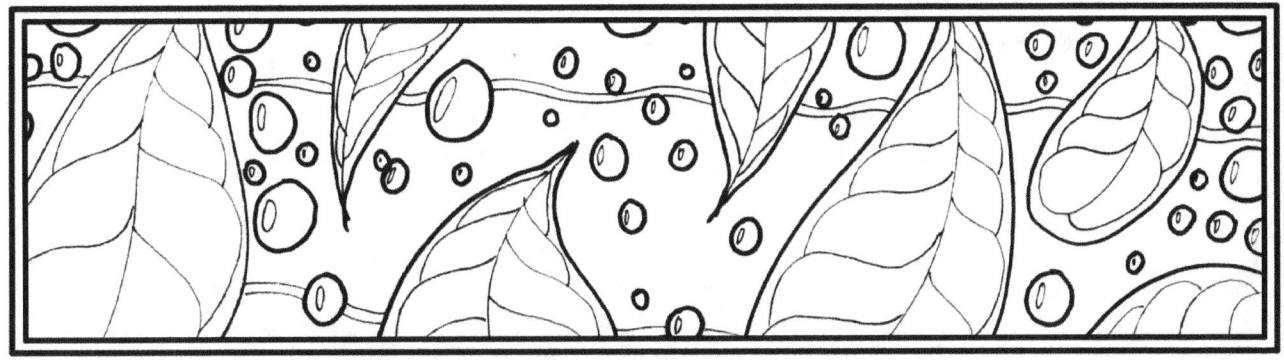

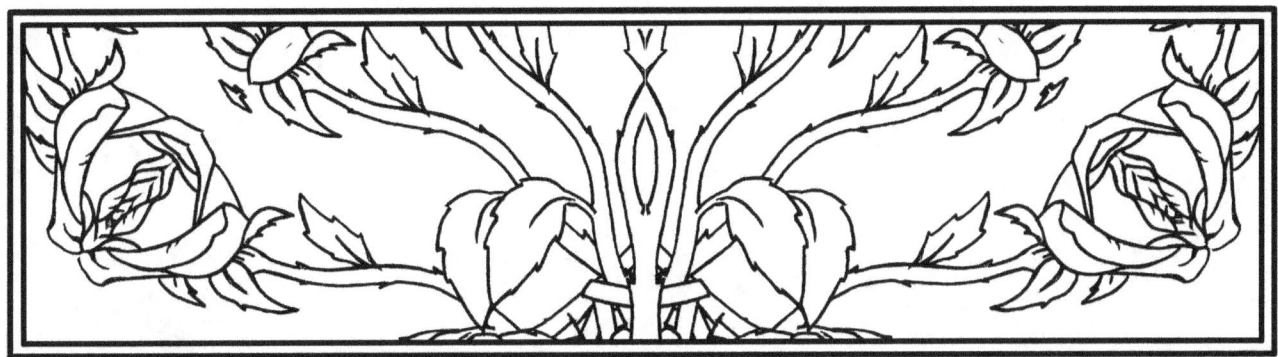

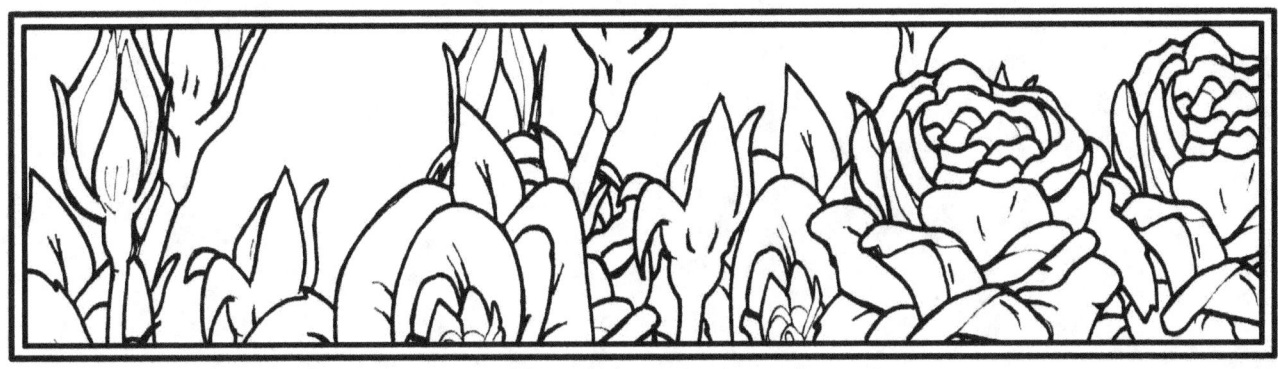

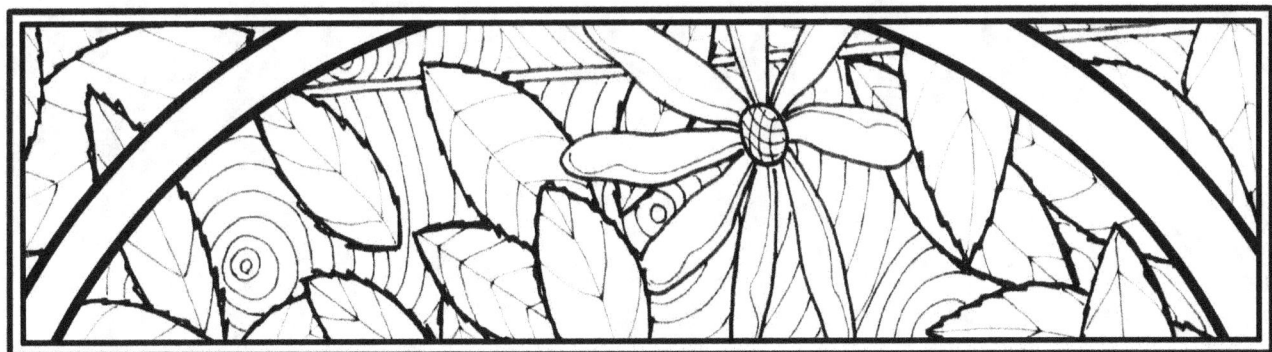

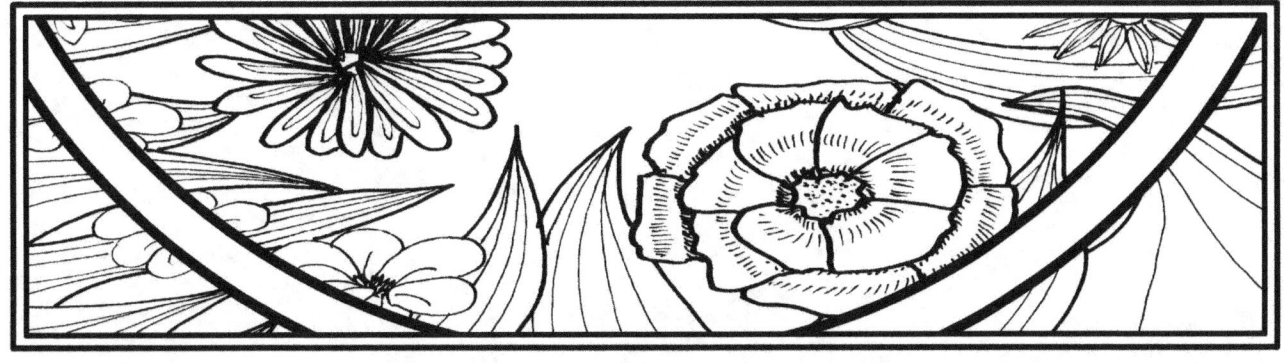

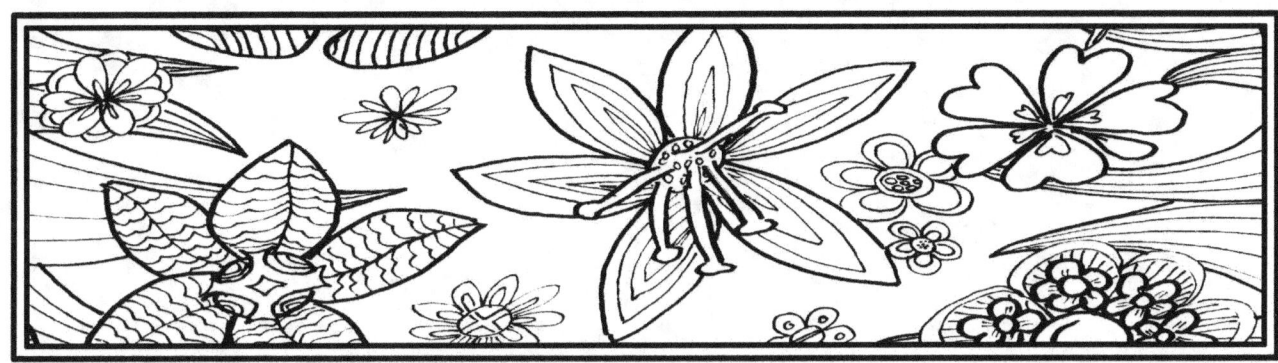

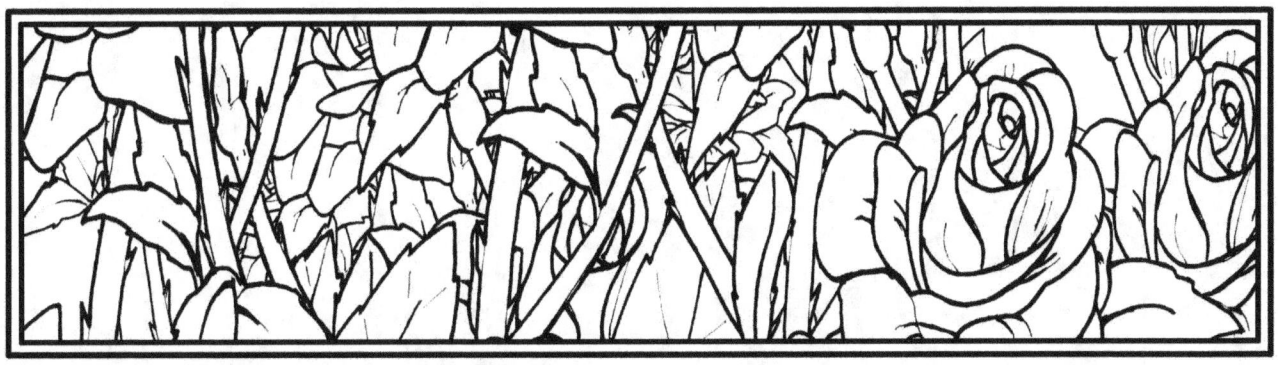

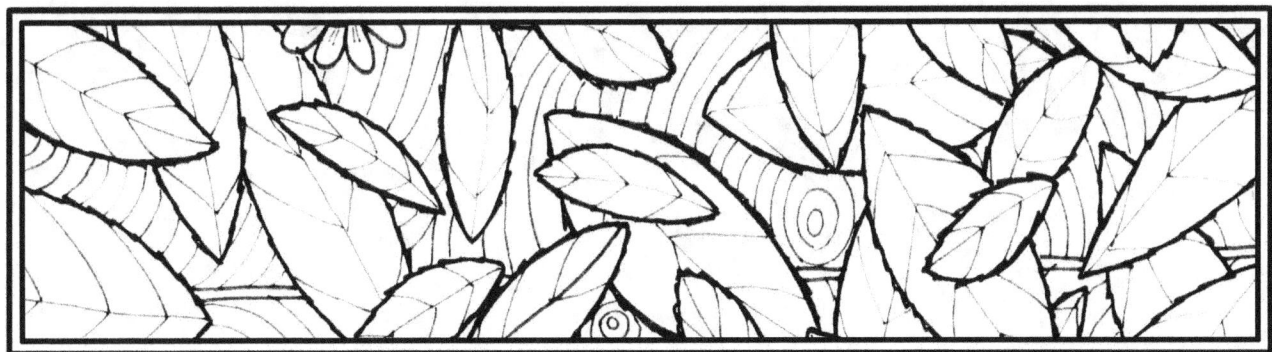

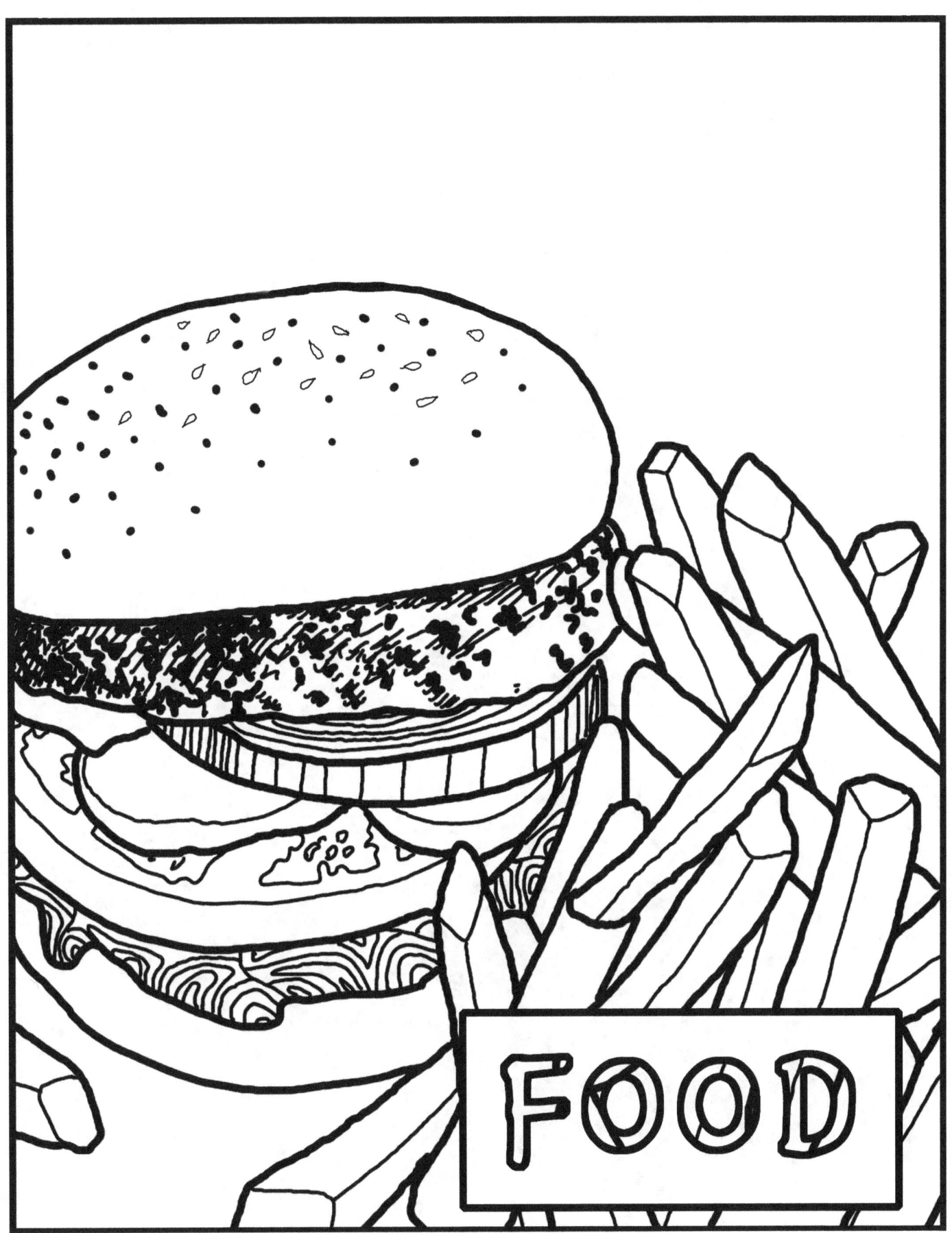

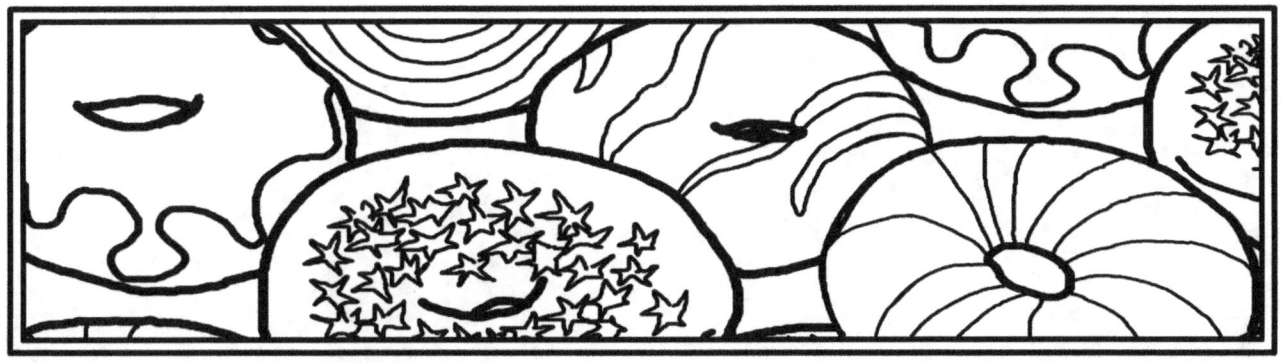

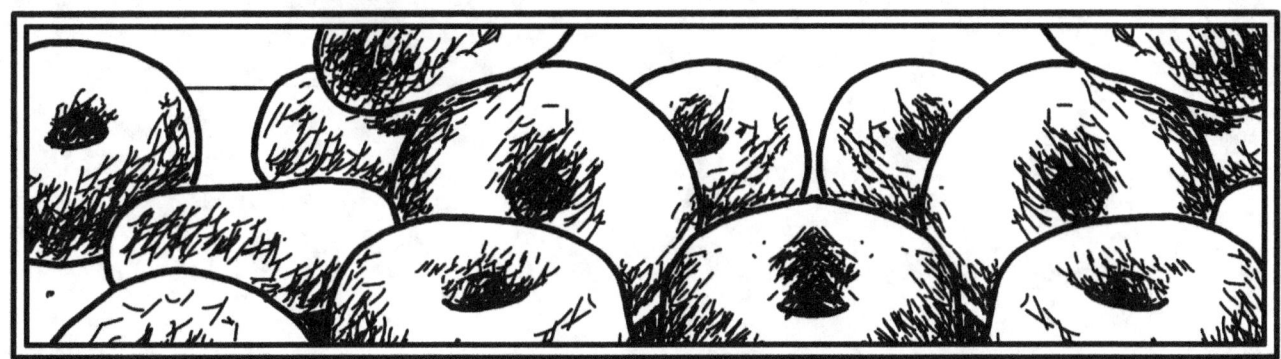

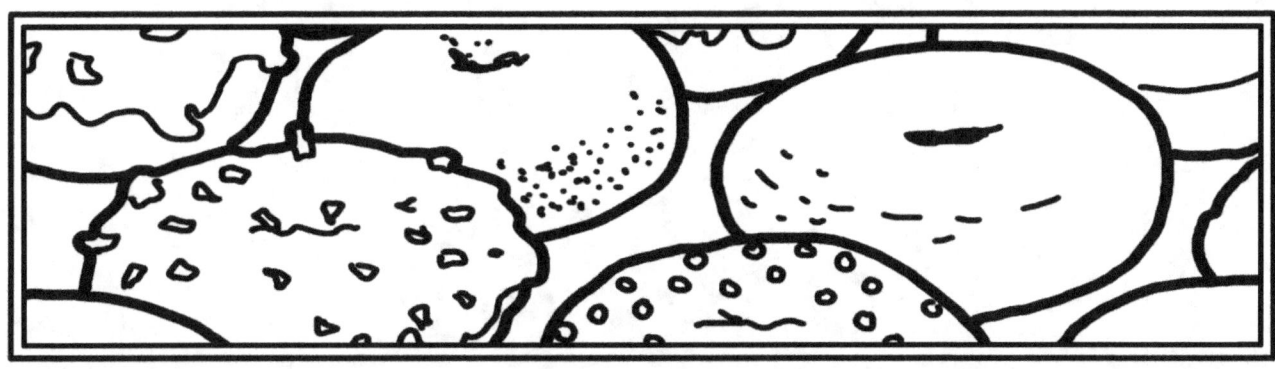

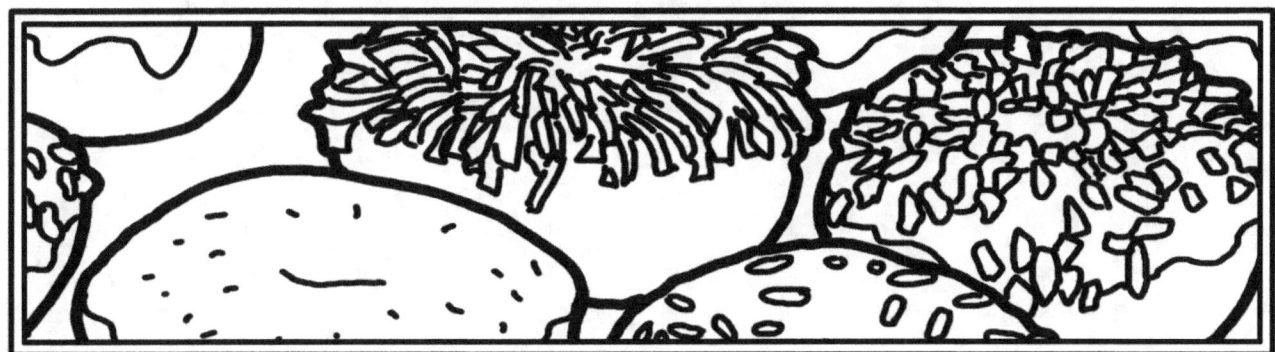

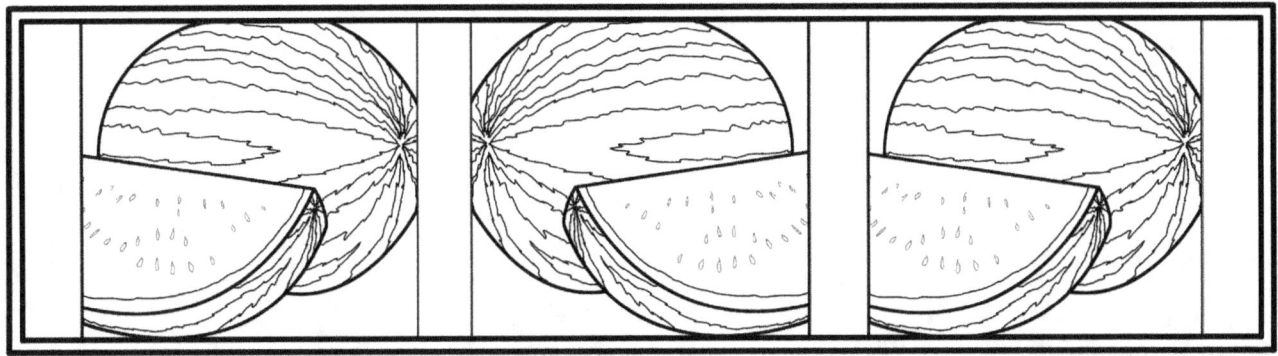

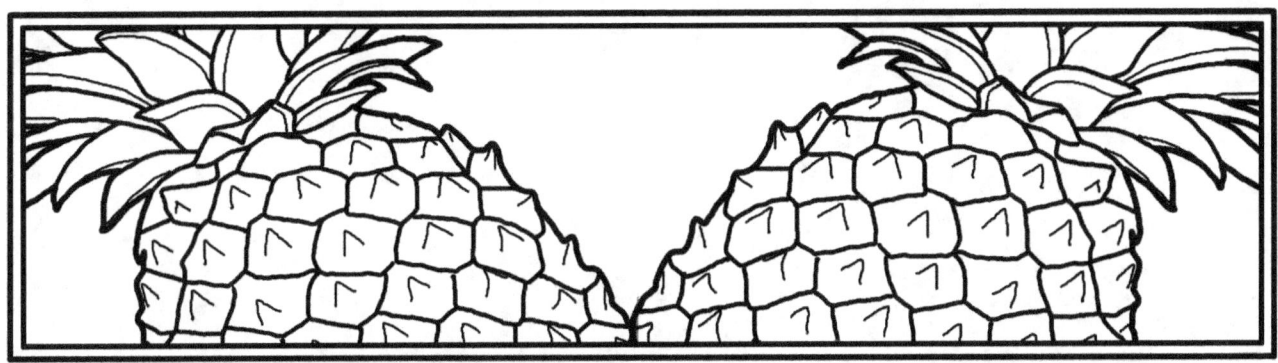

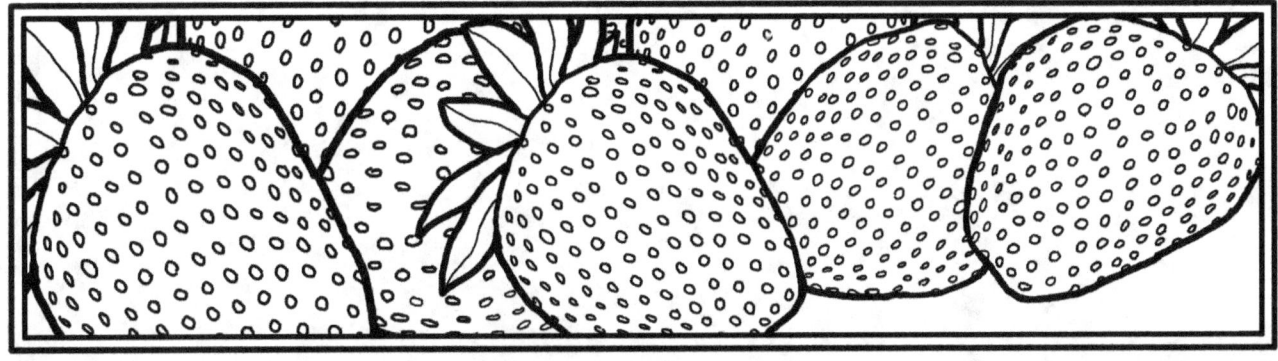

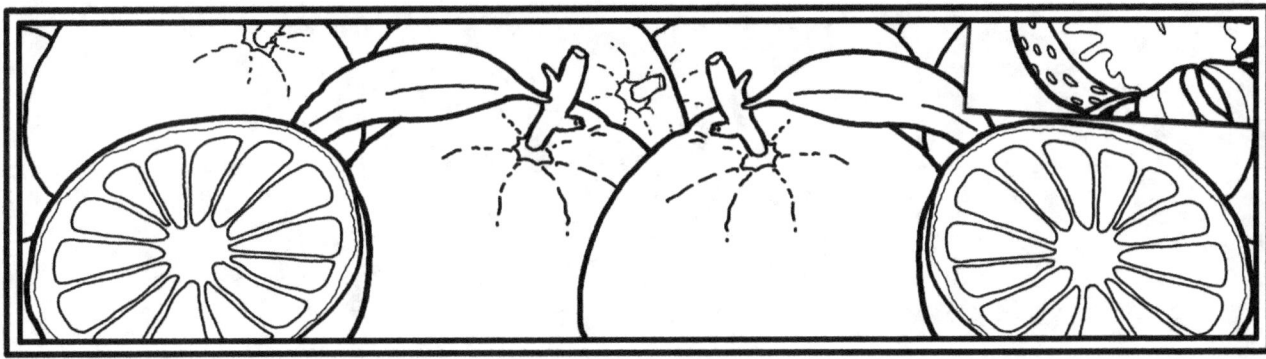

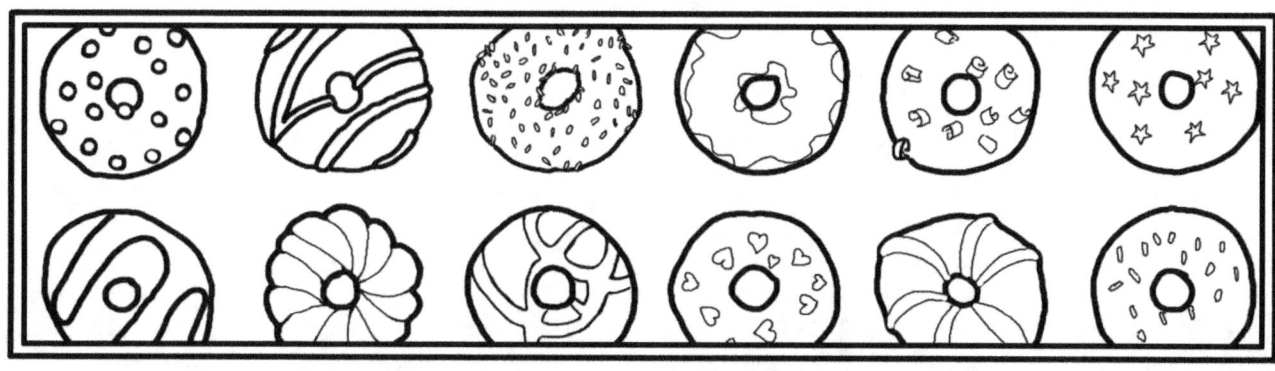
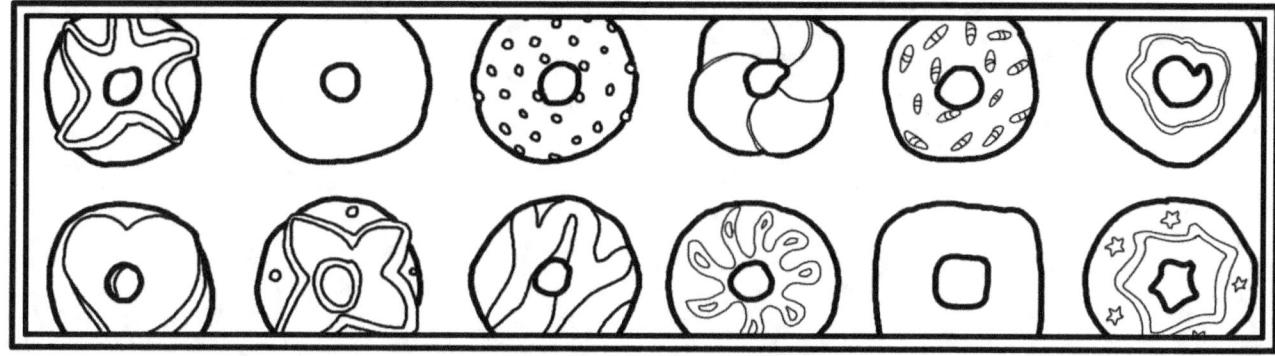
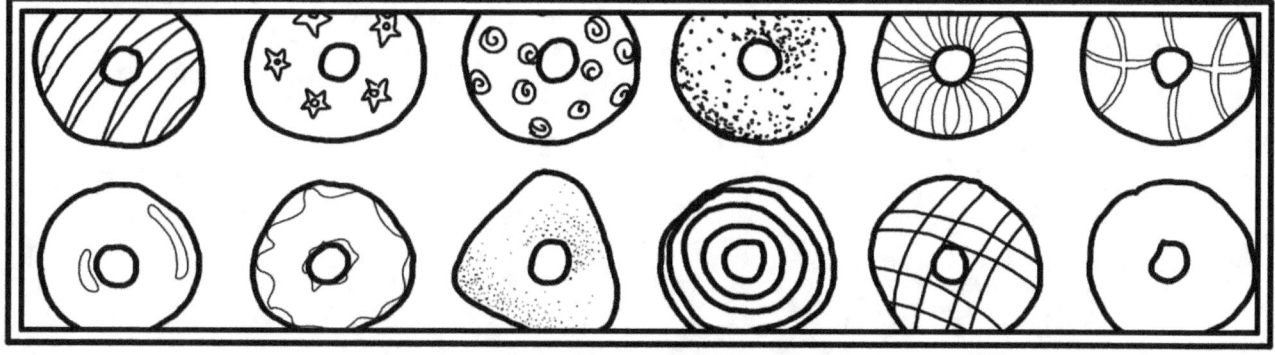
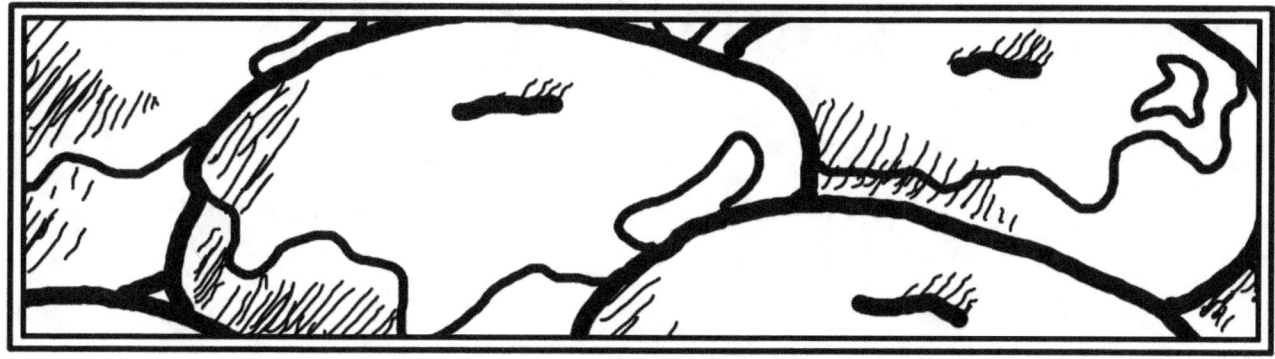

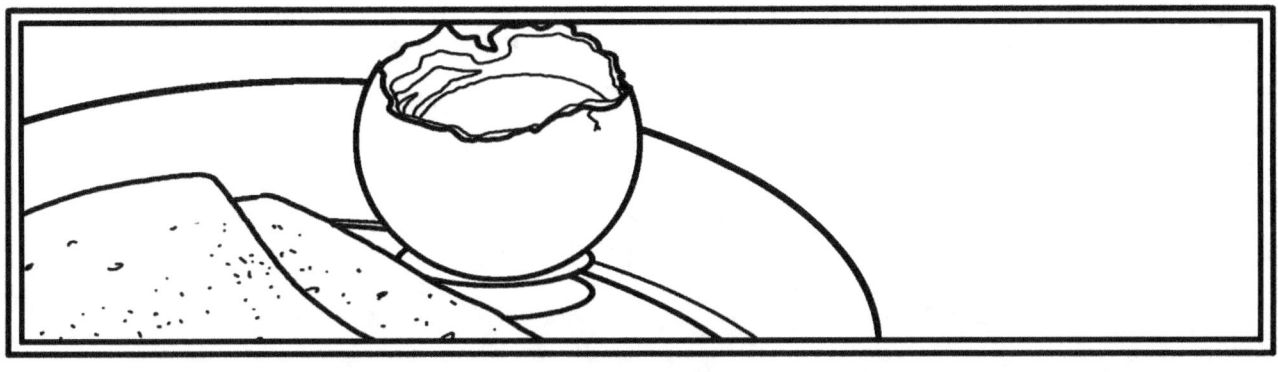
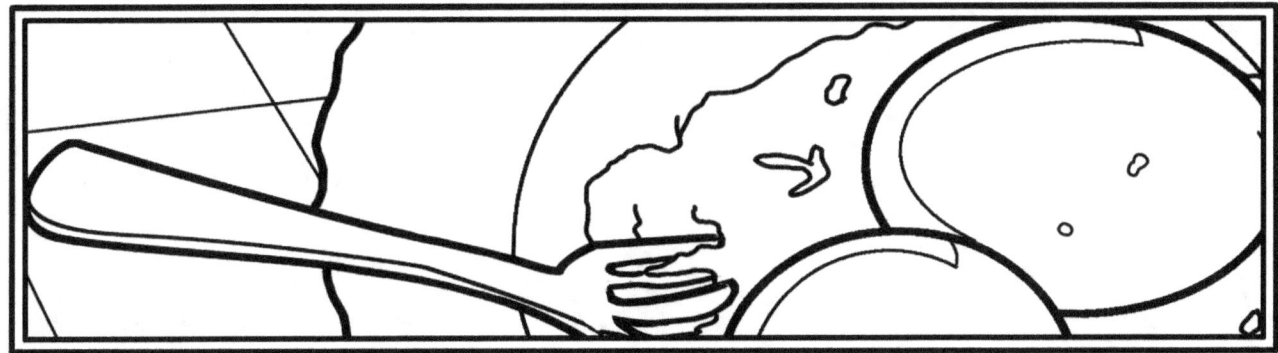
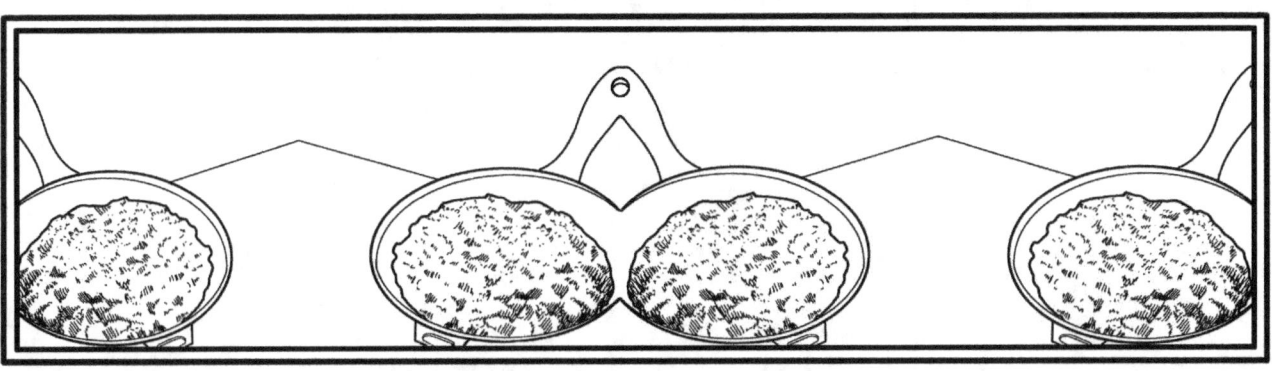
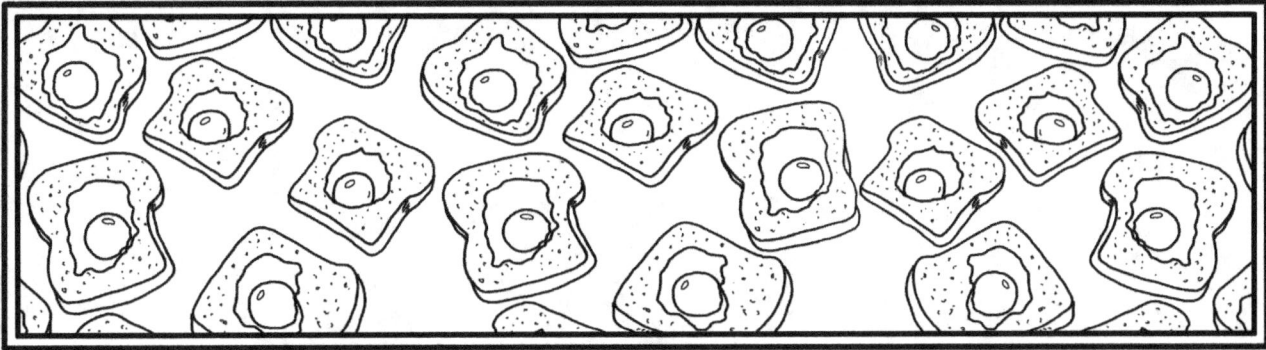

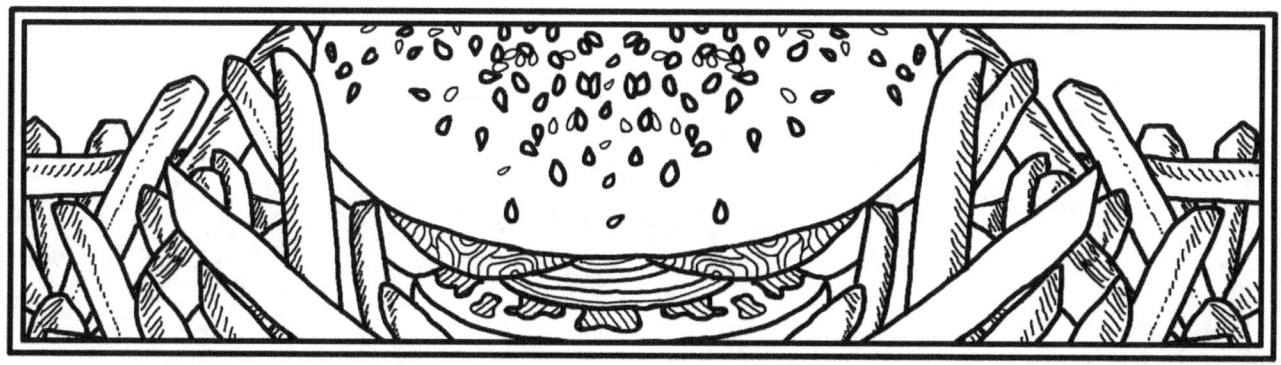

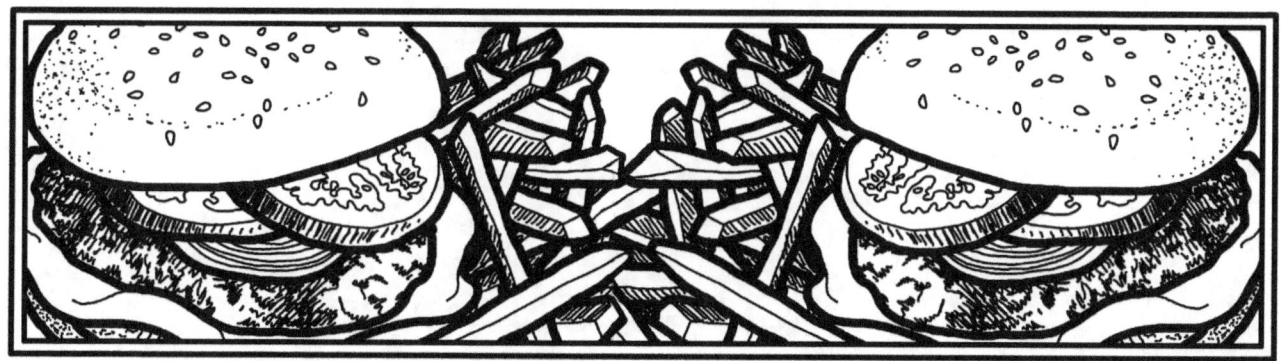

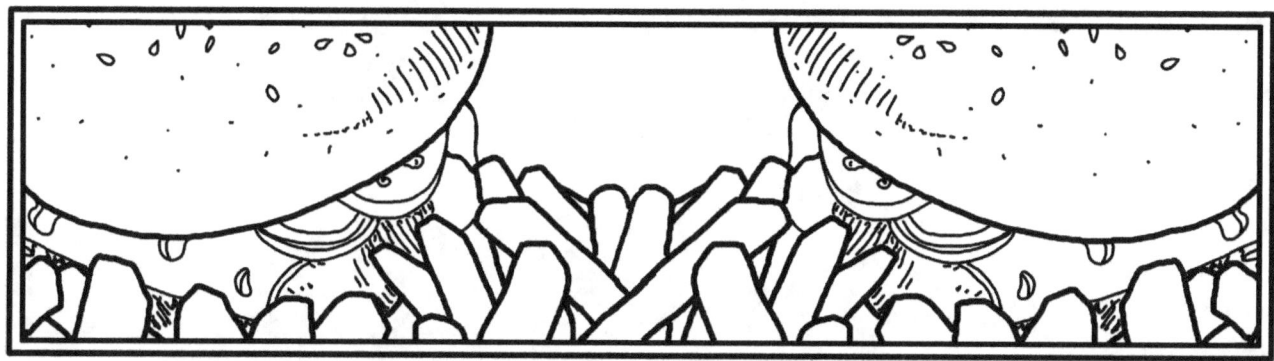

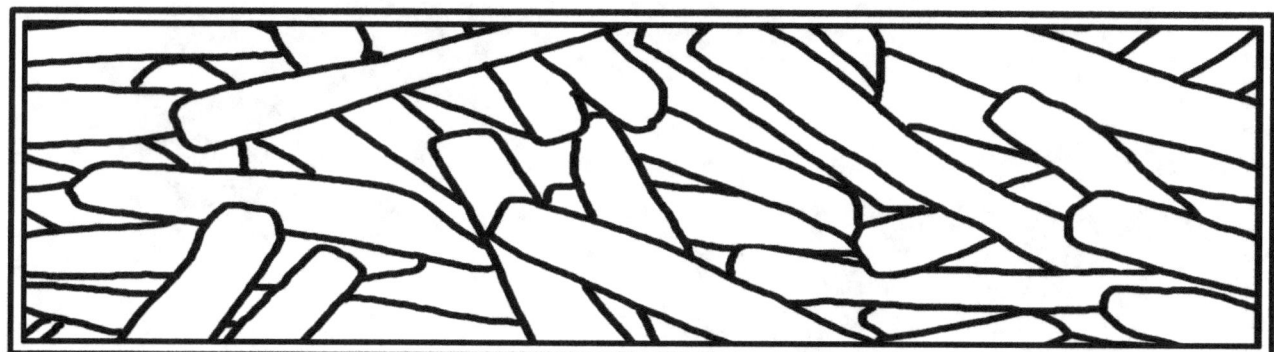

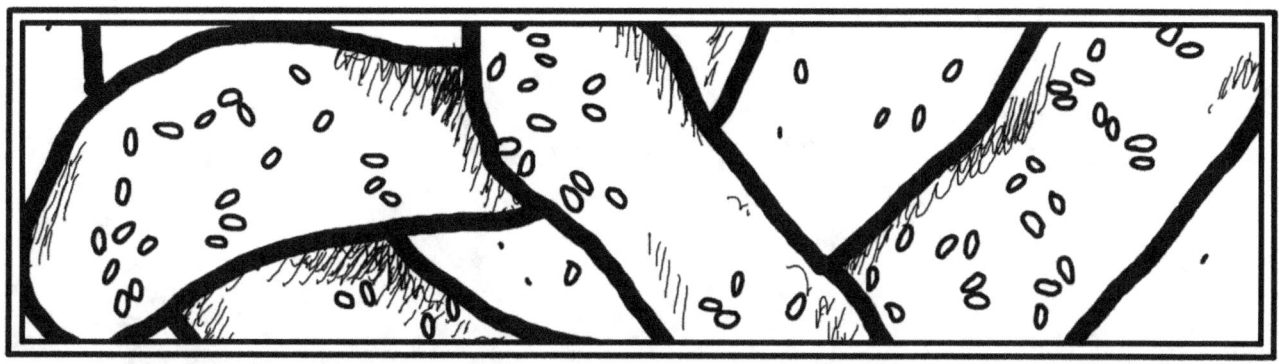
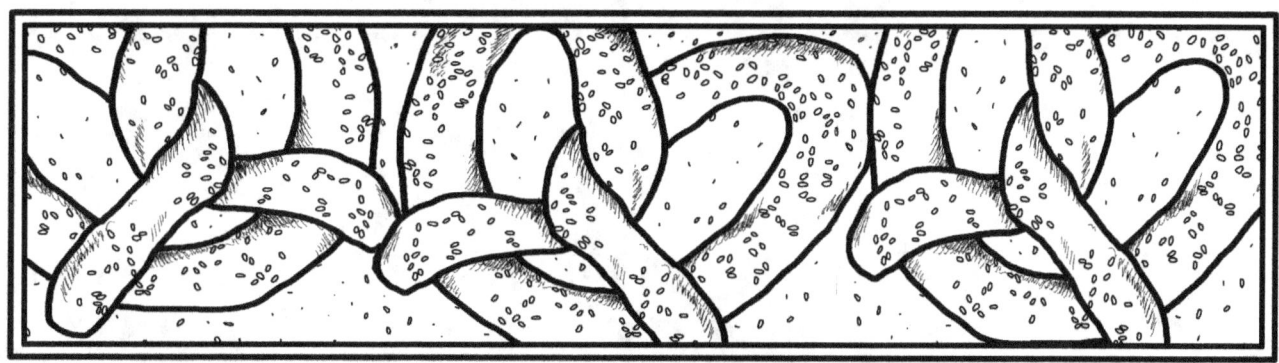
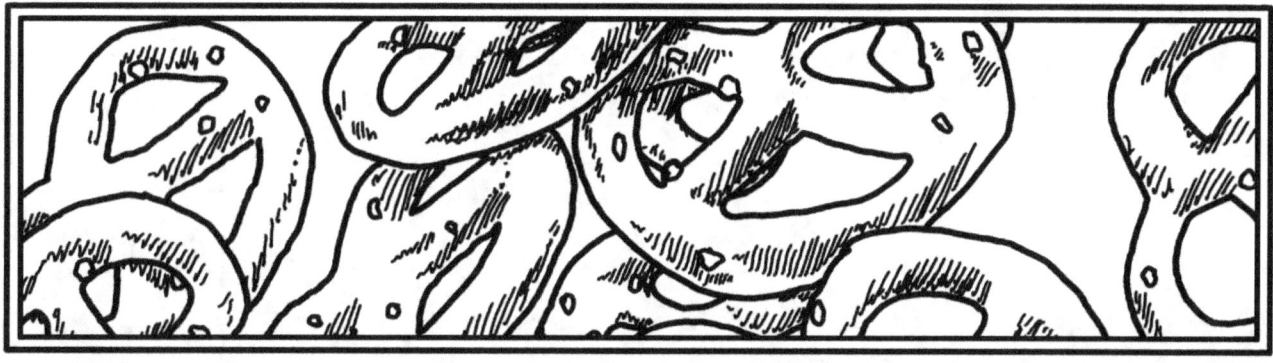
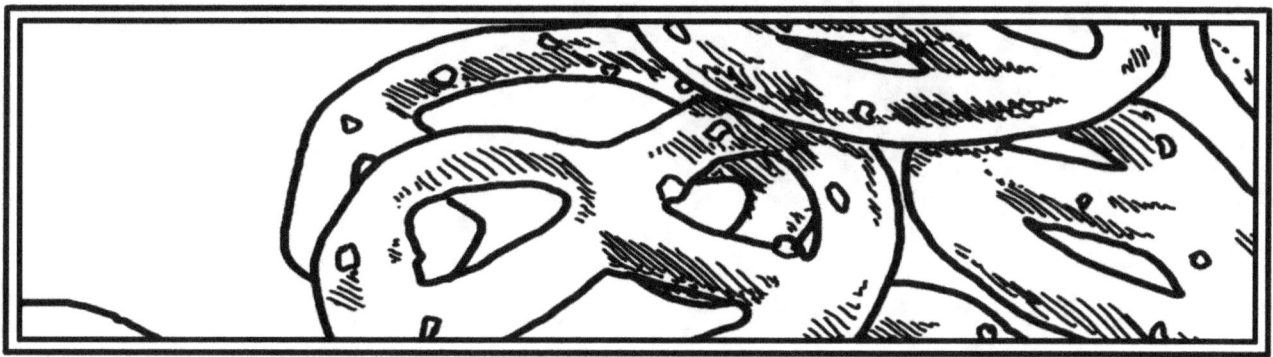

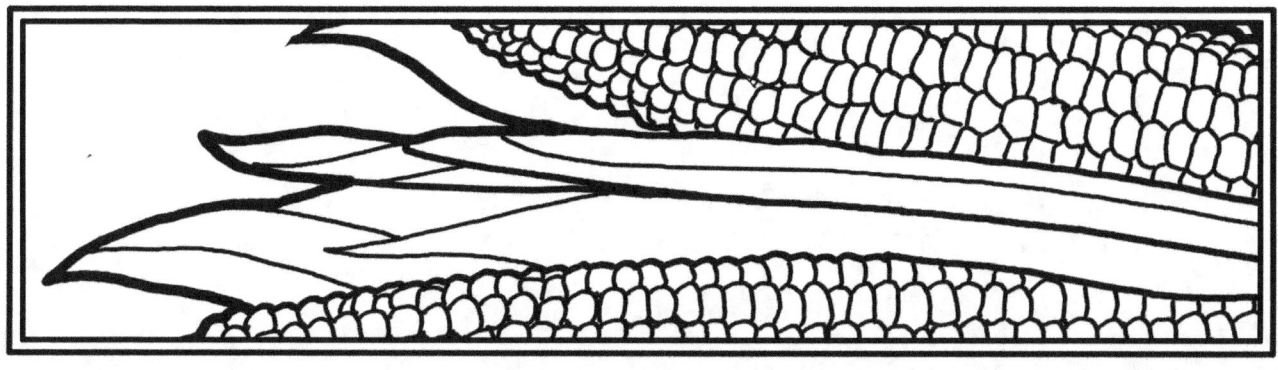
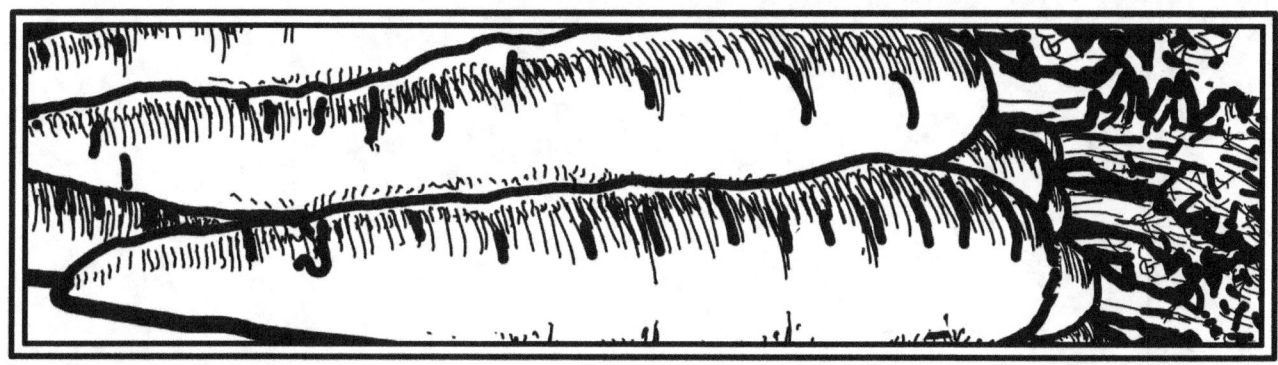
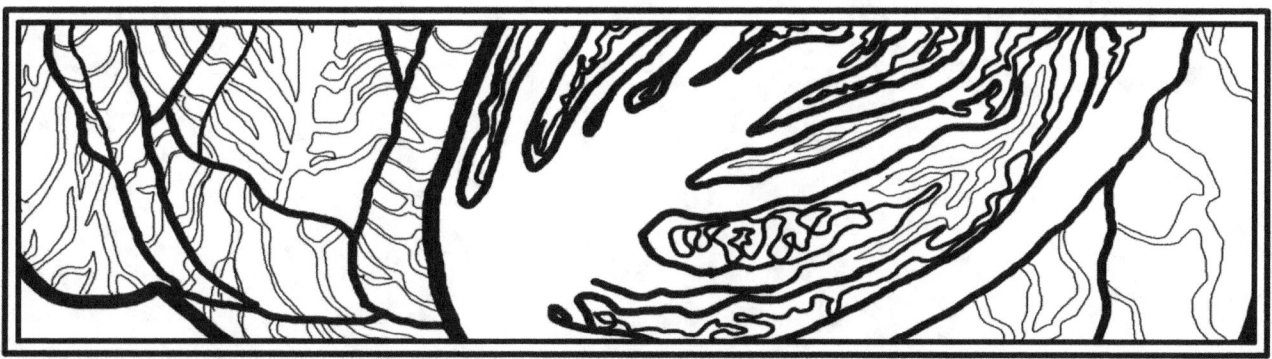
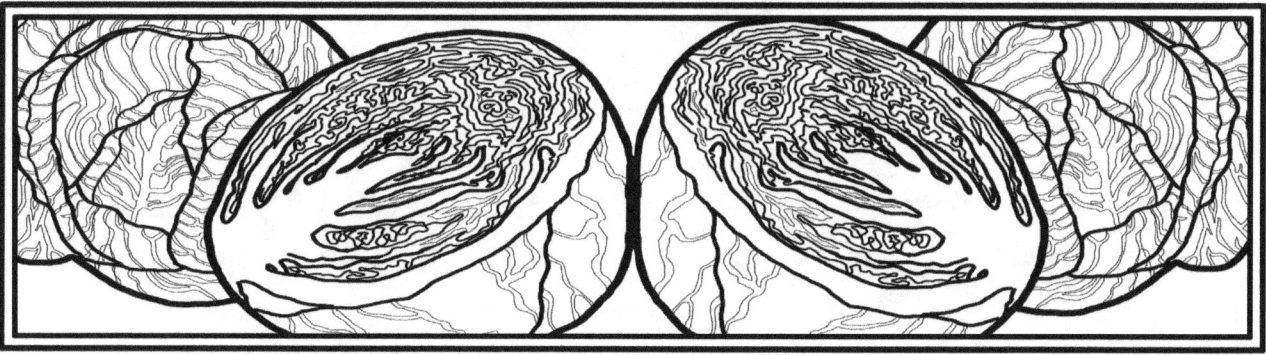

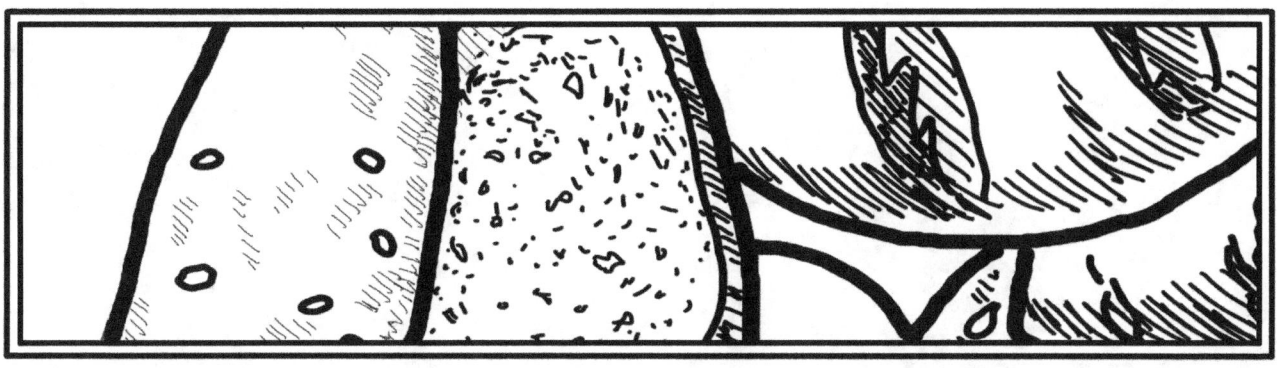

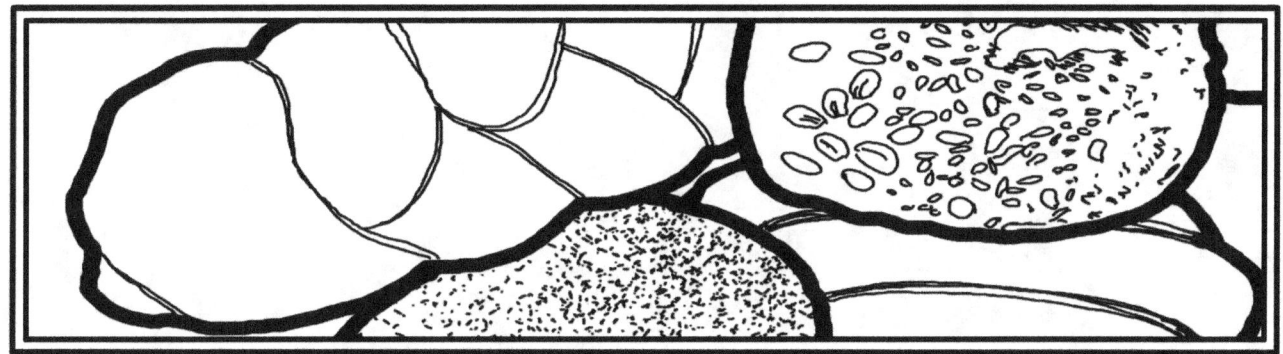

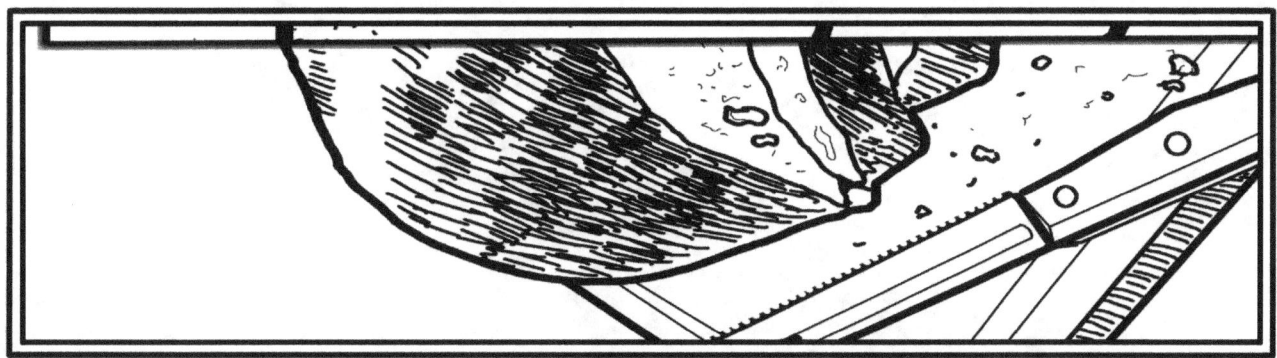

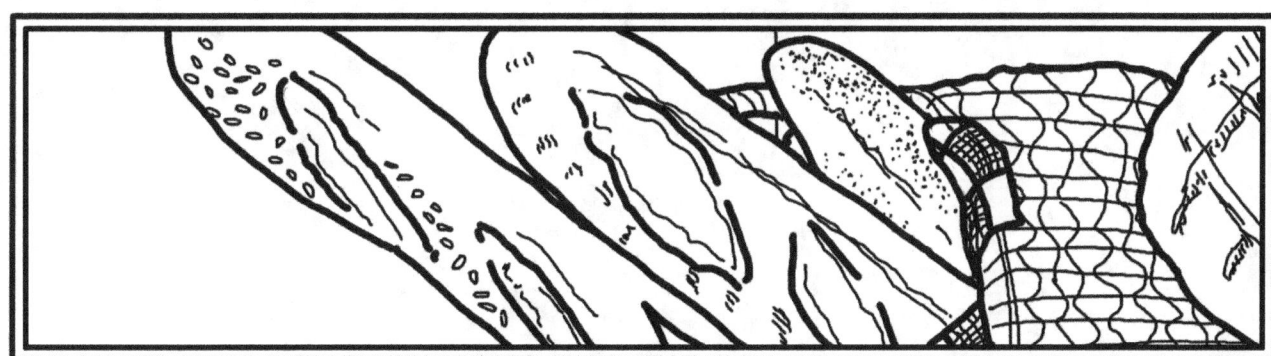

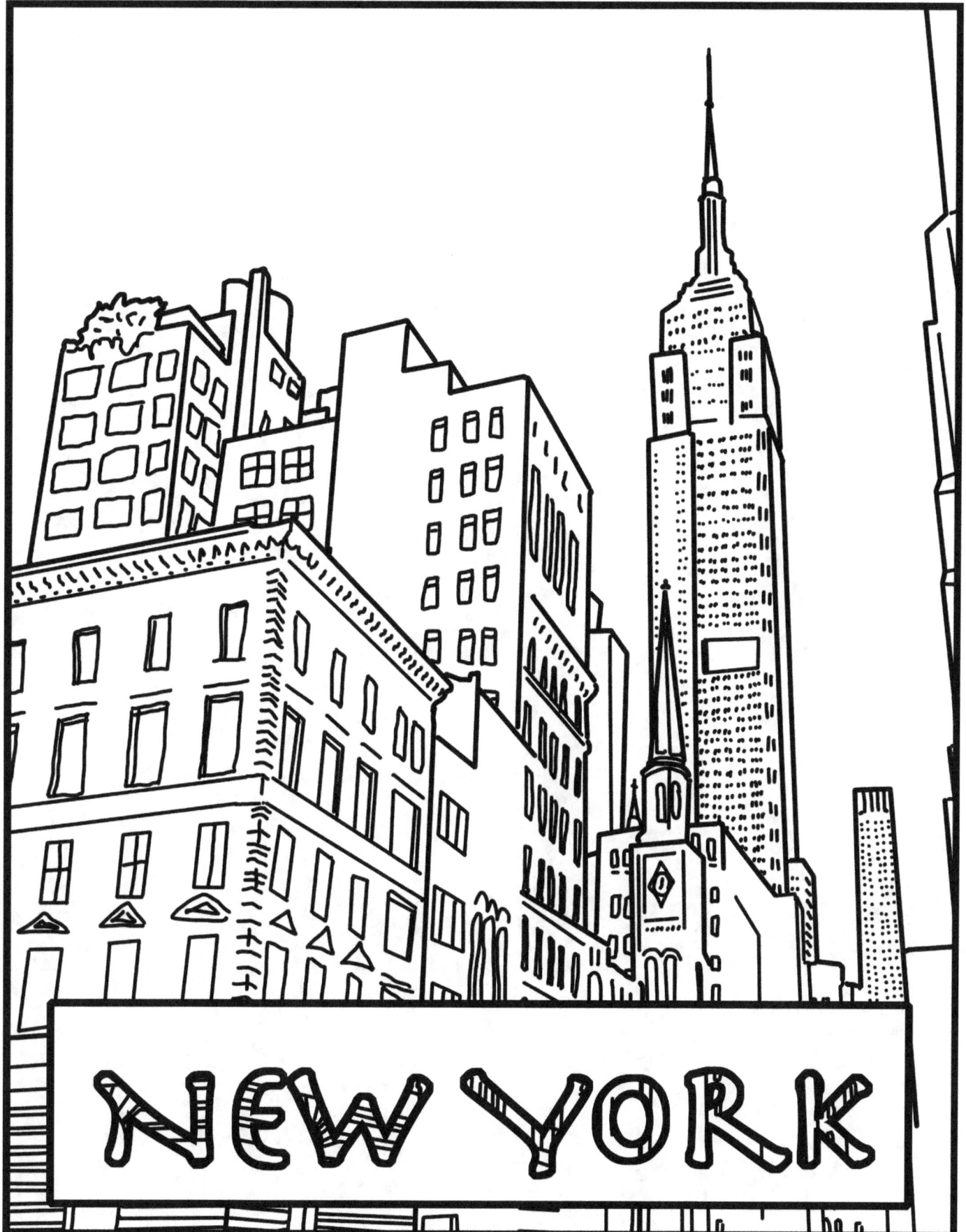

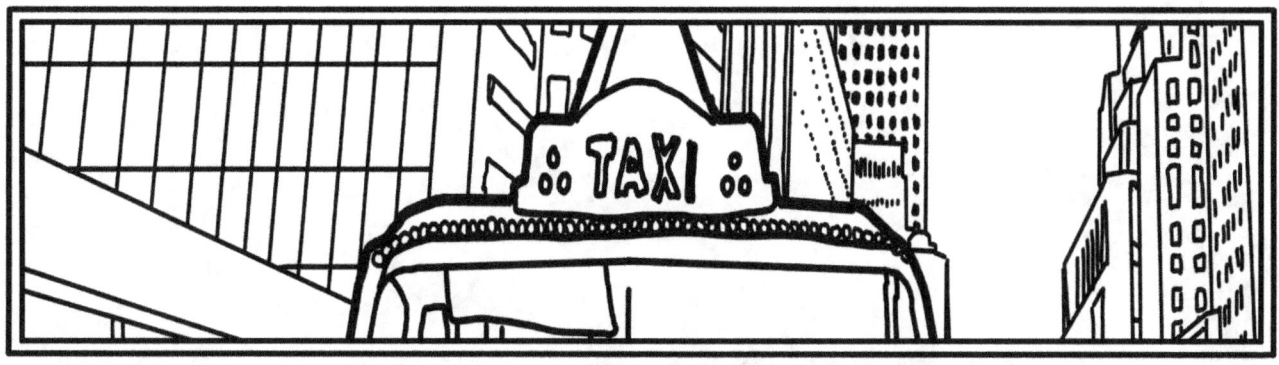
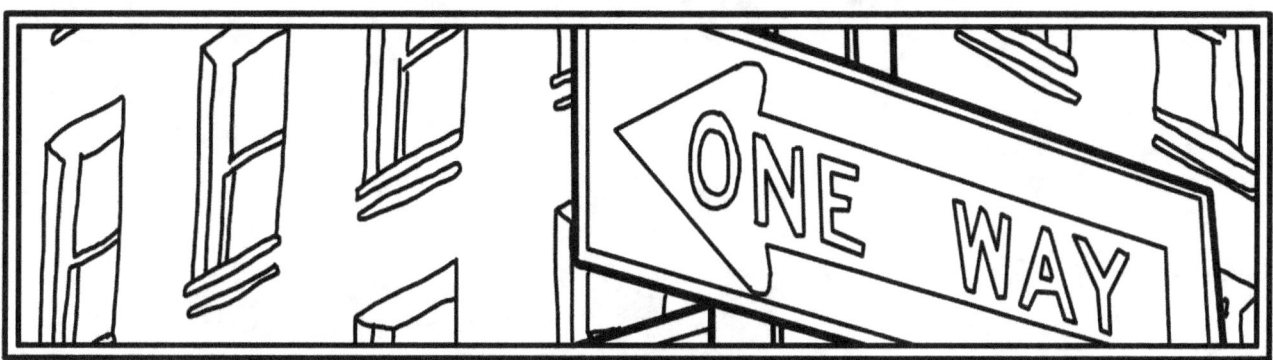
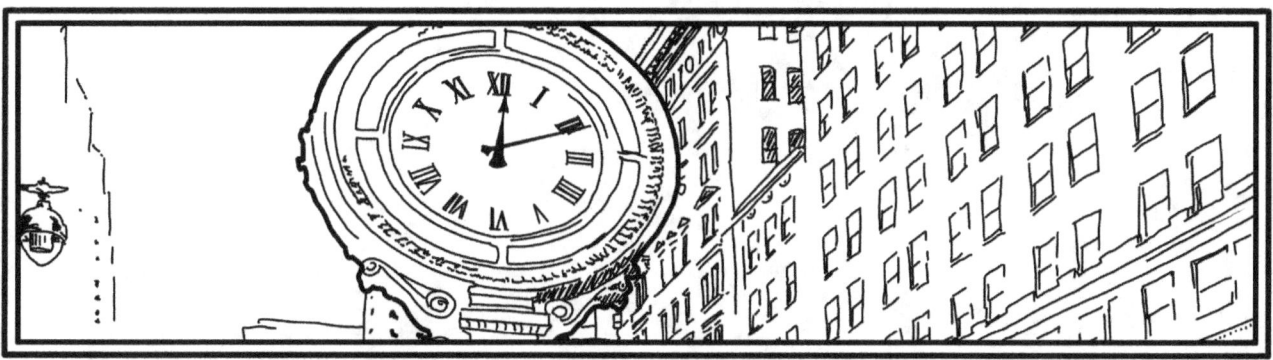
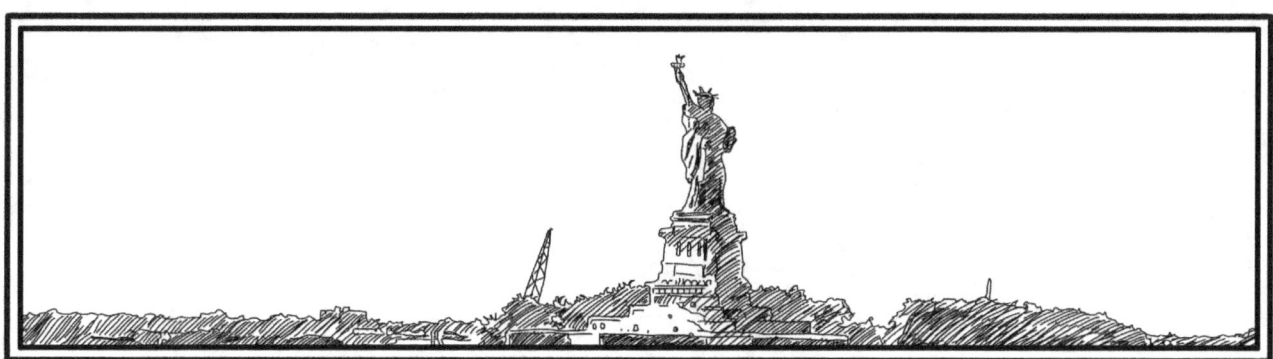

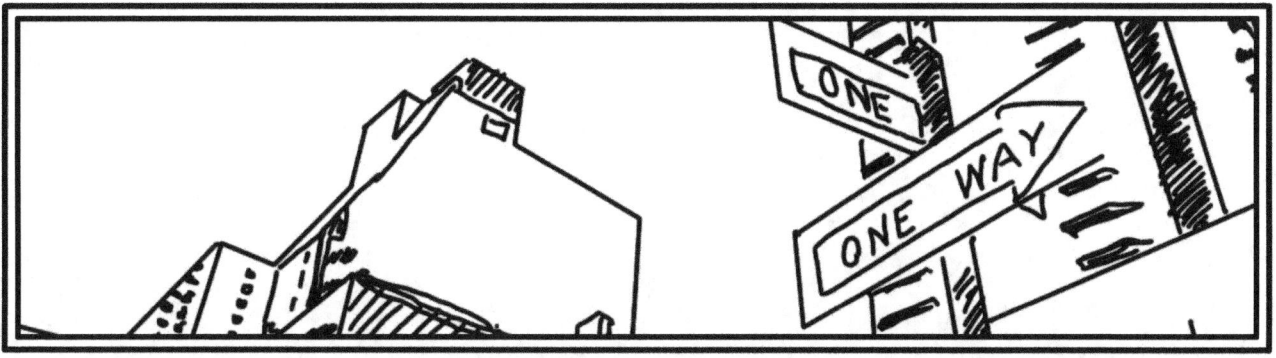

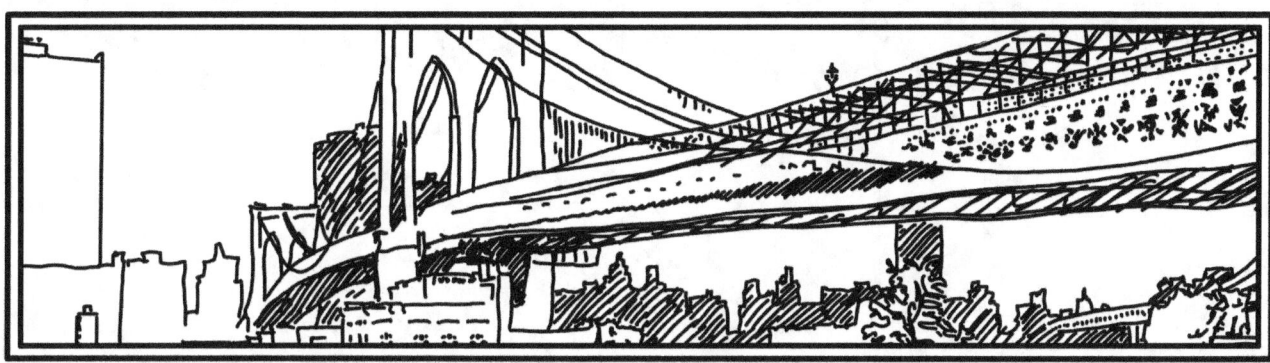

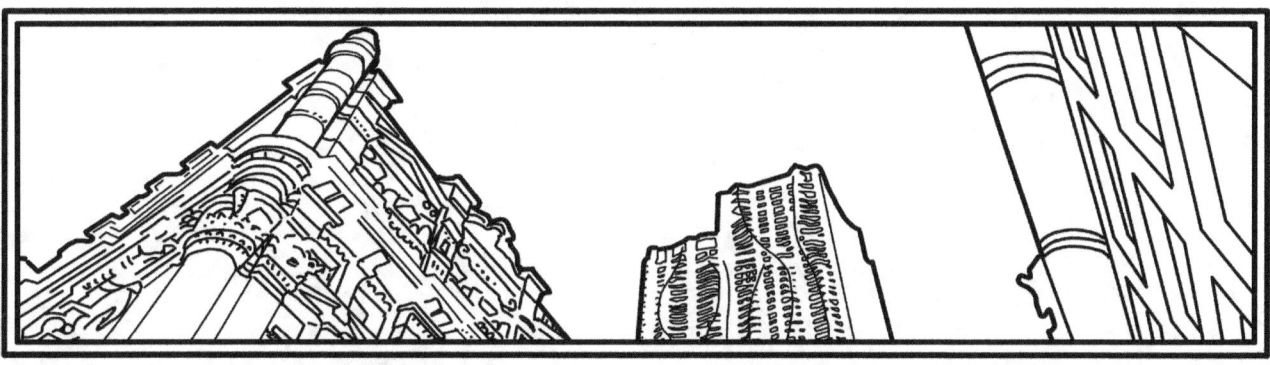

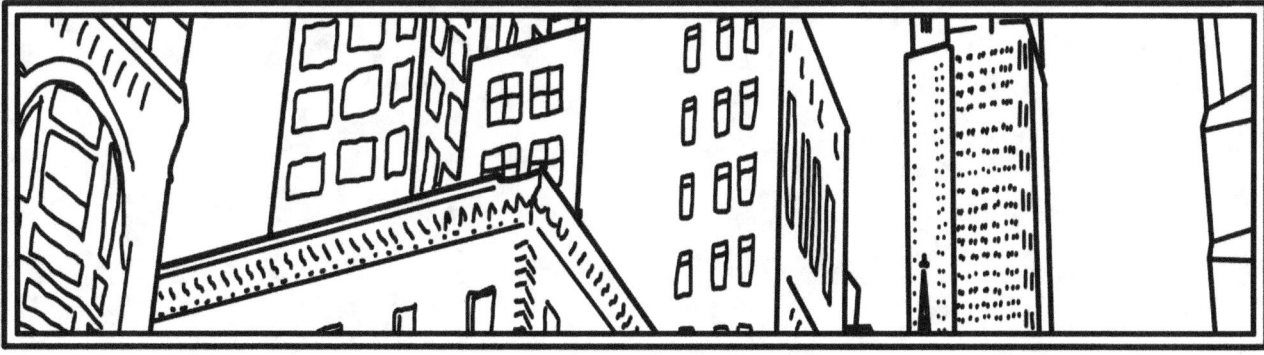

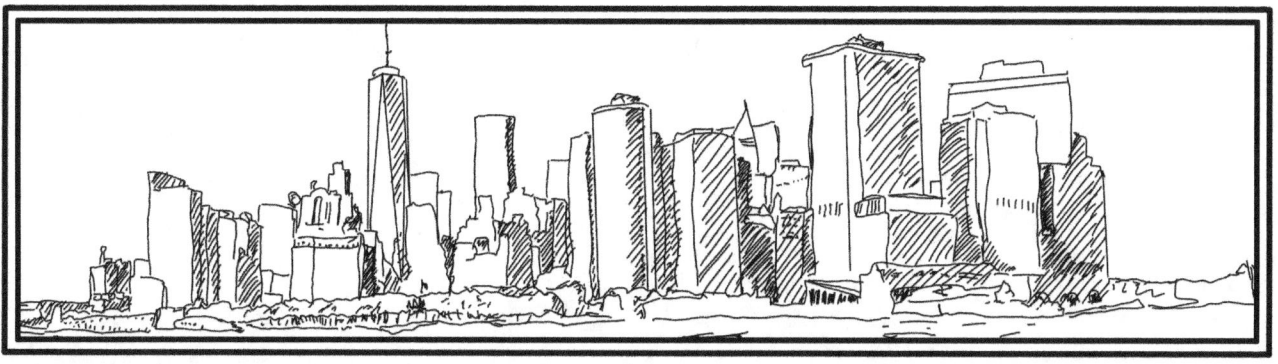

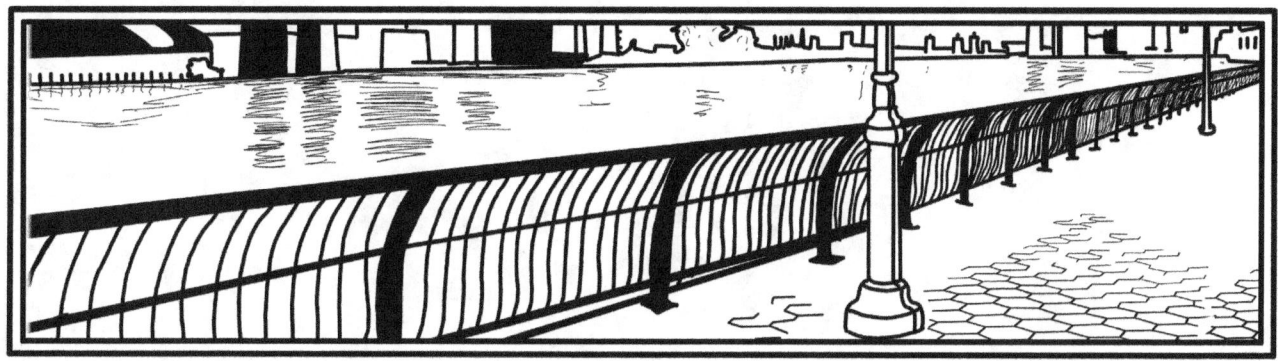

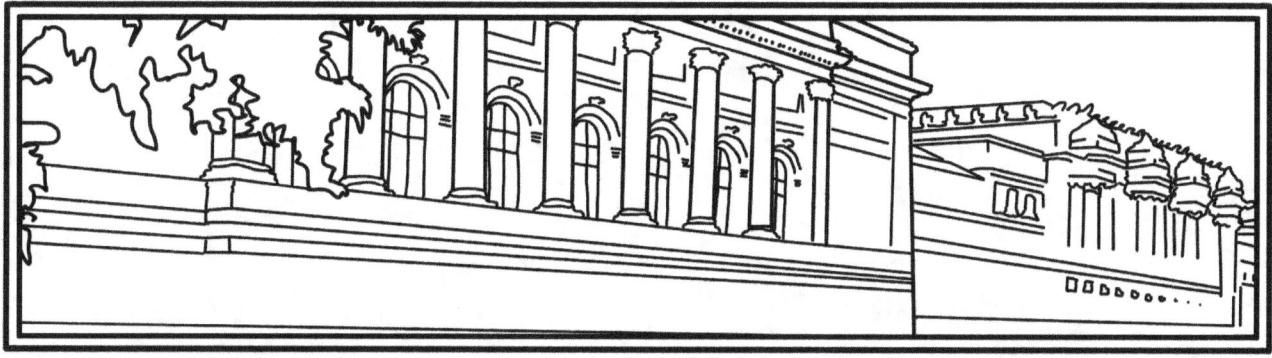

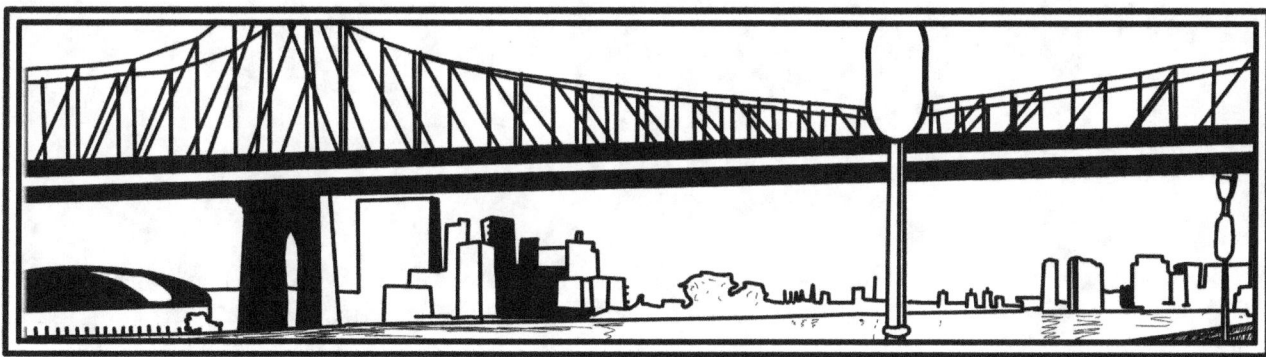

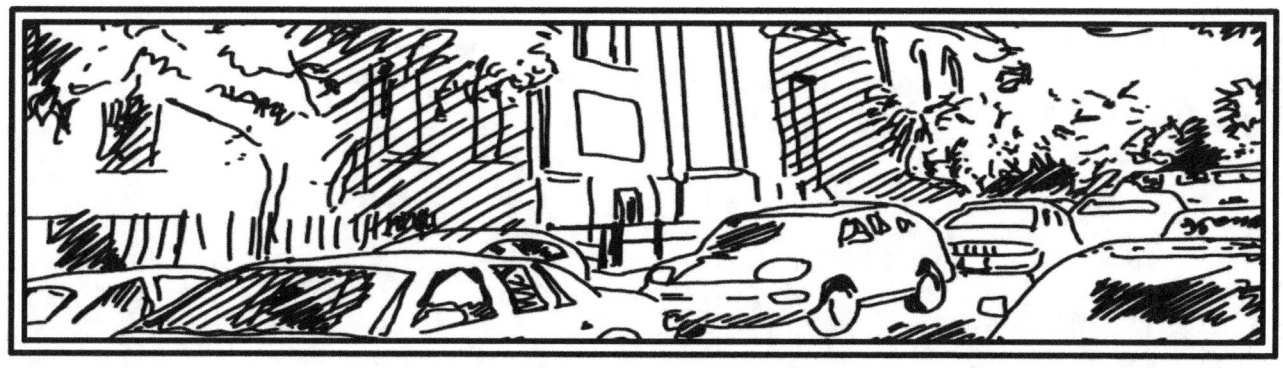

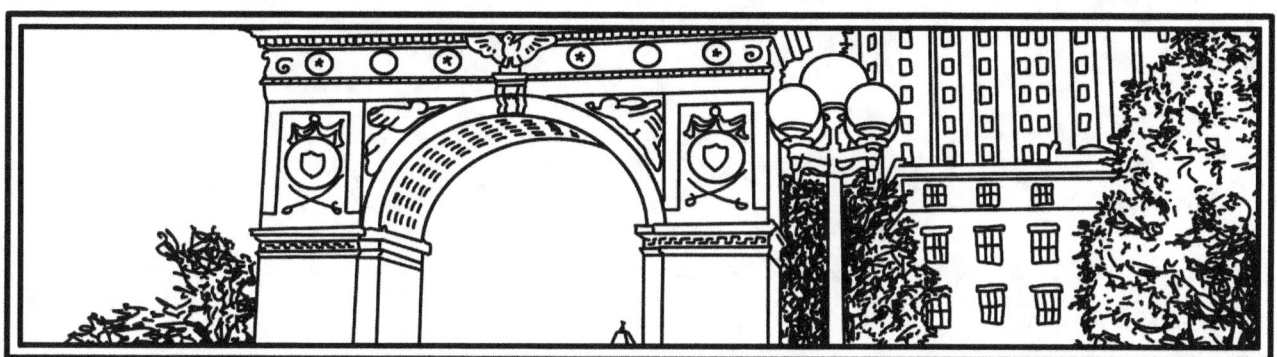

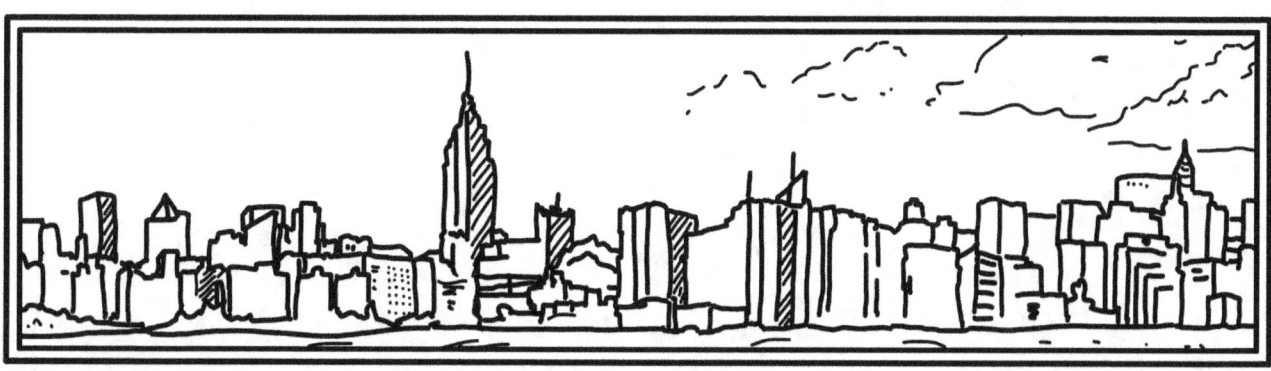

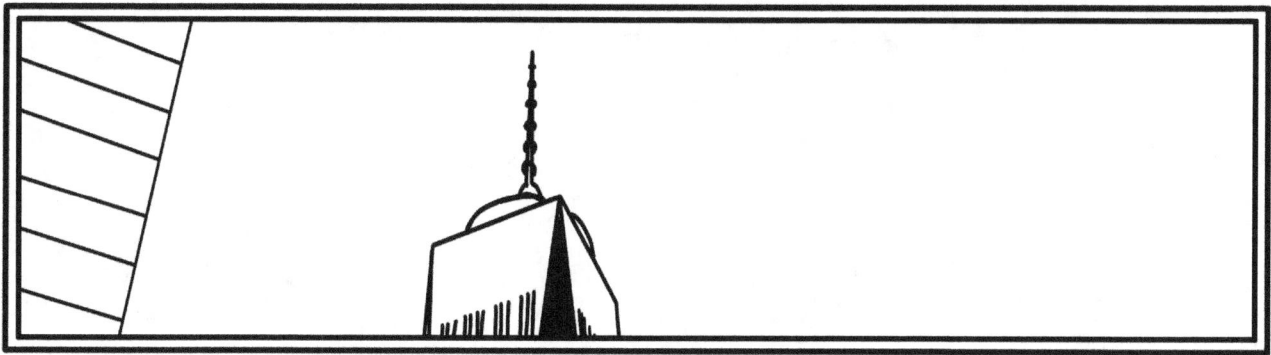

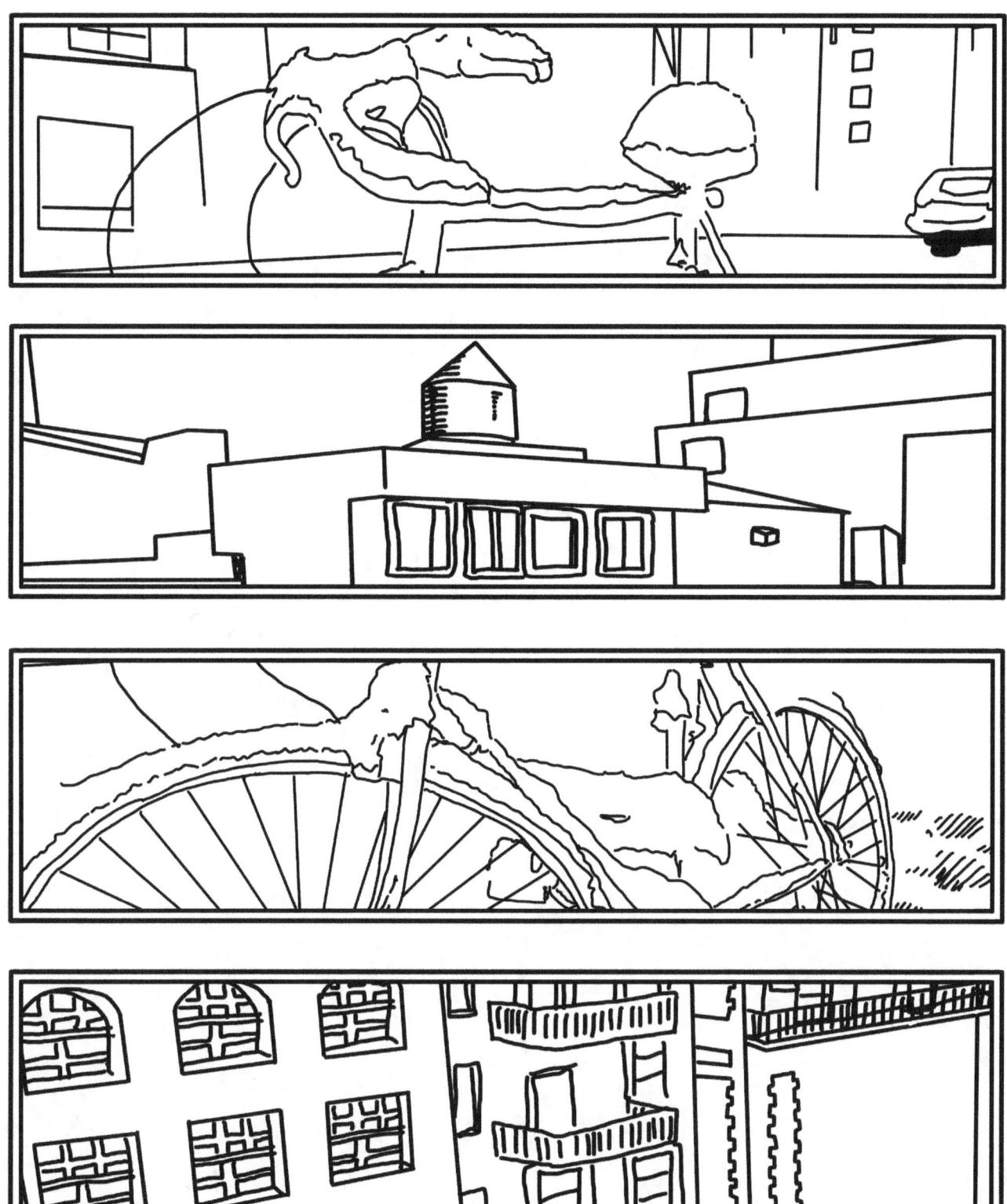

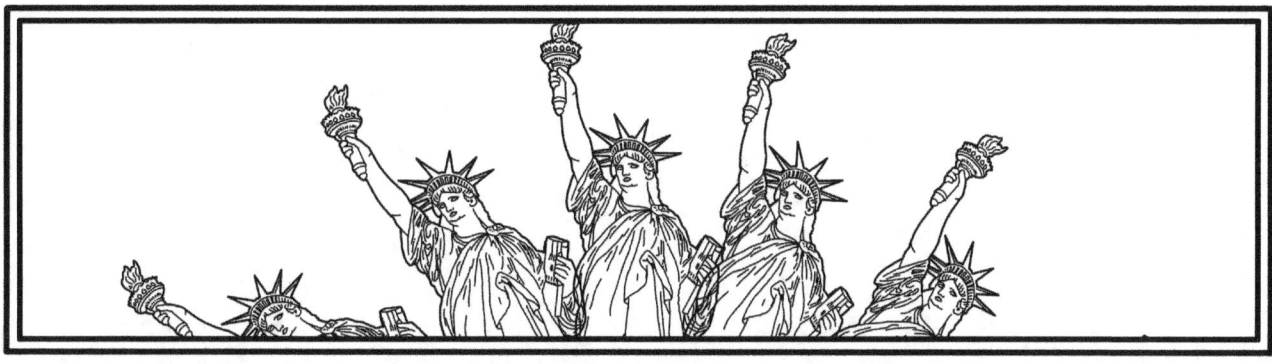
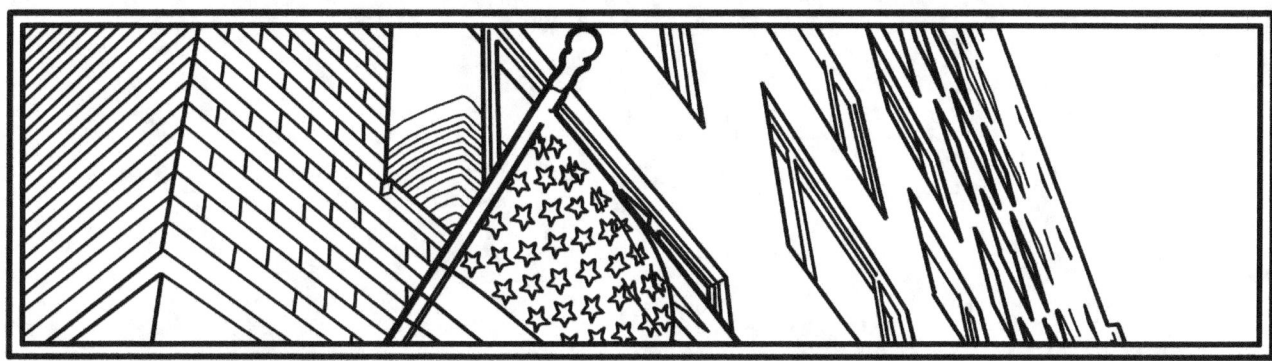
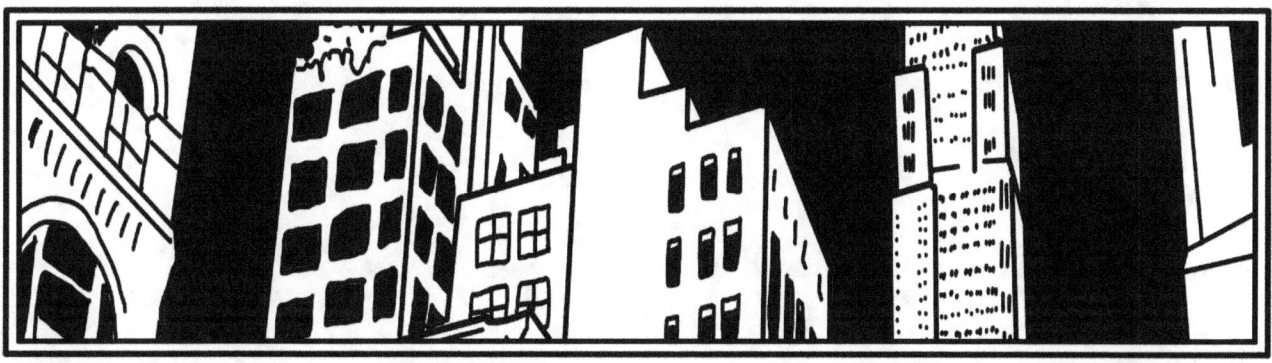
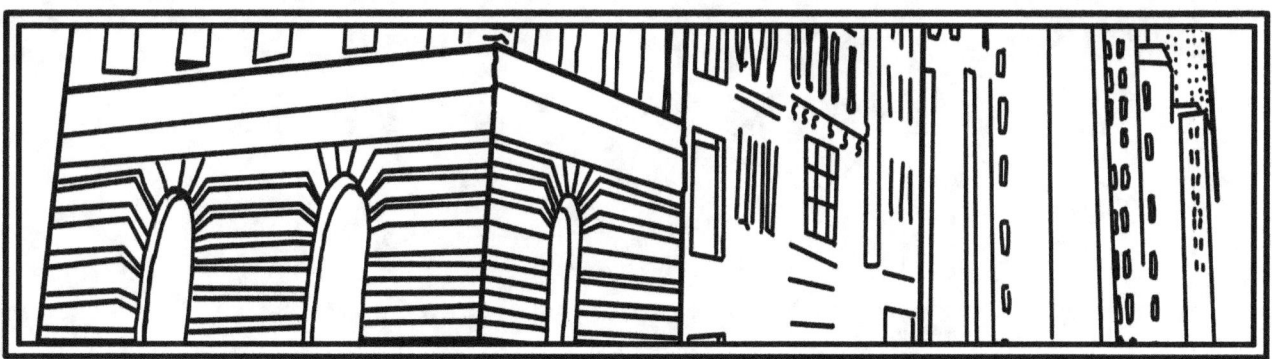

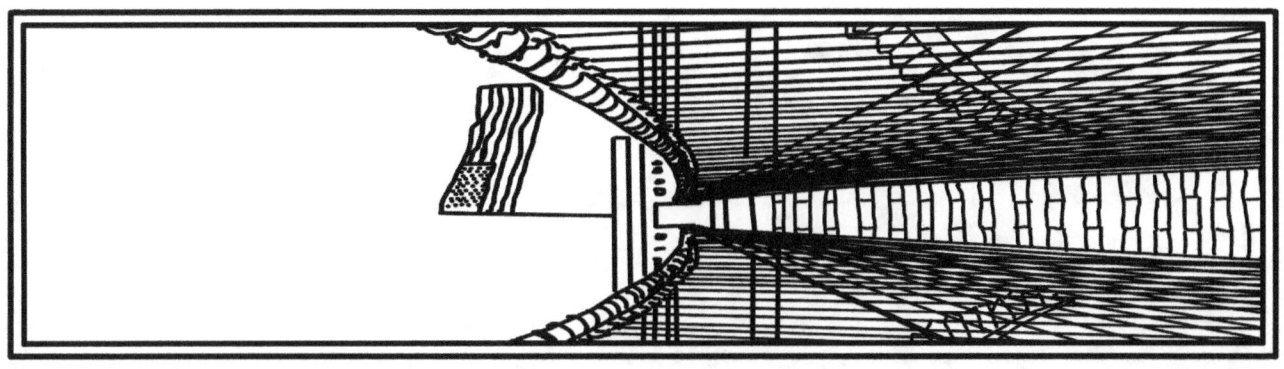
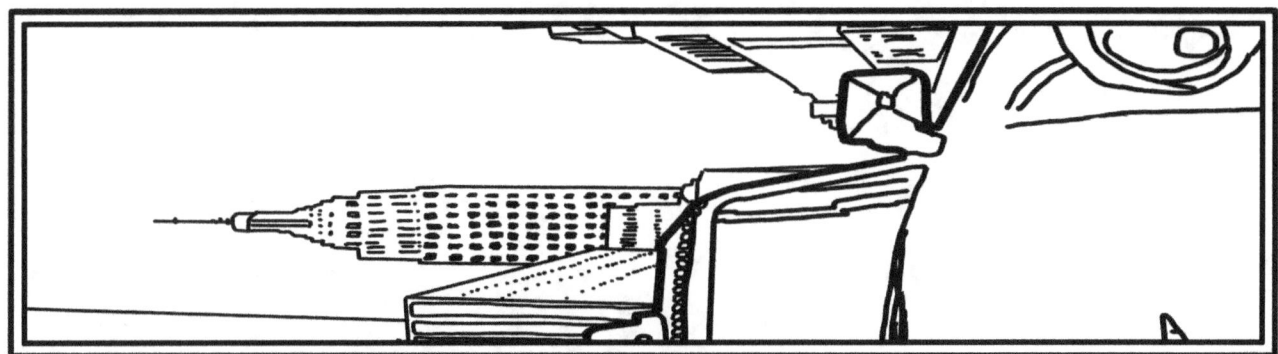
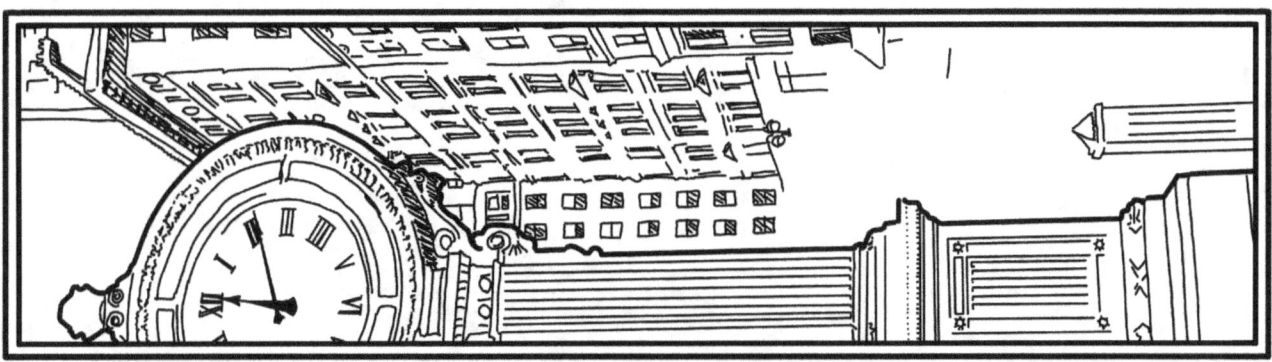
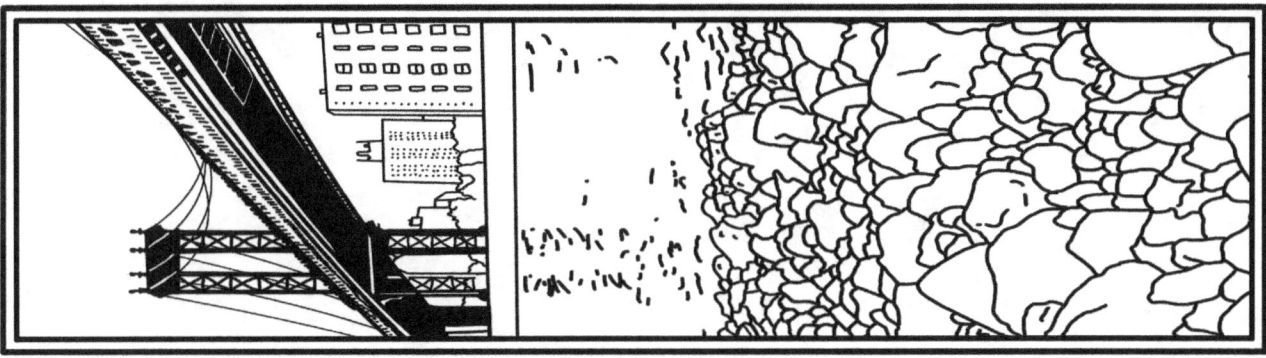

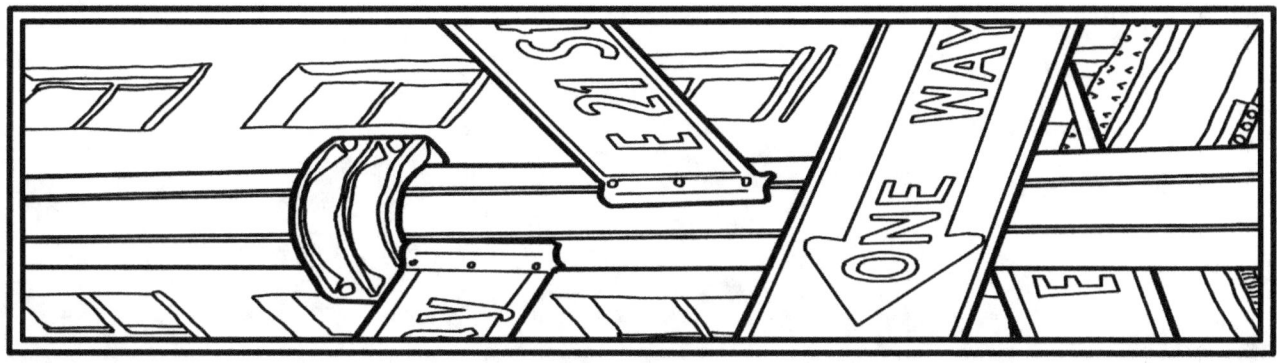

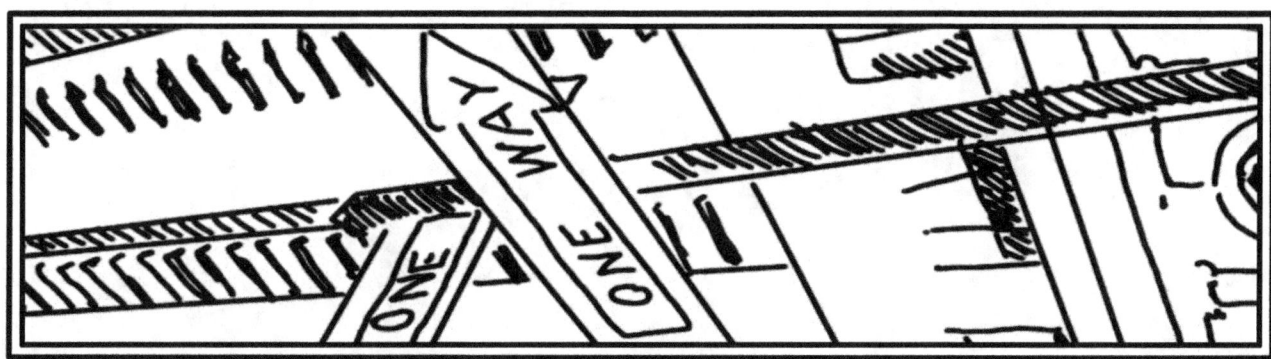

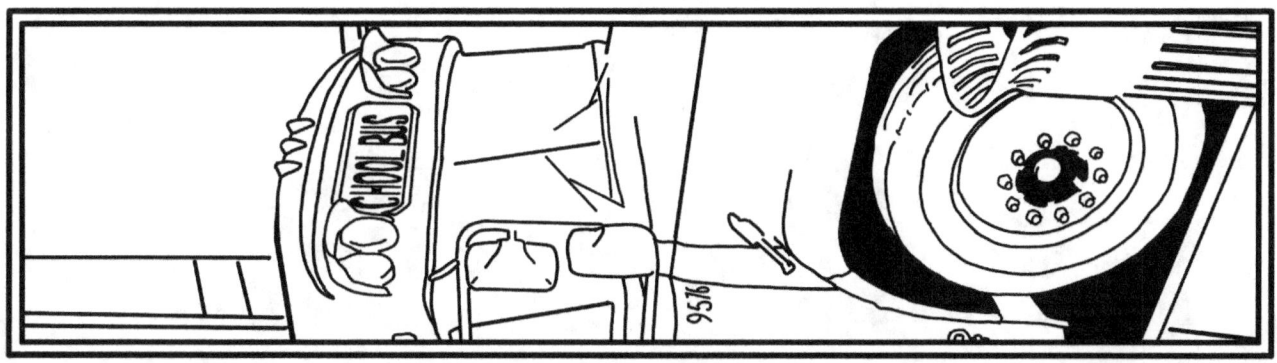

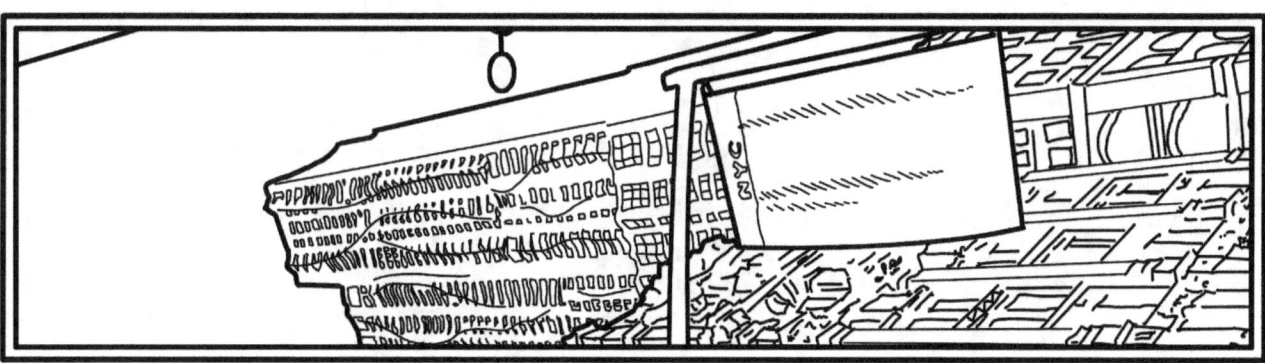

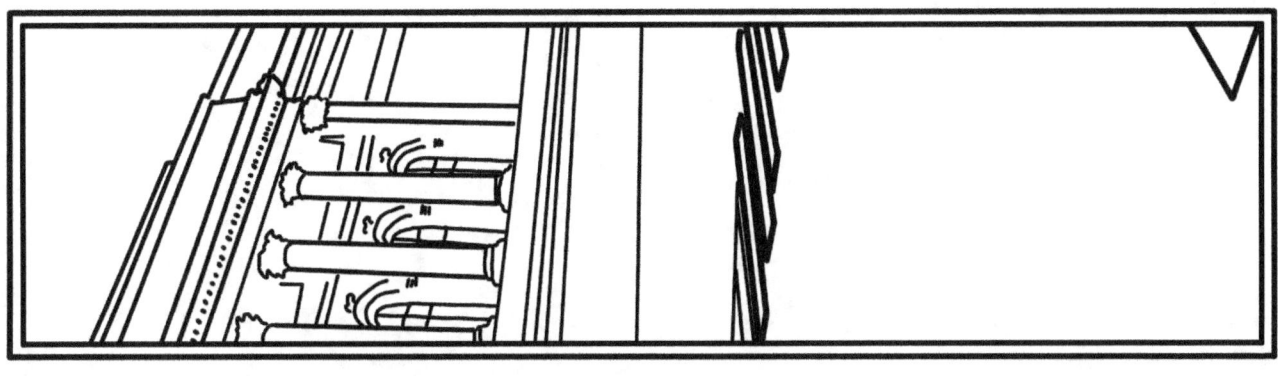

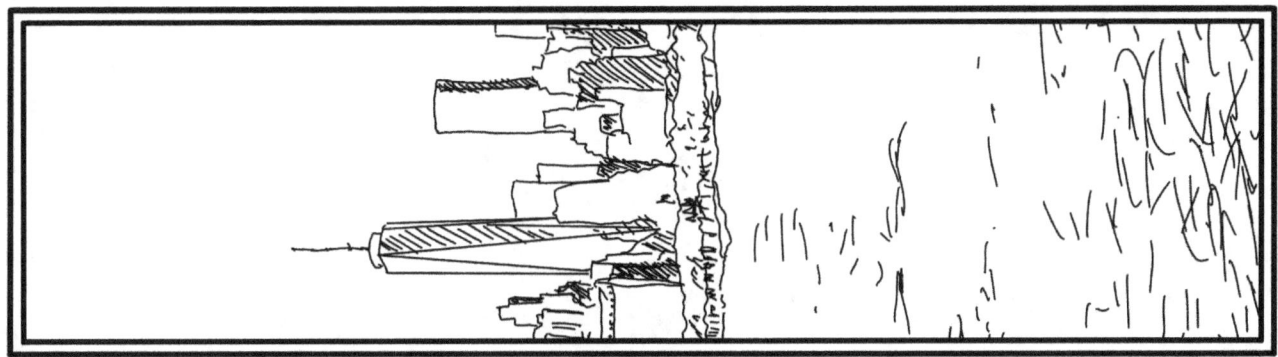

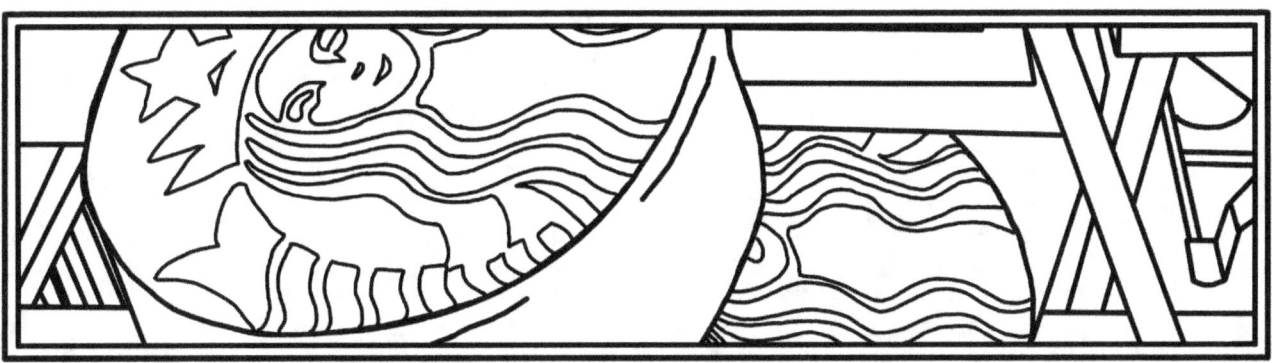

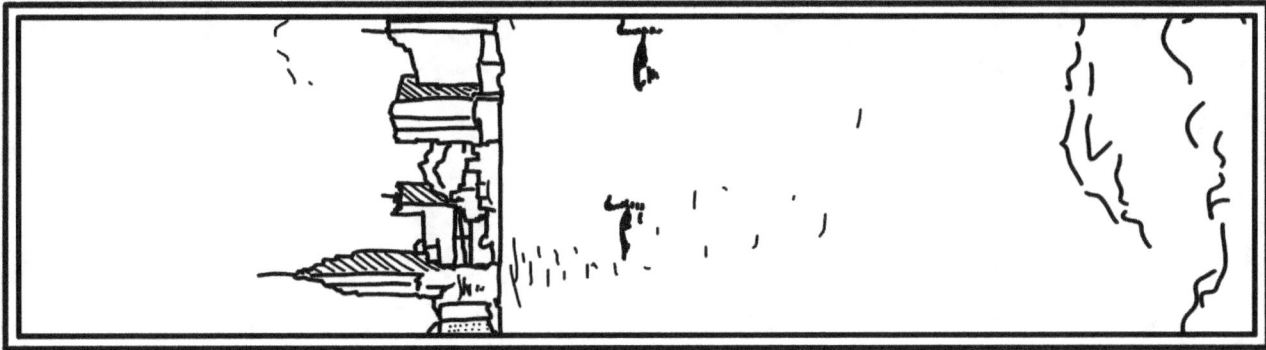

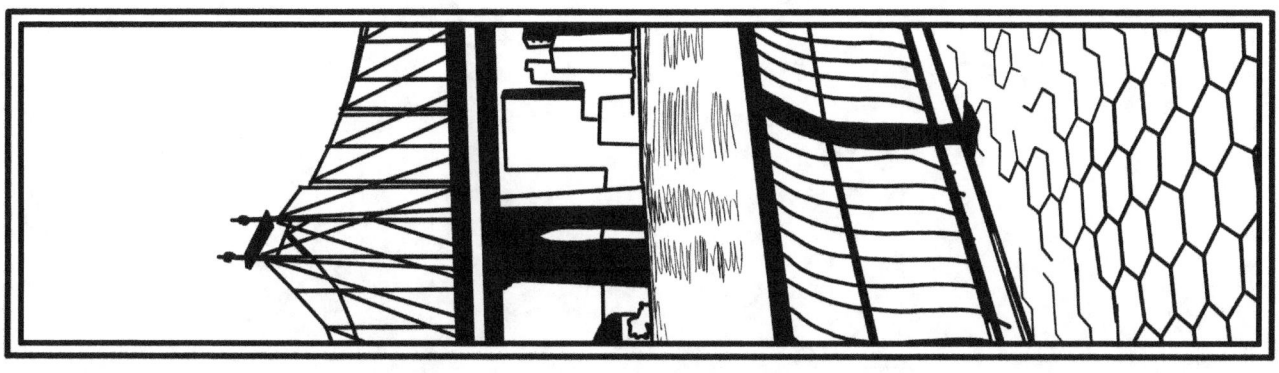
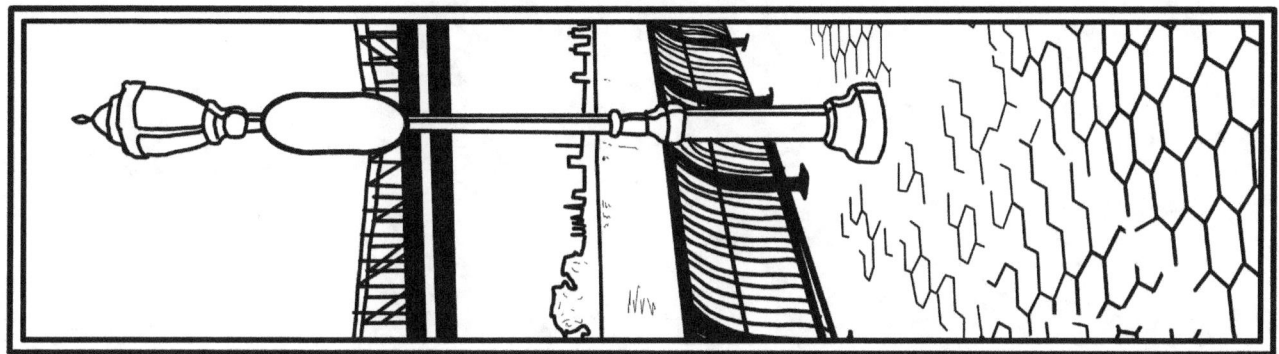
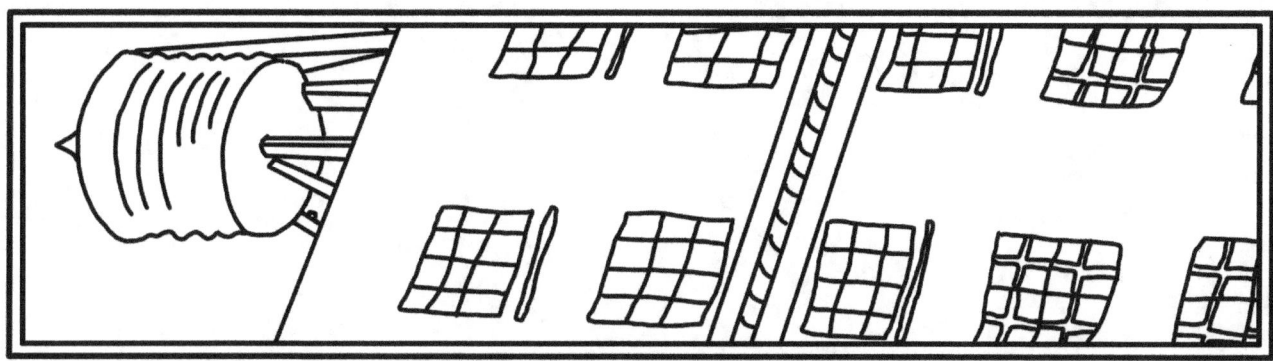
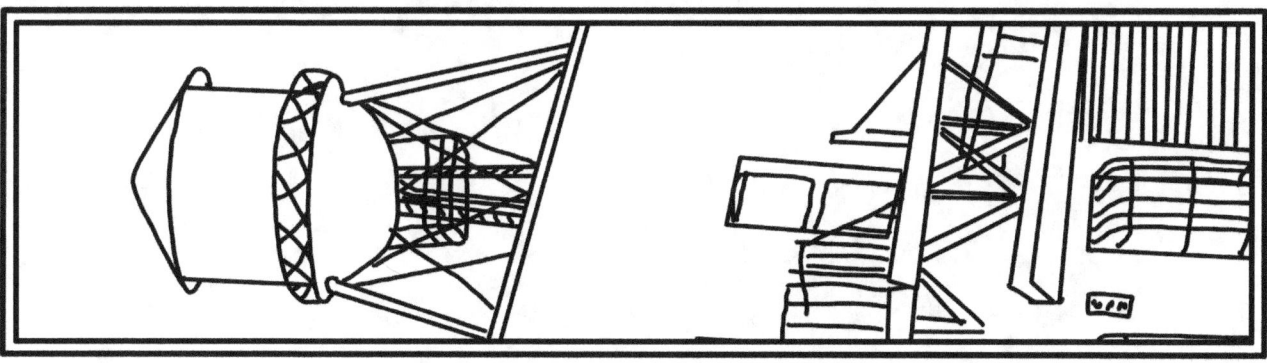

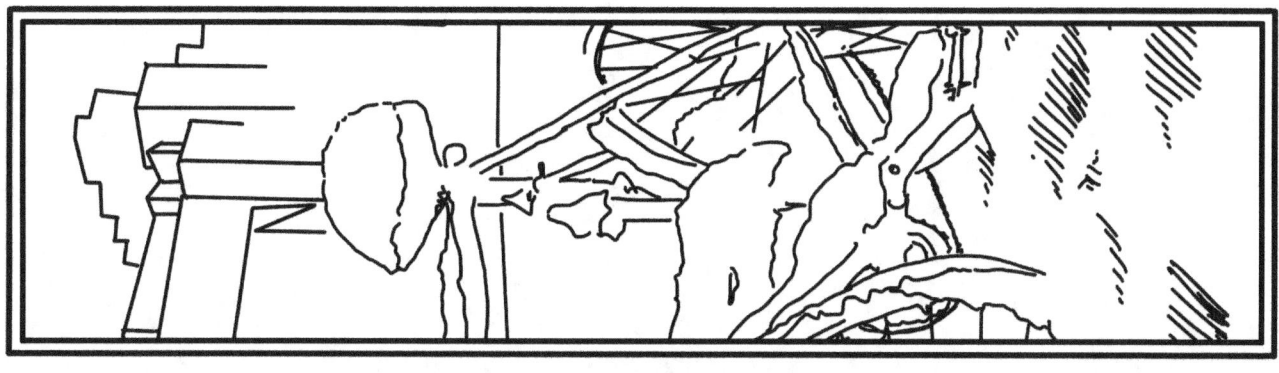

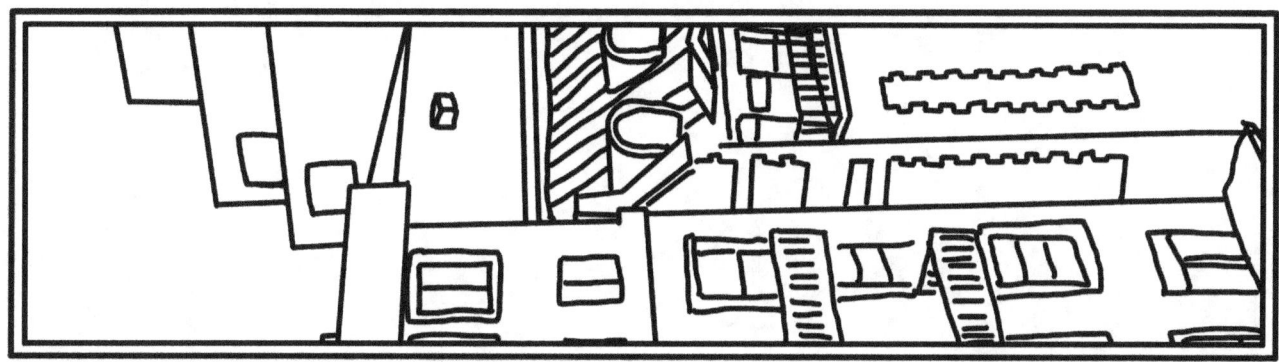

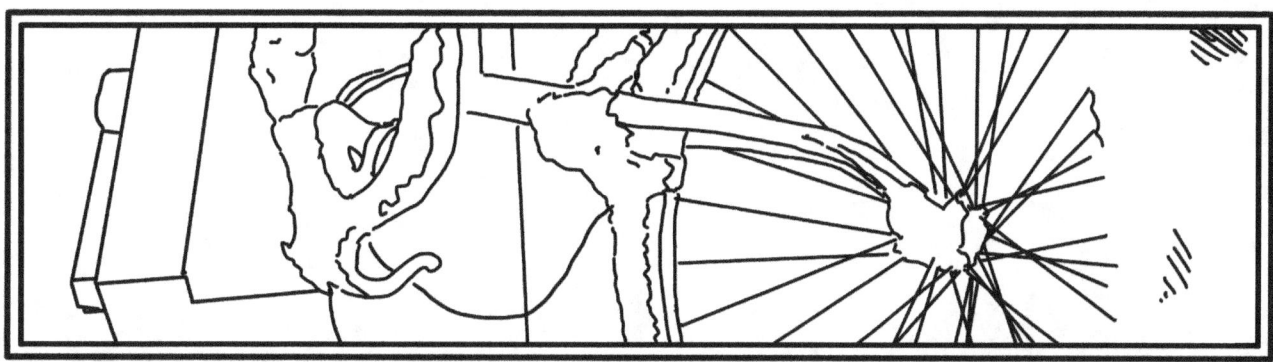

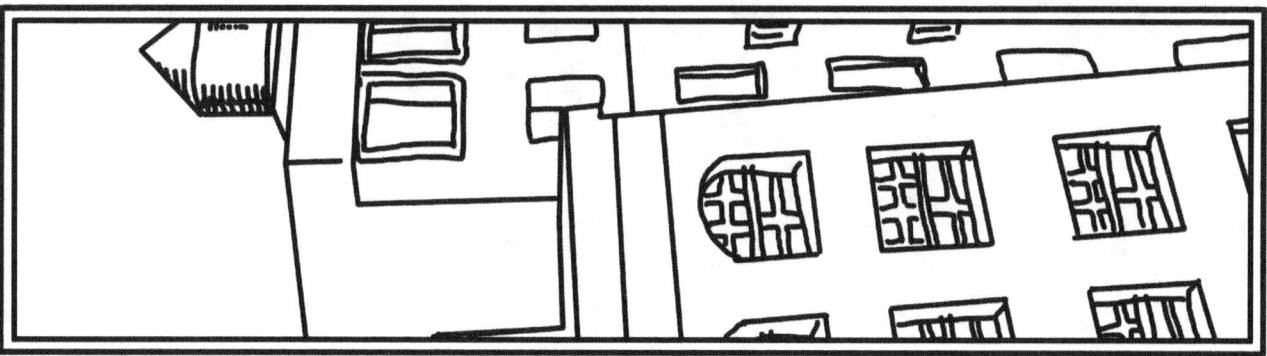

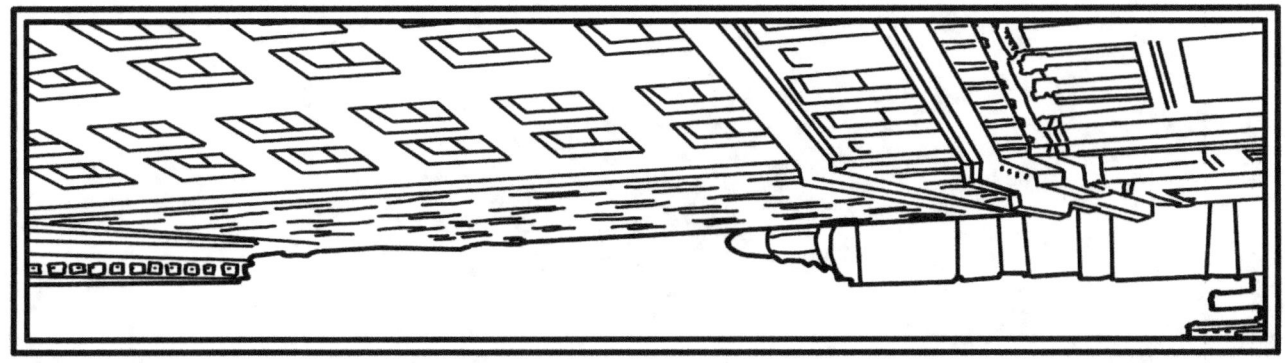

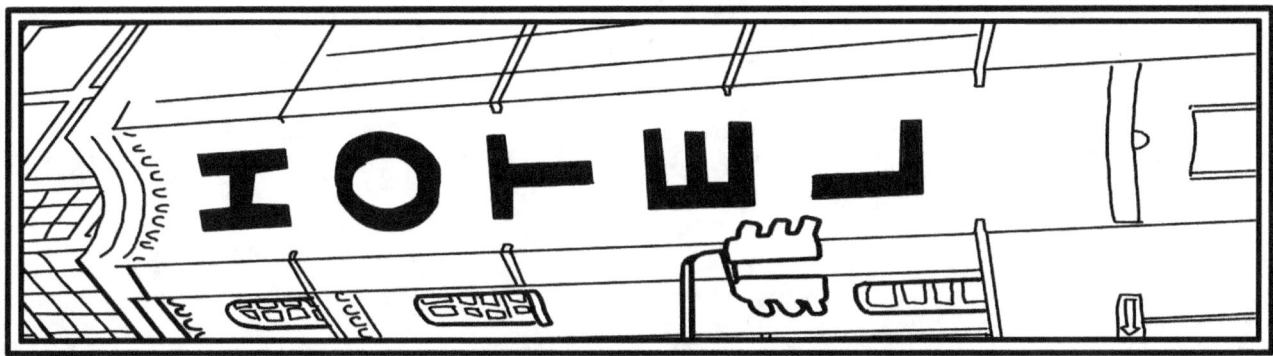

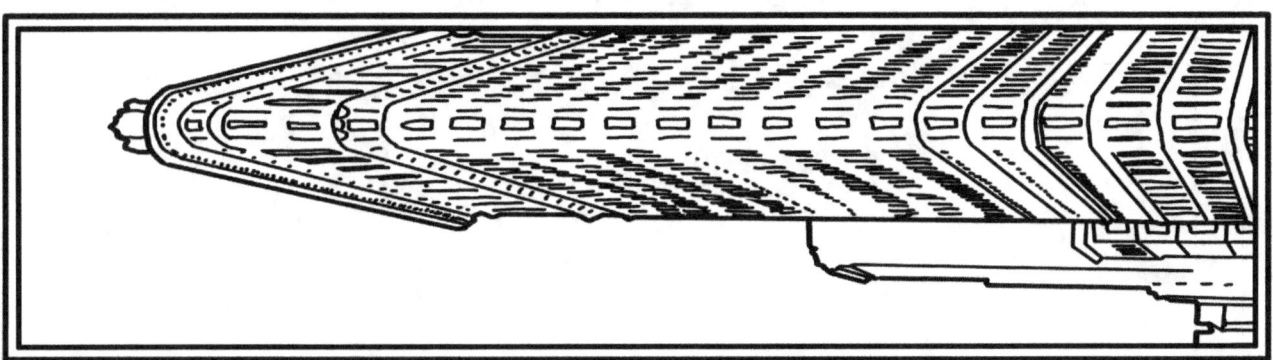

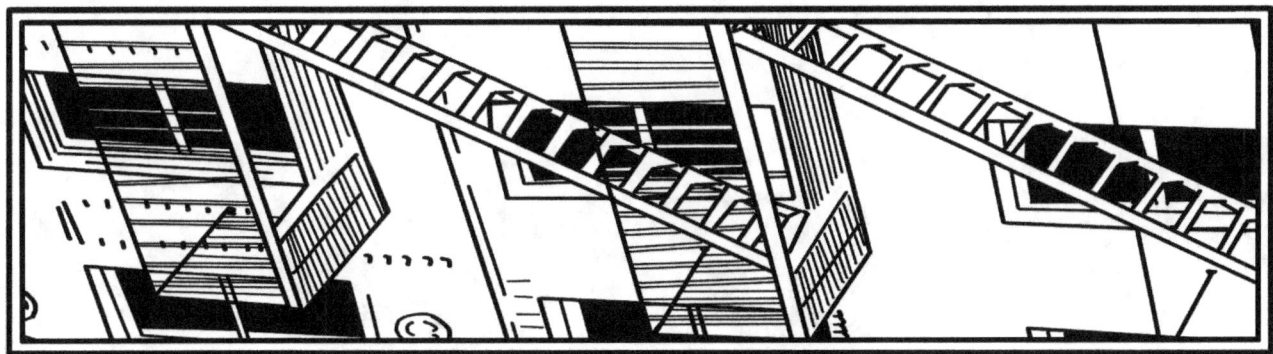

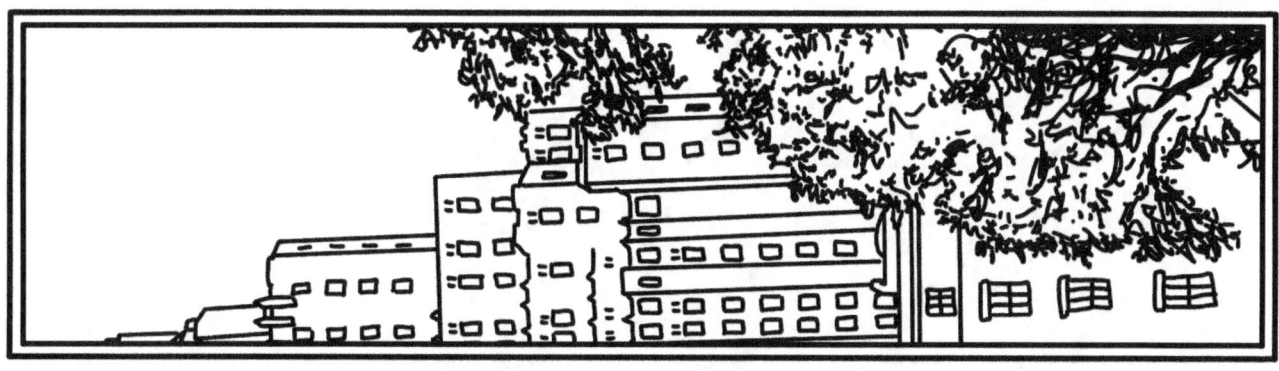

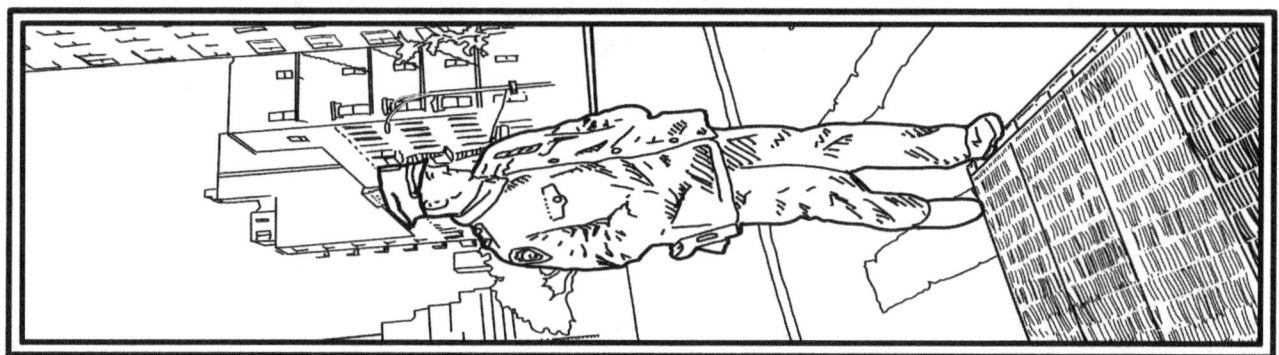

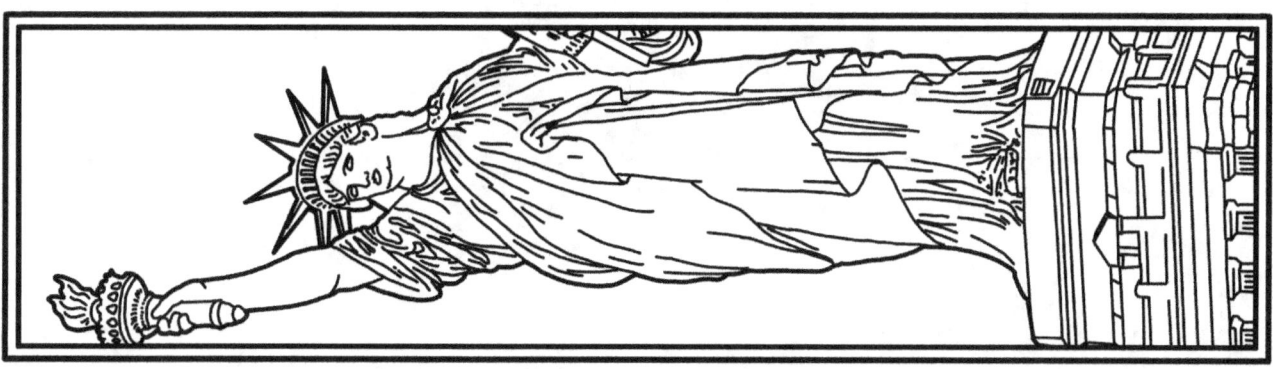

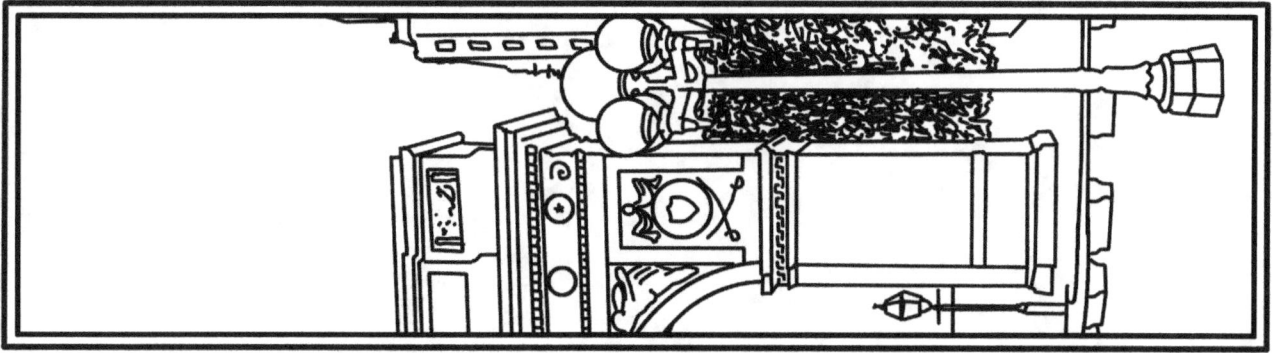

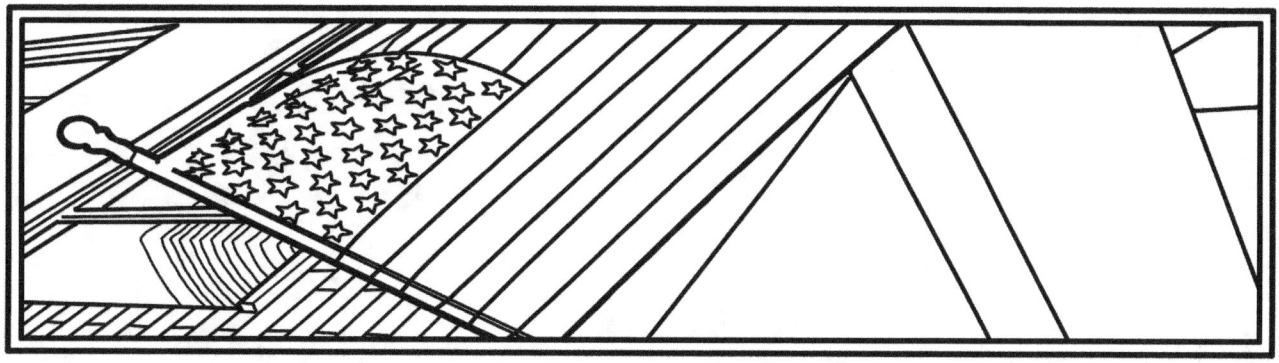
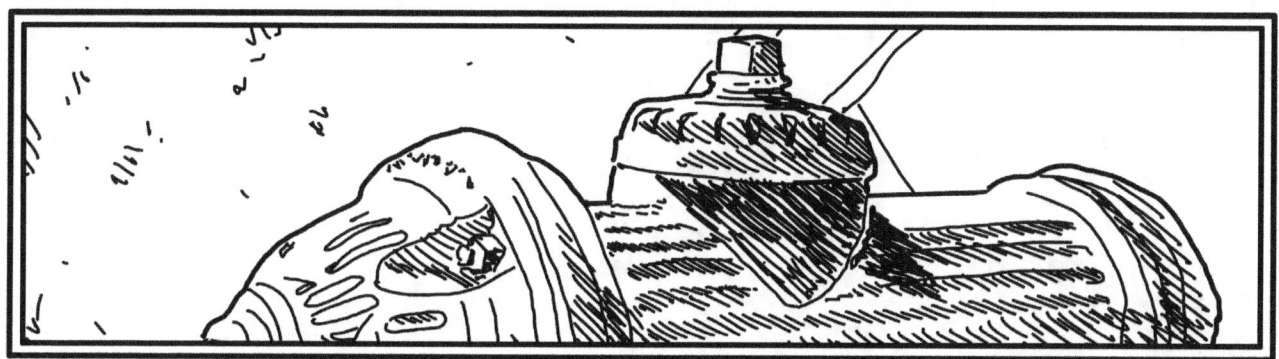
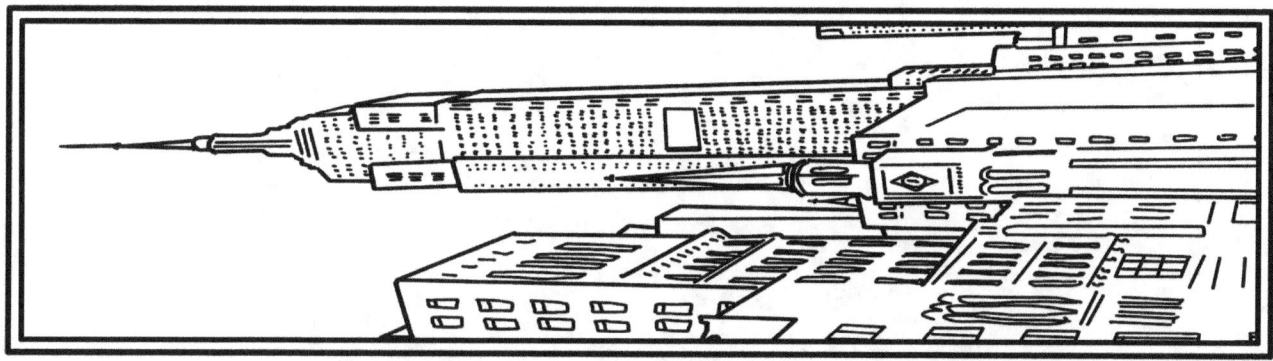
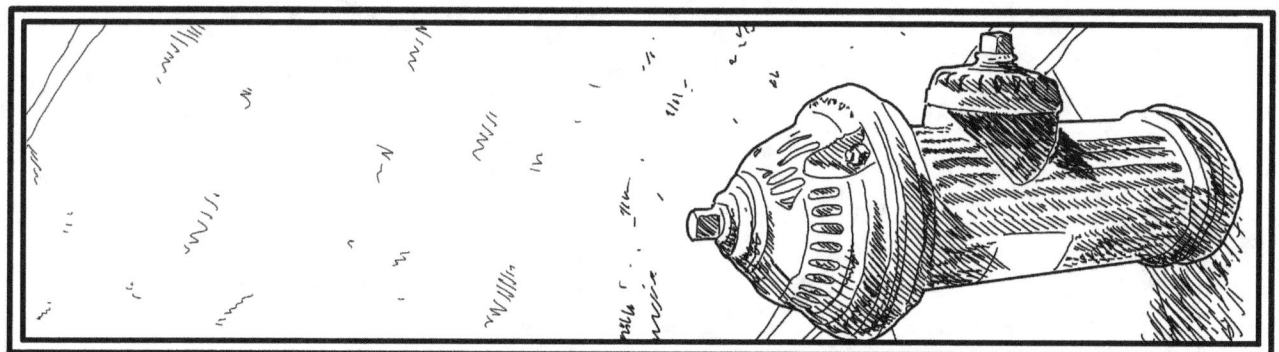

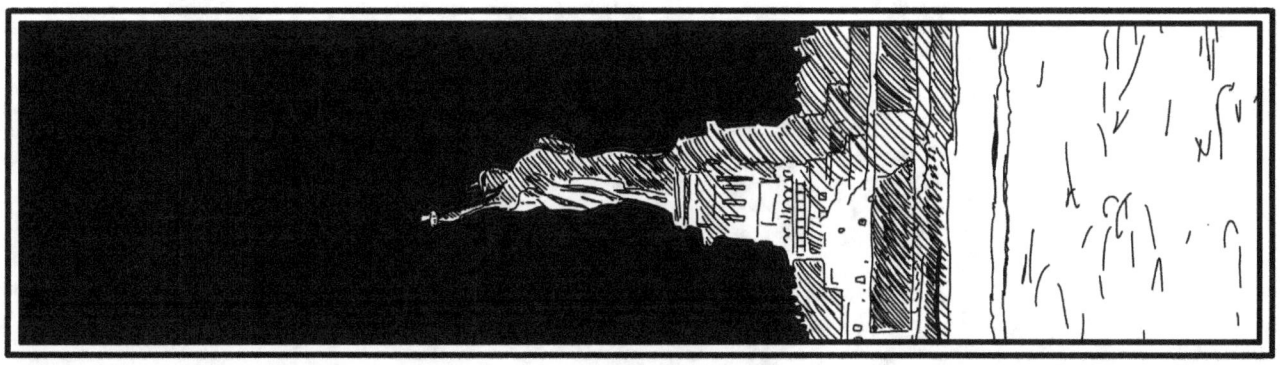

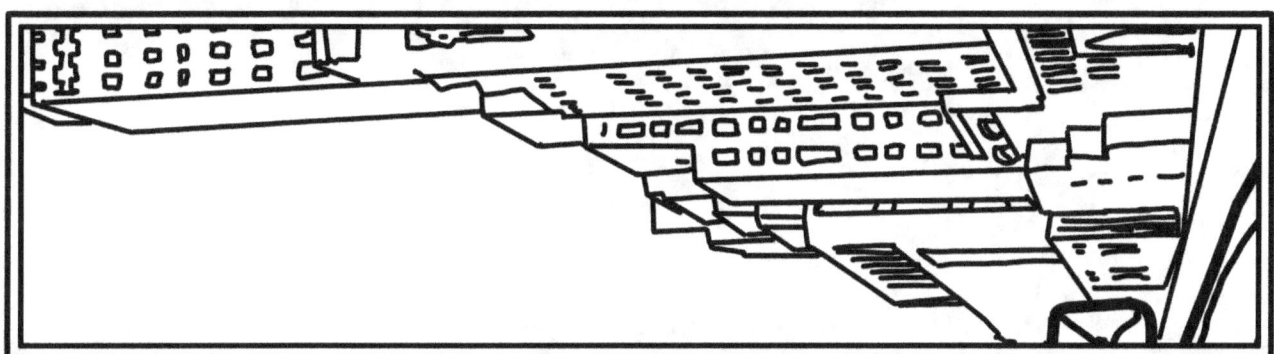

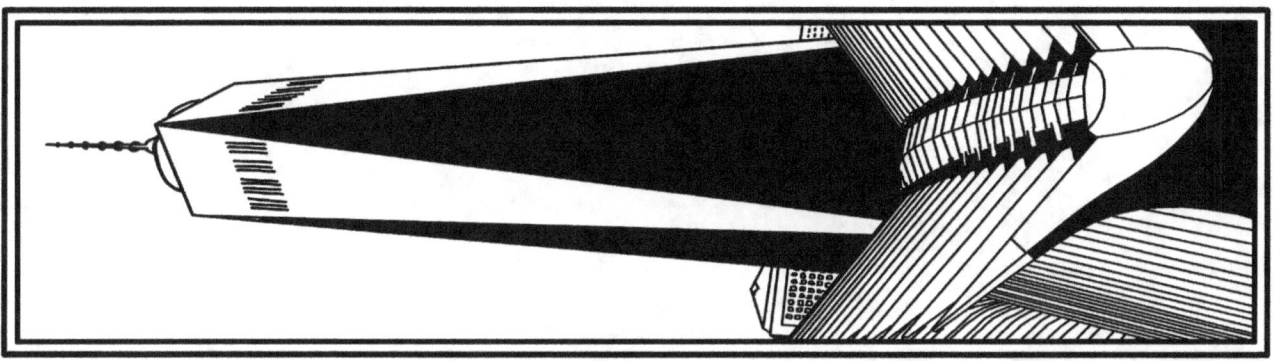

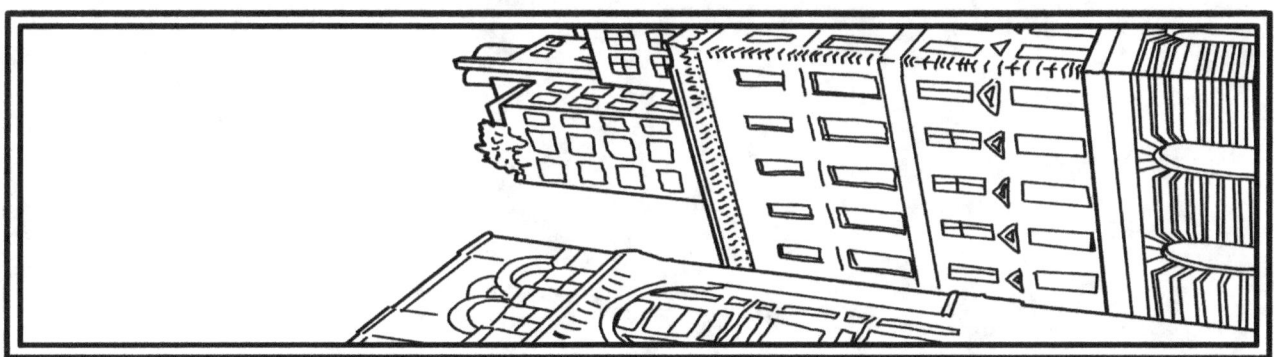

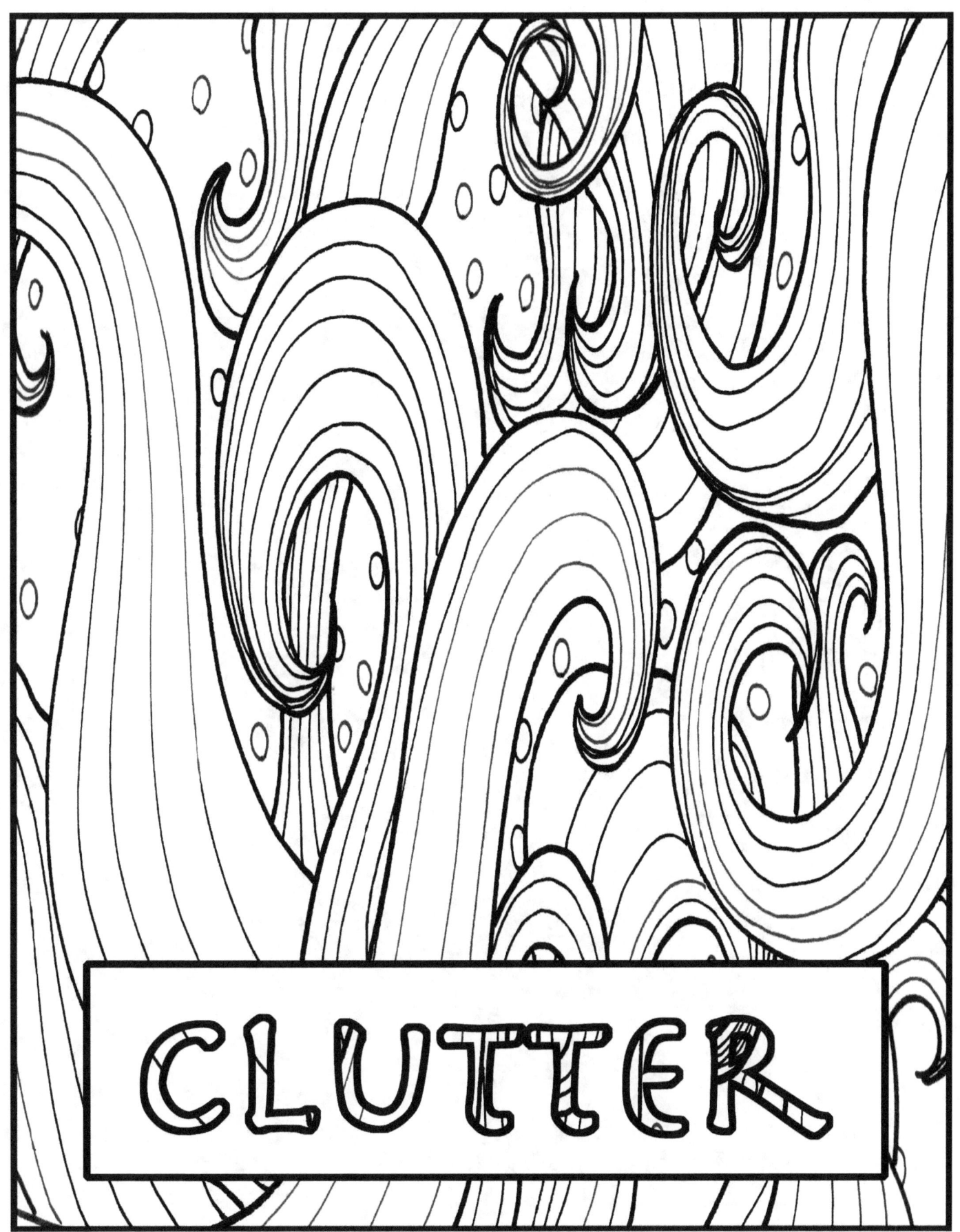

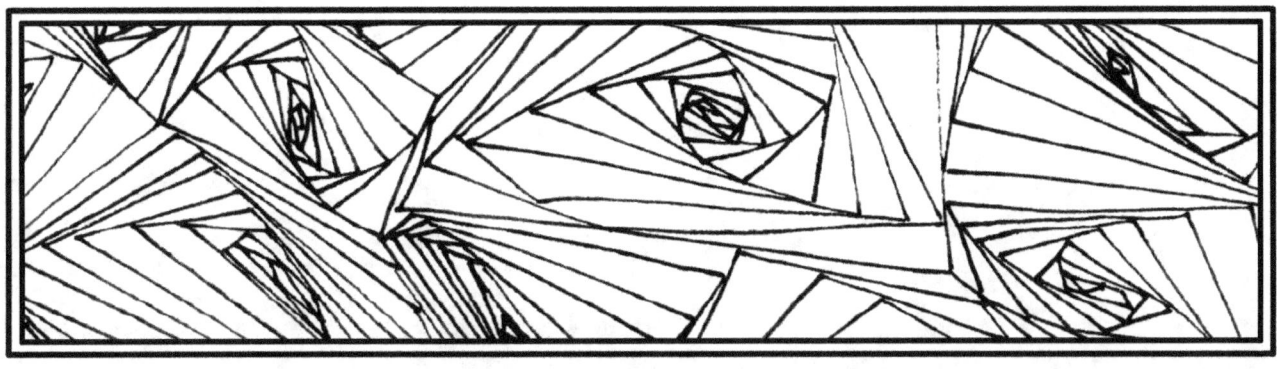

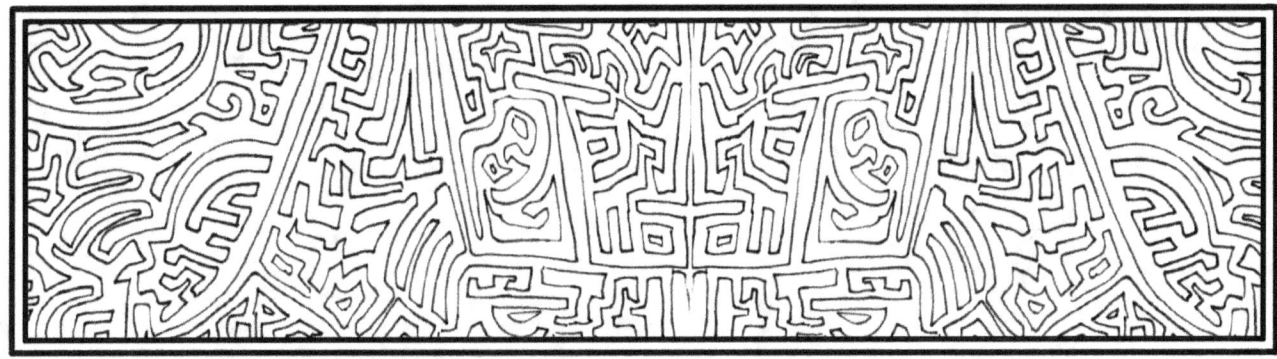

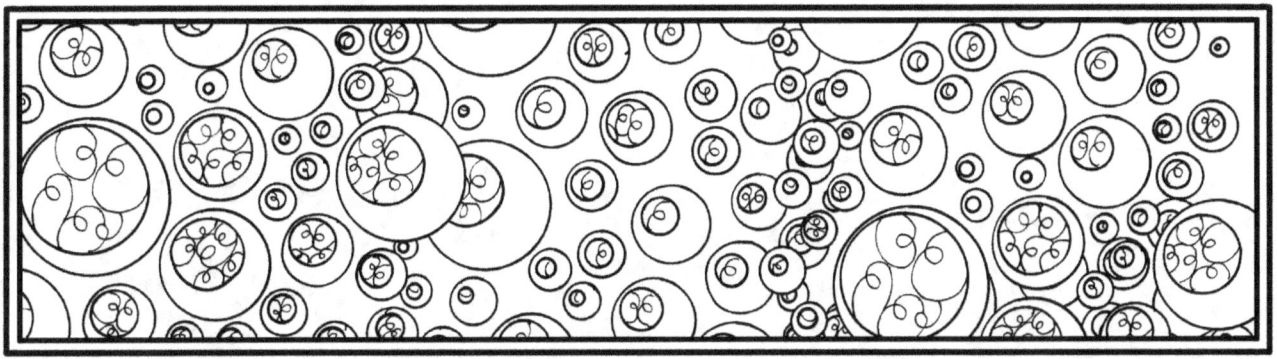

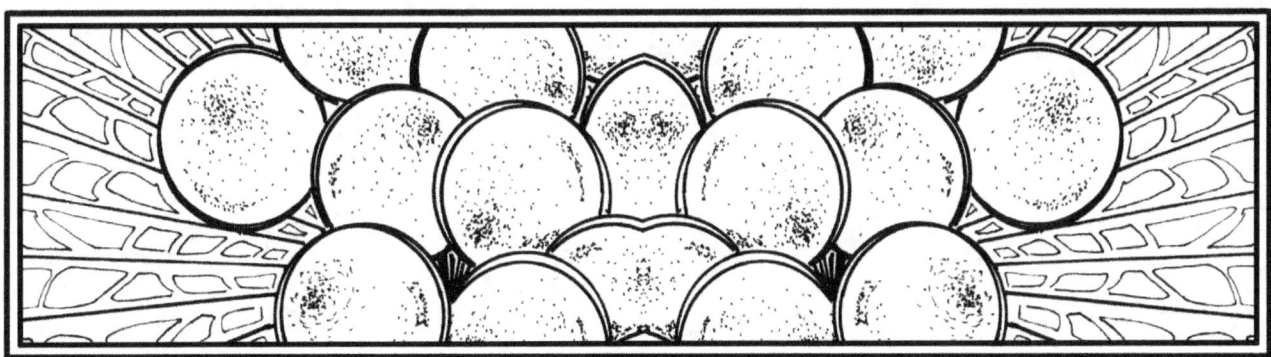

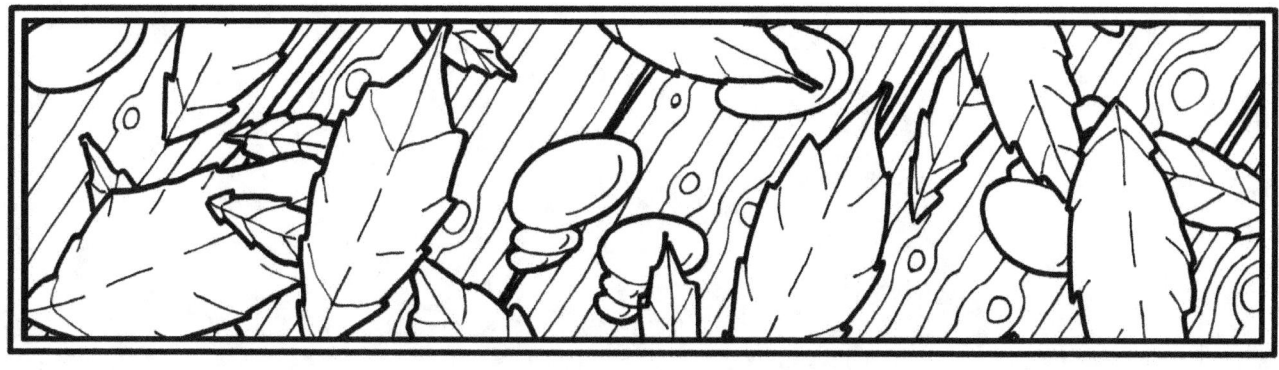

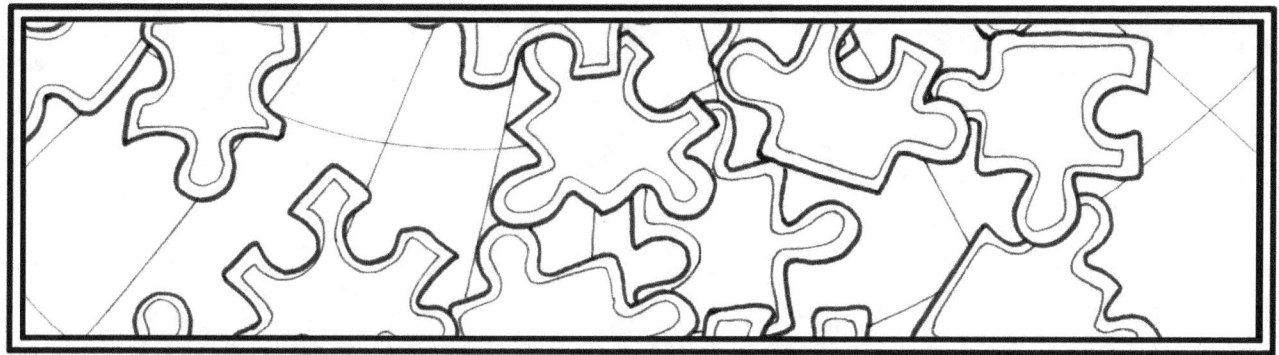

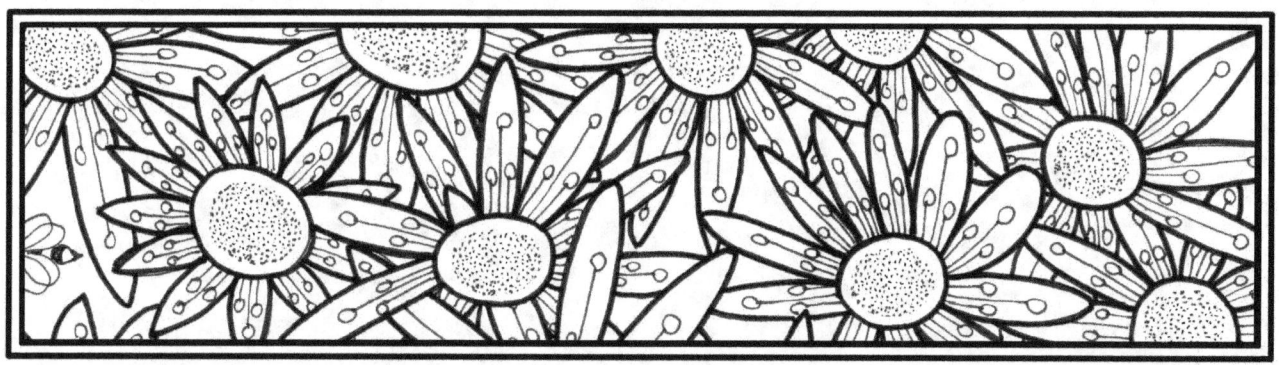

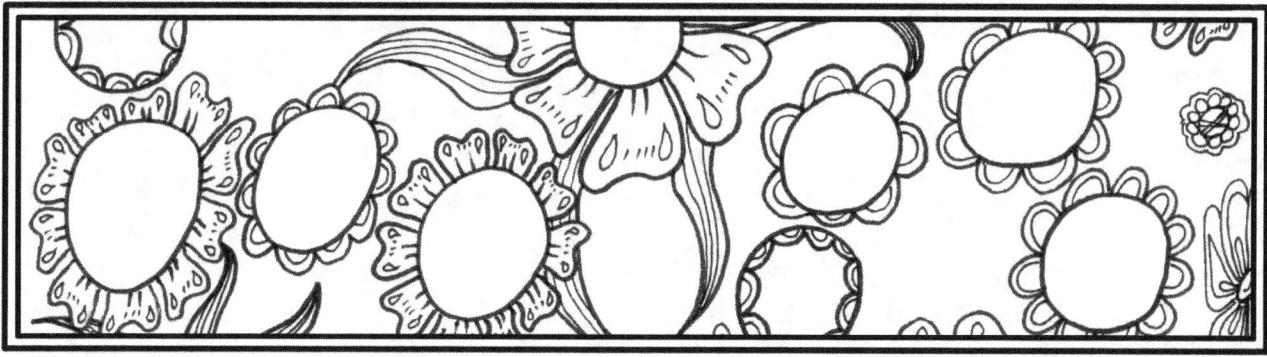

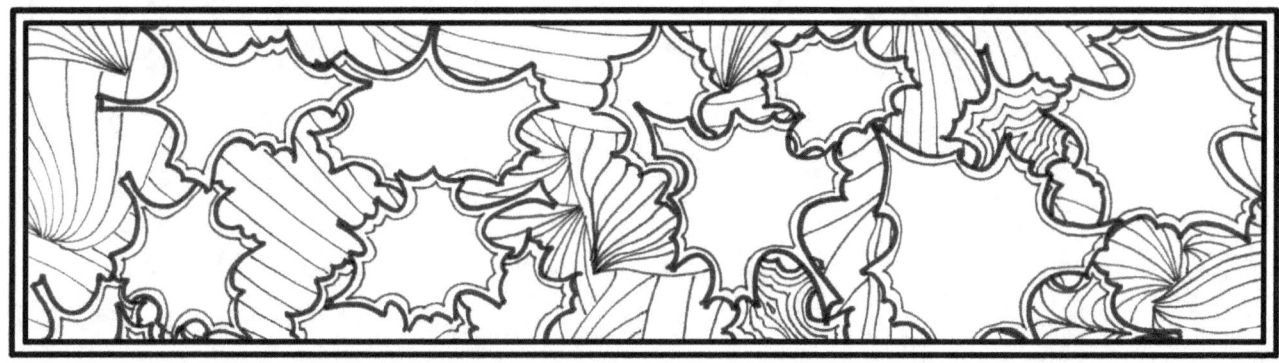

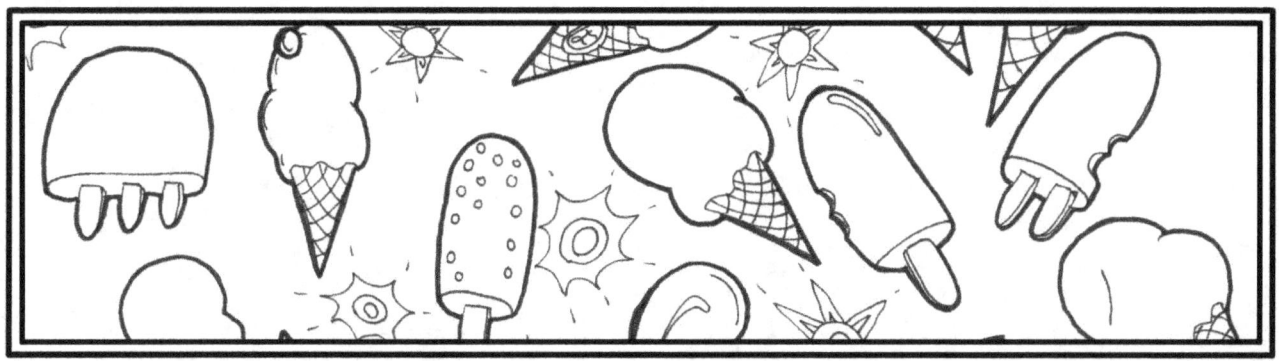

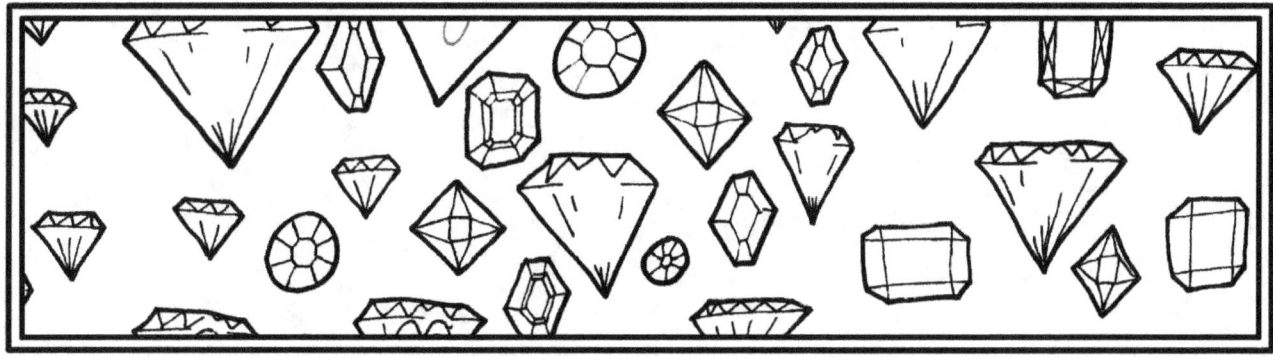

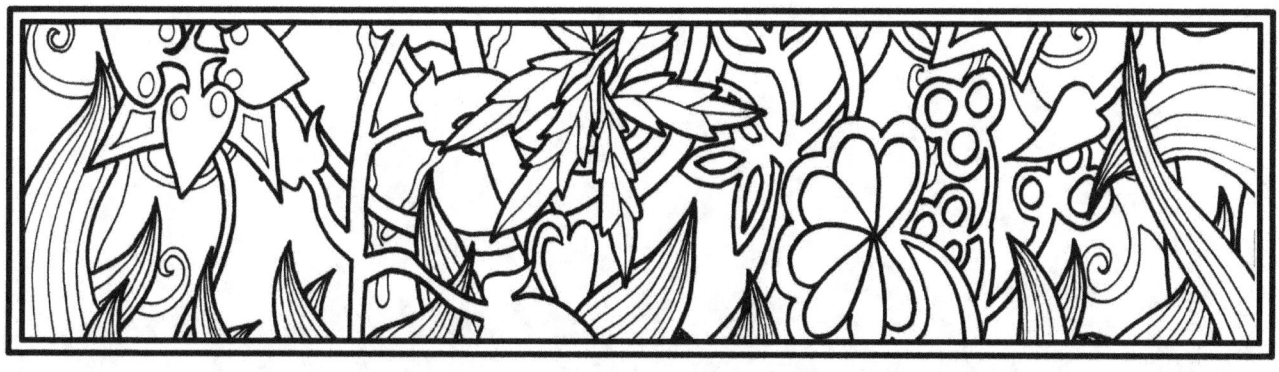

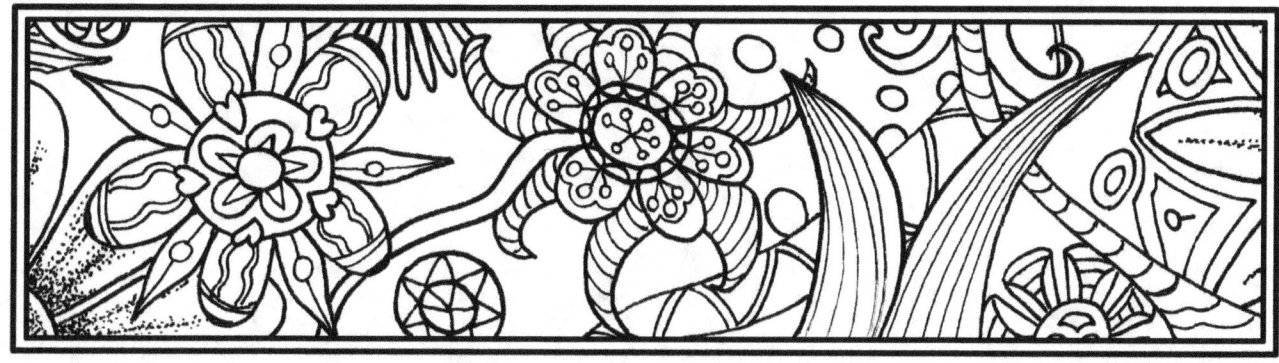

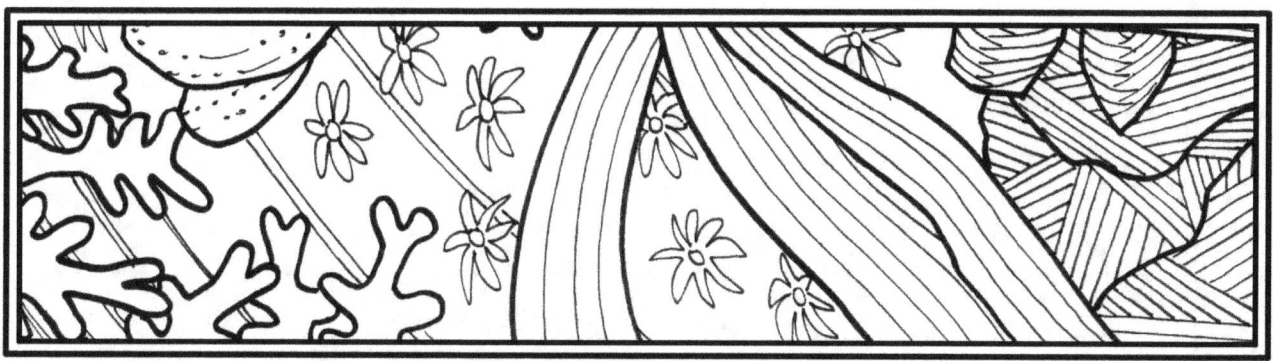

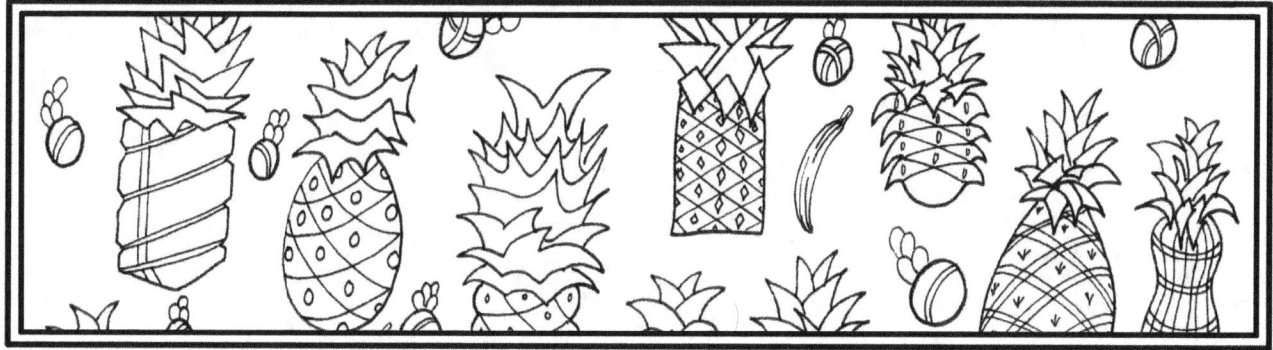

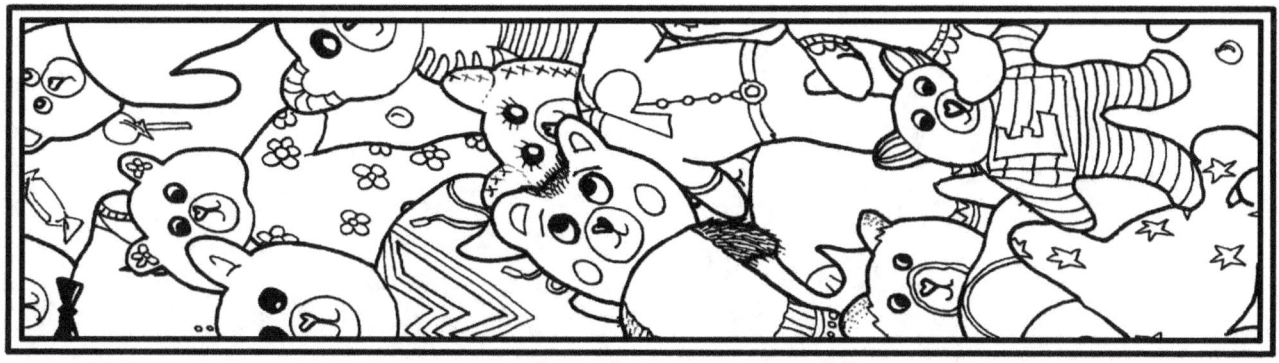

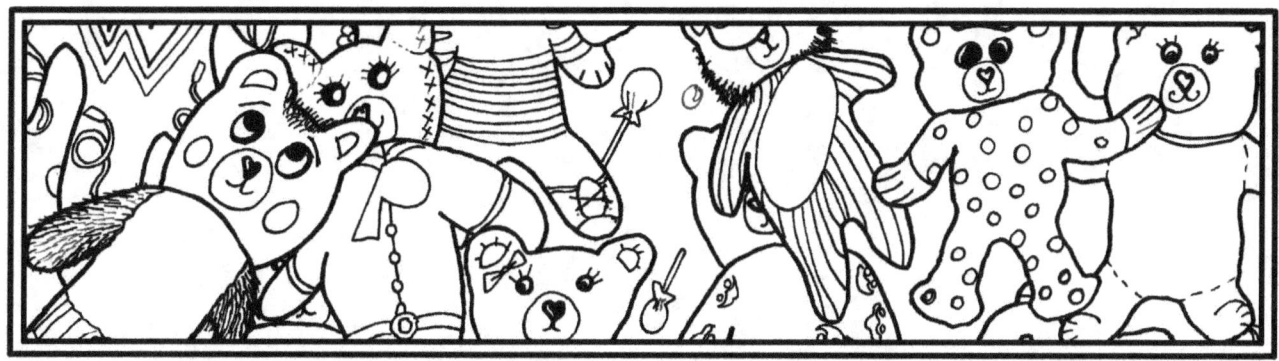

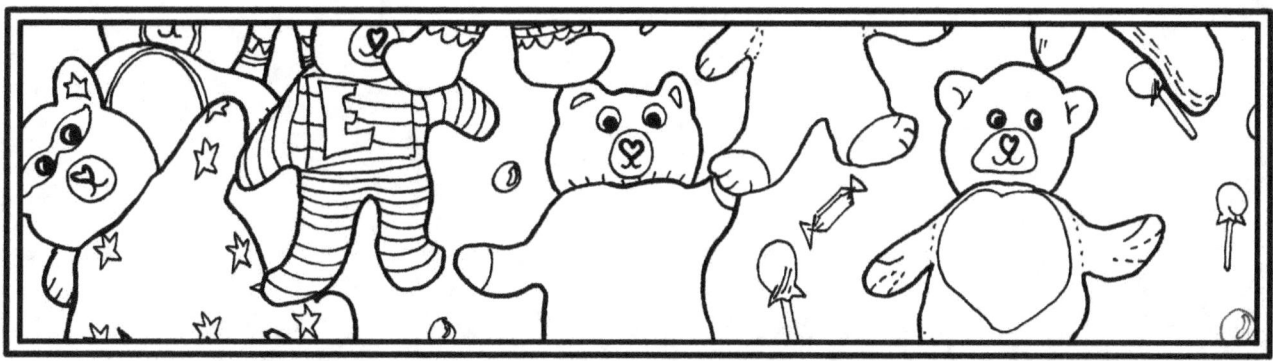

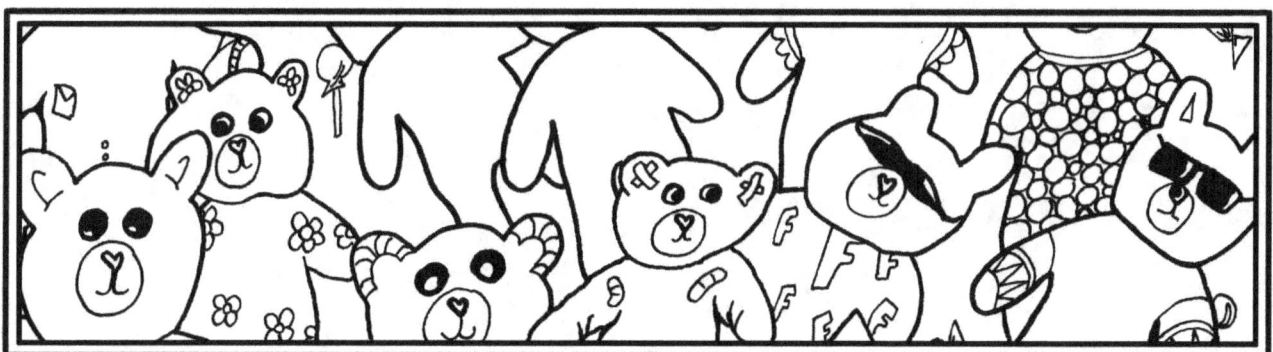

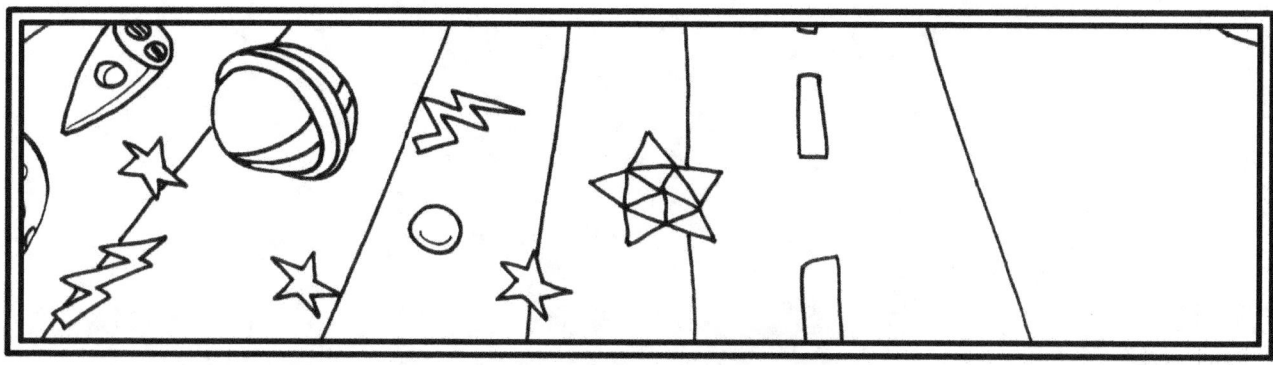

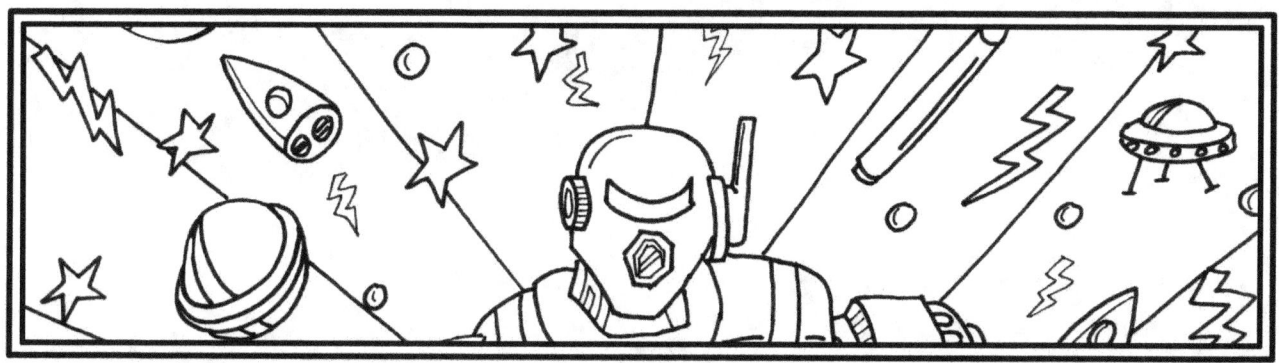

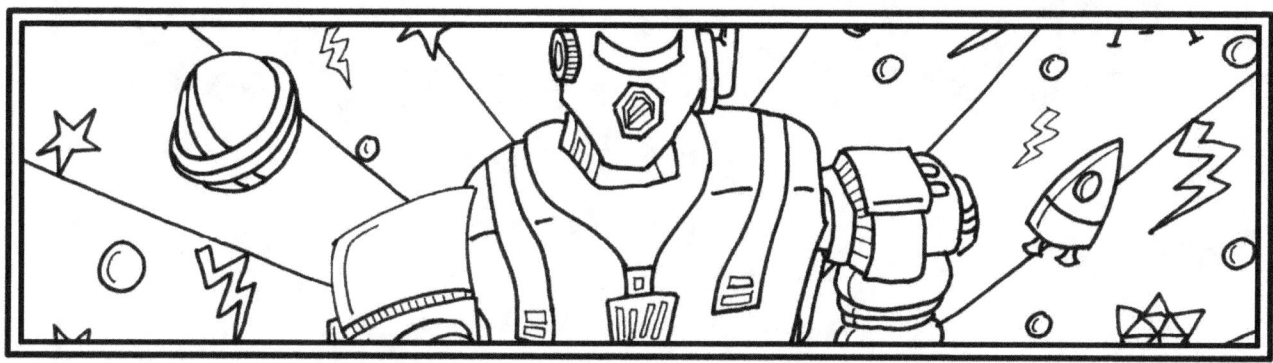

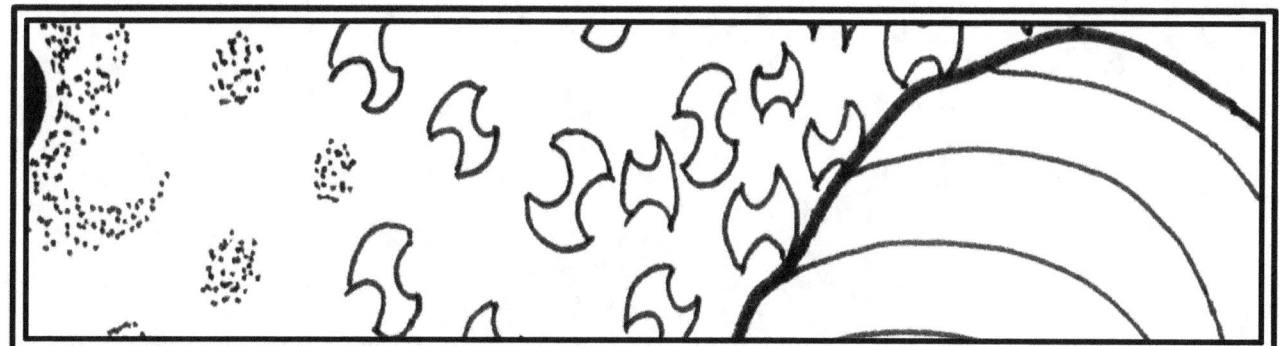

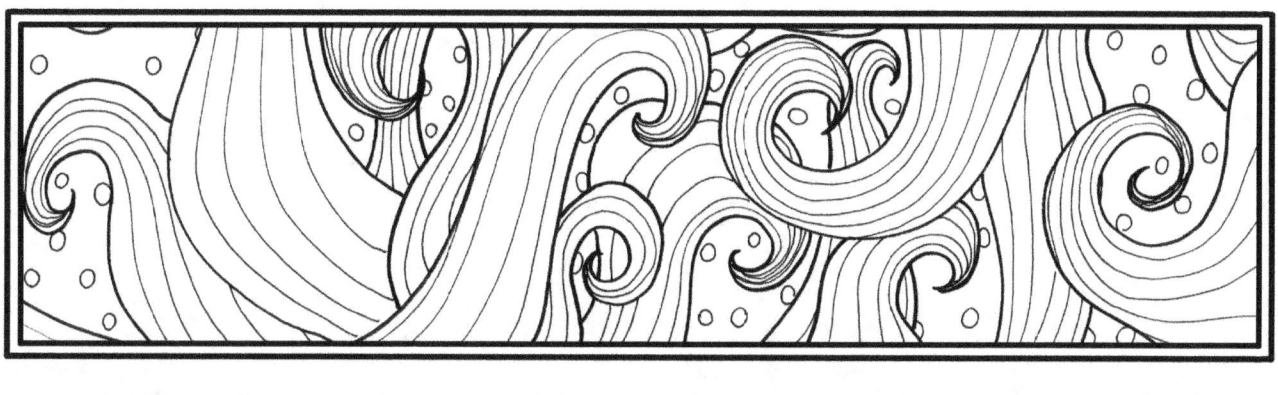
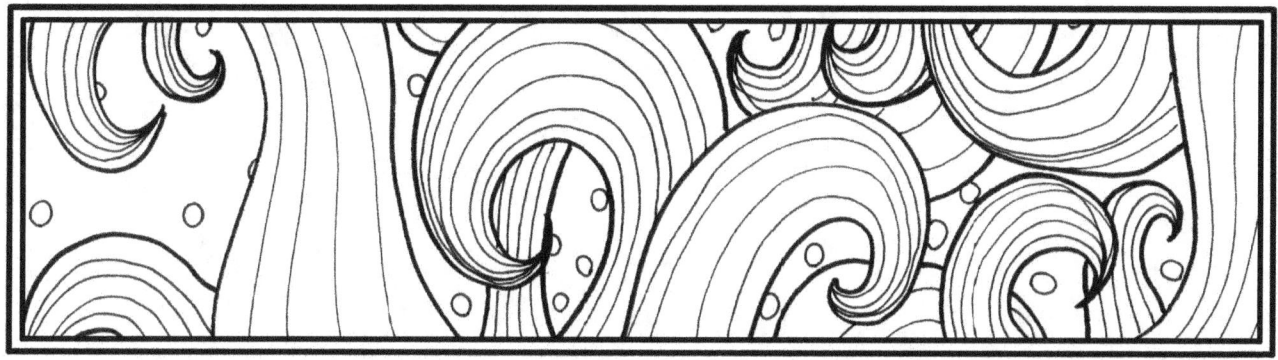
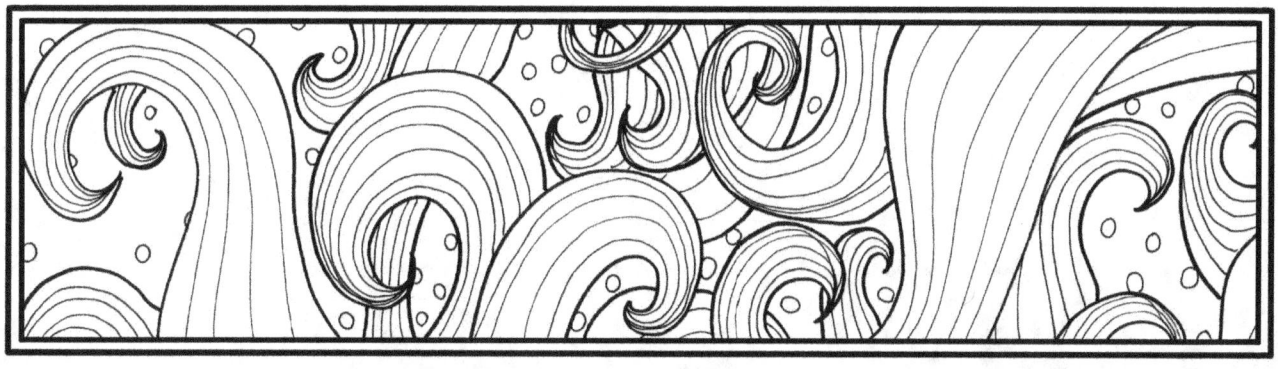
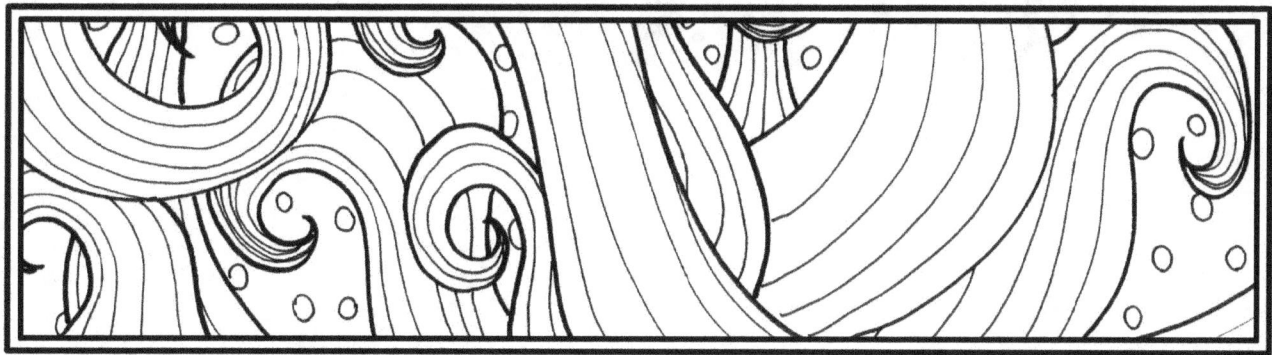

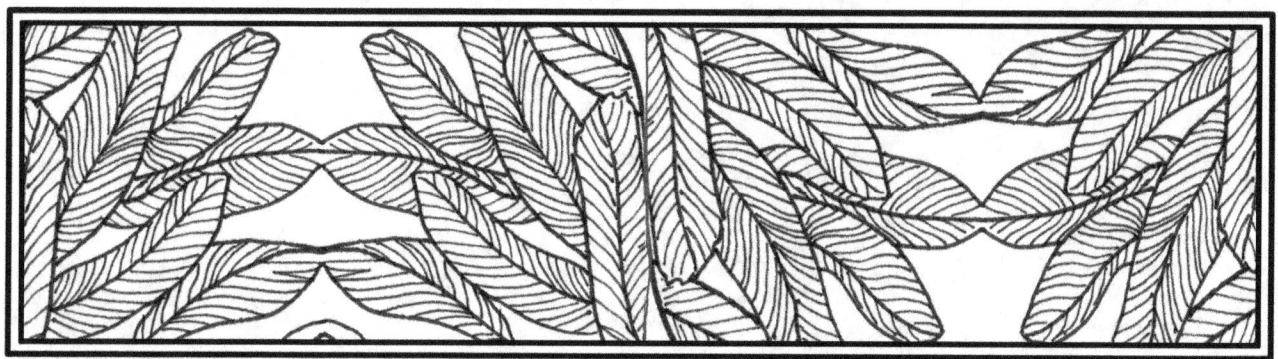

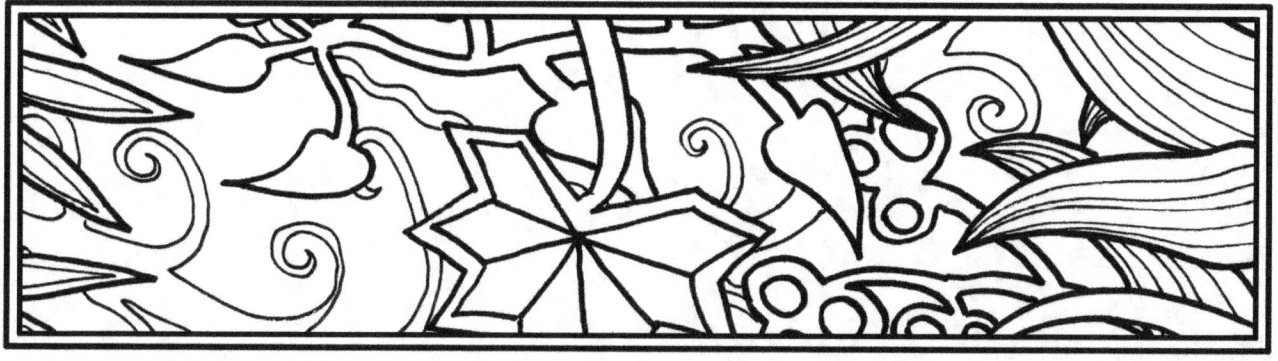

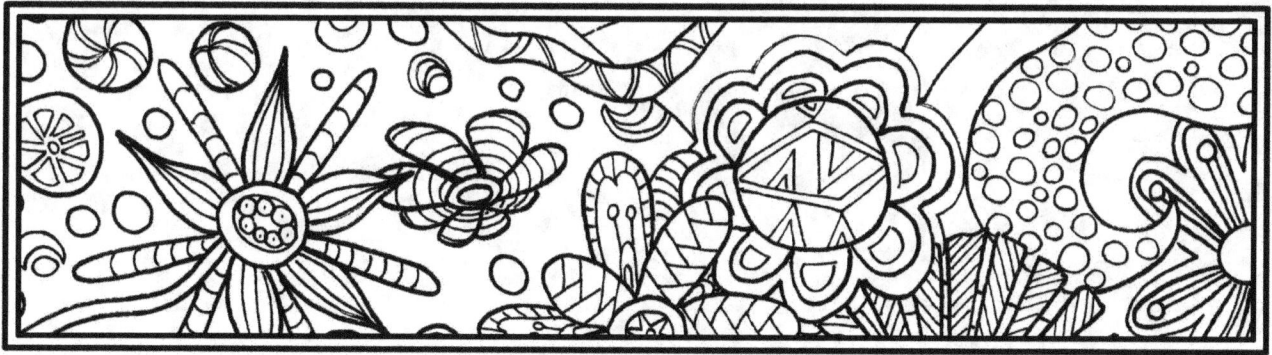

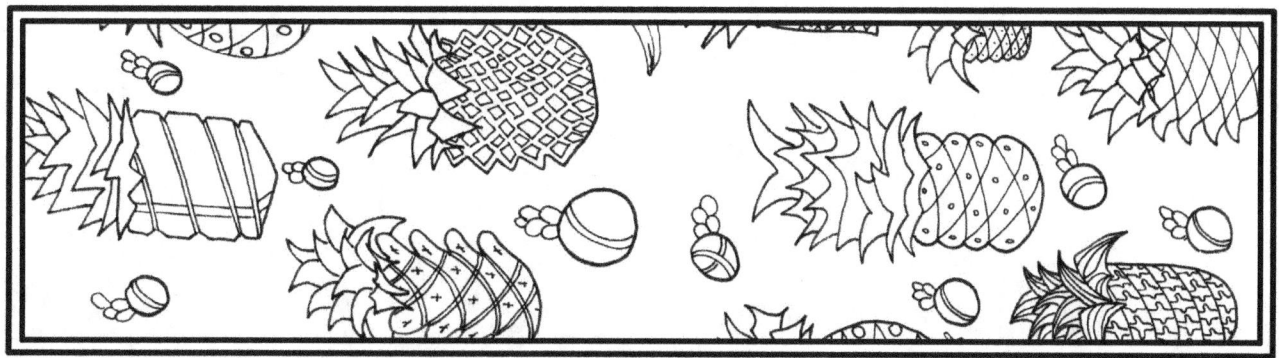

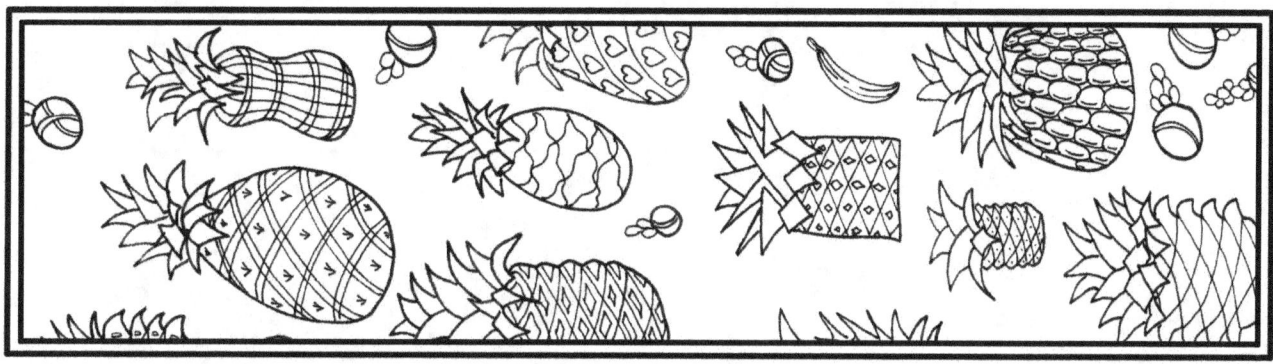

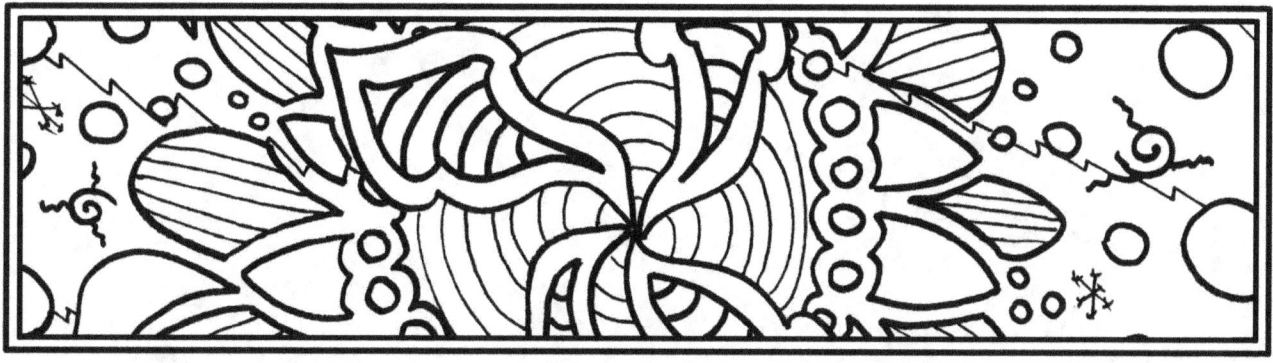

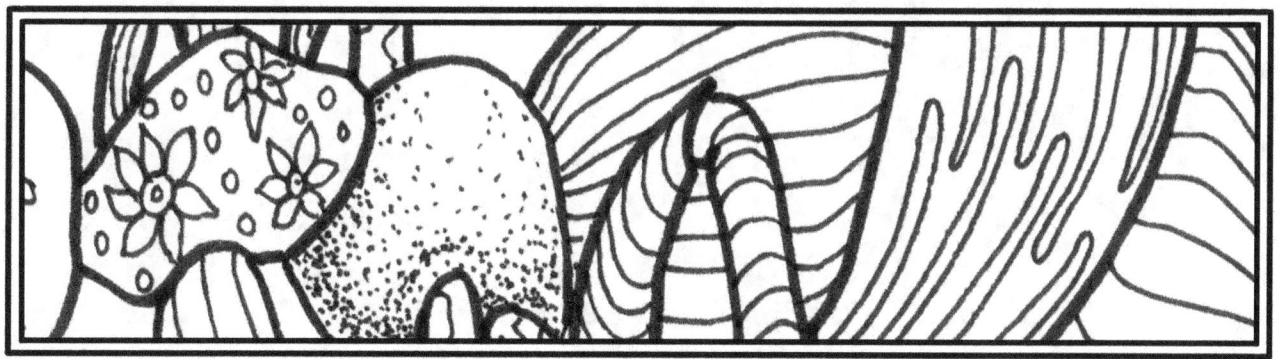

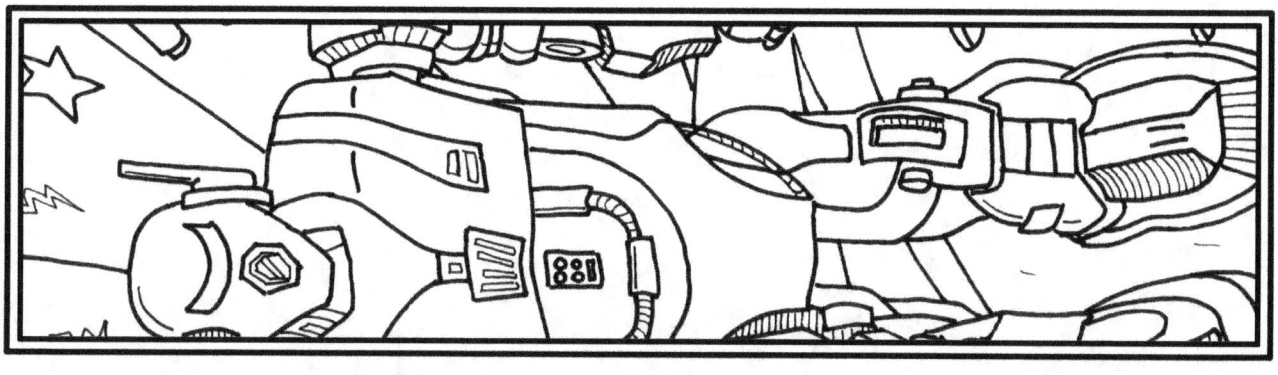

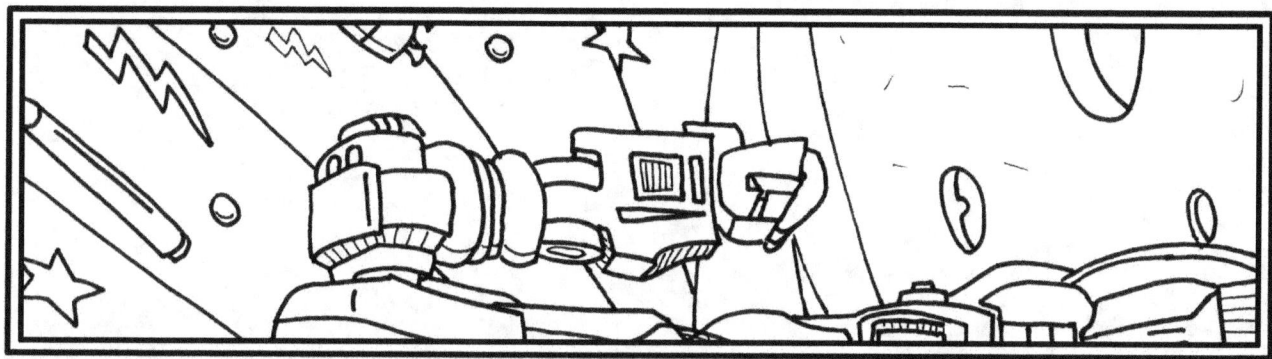

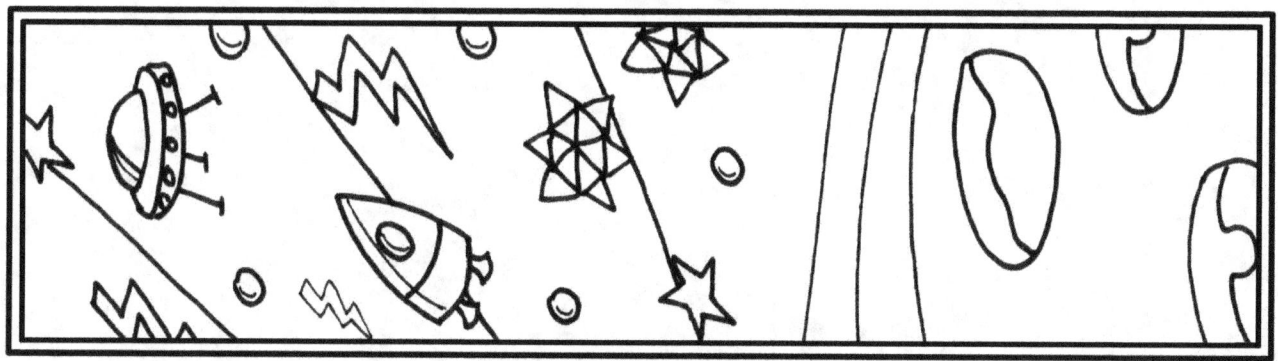

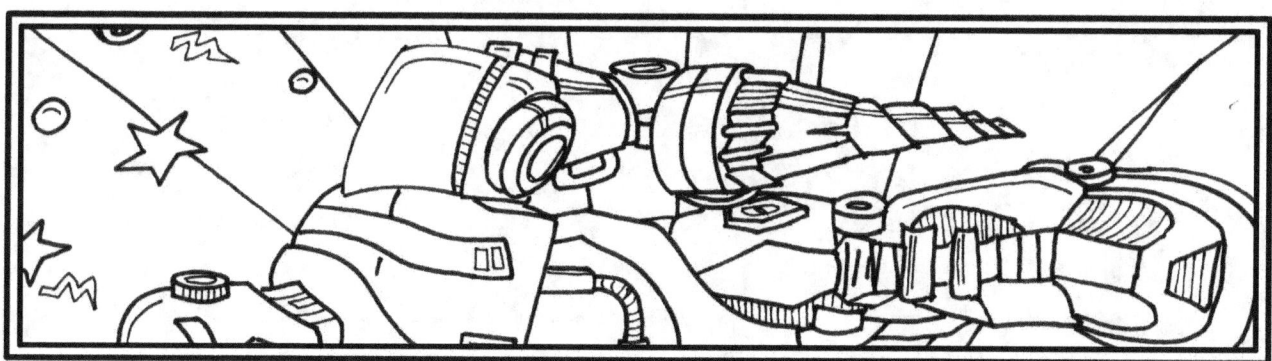

HOLIDAYS

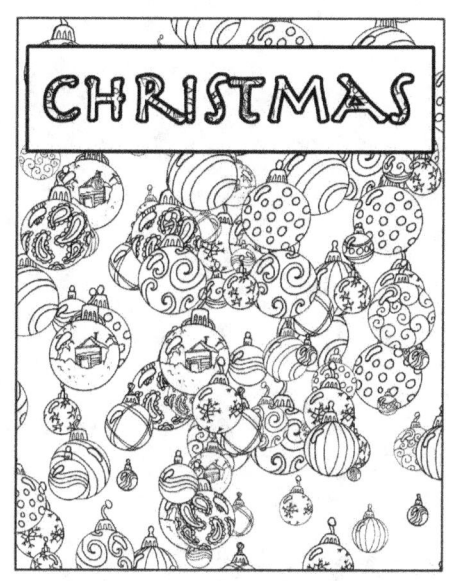

CHRISTMAS

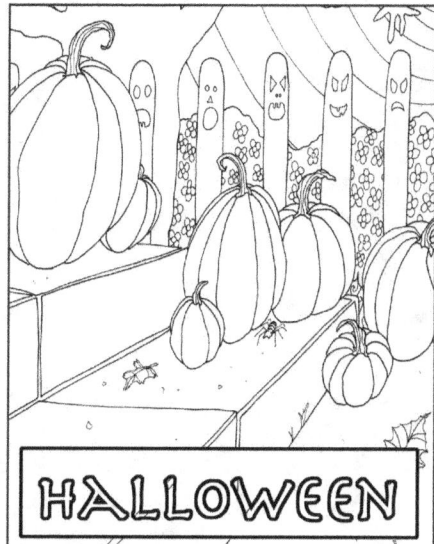

HALLOWEEN

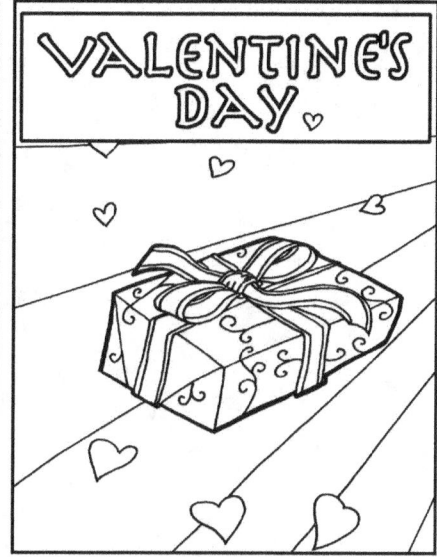

VALENTINE'S DAY

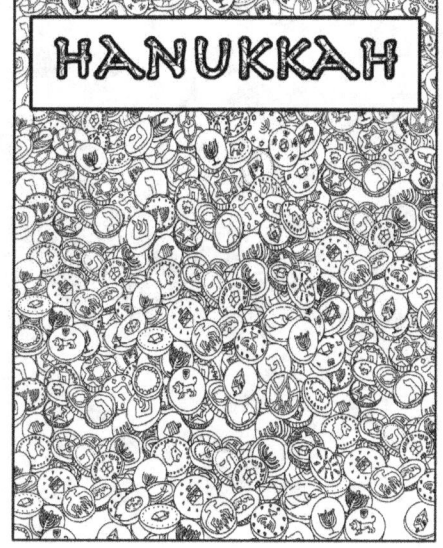

HANUKKAH

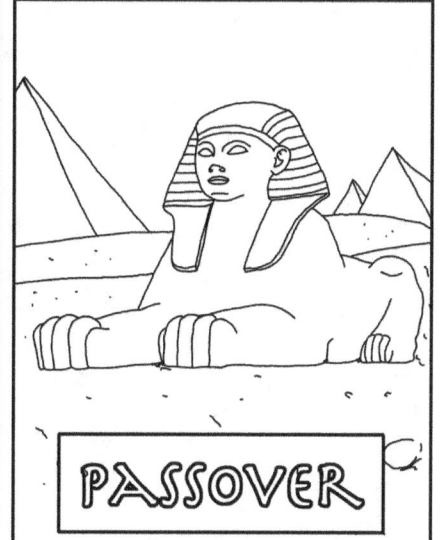

PASSOVER

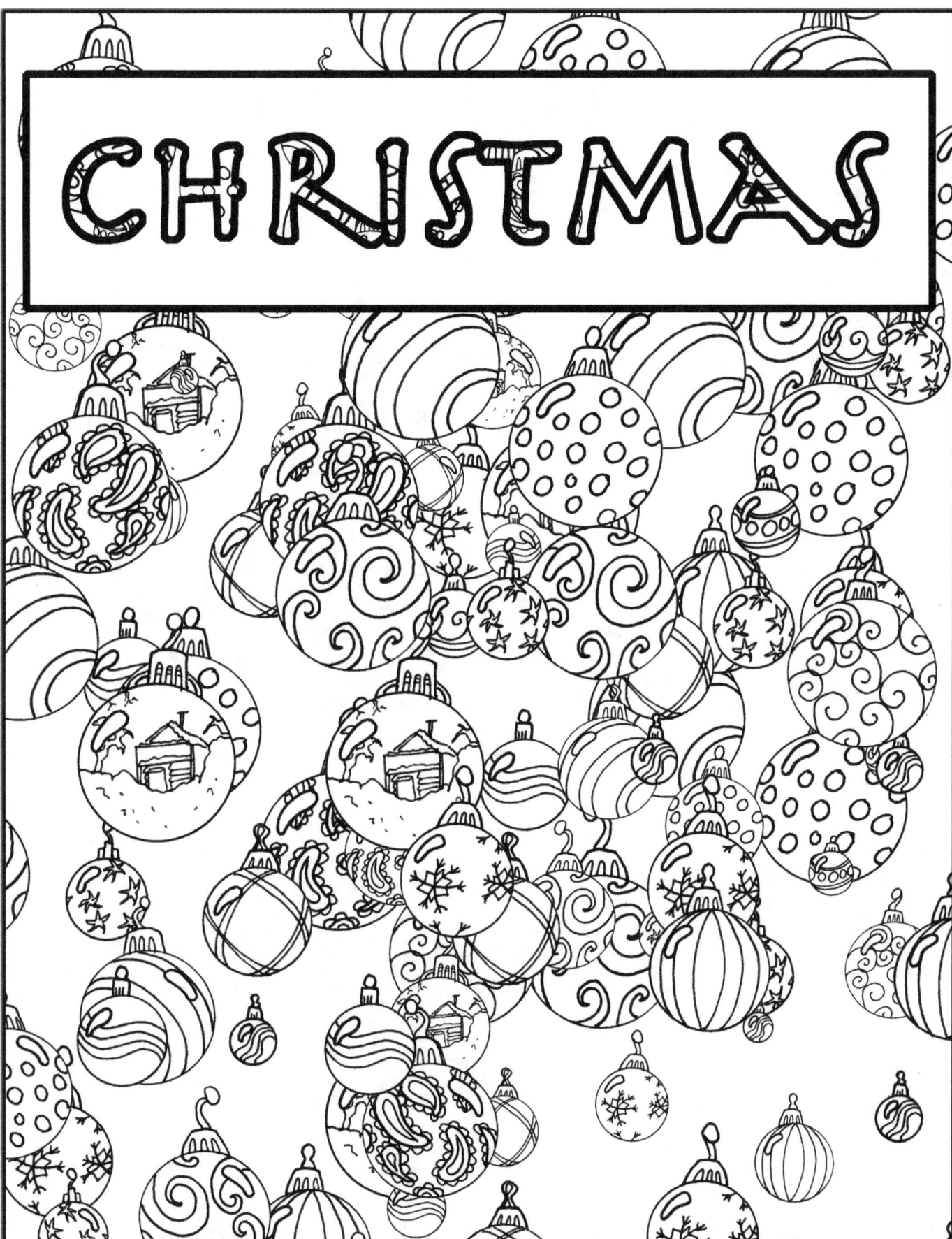

CHRISTMAS

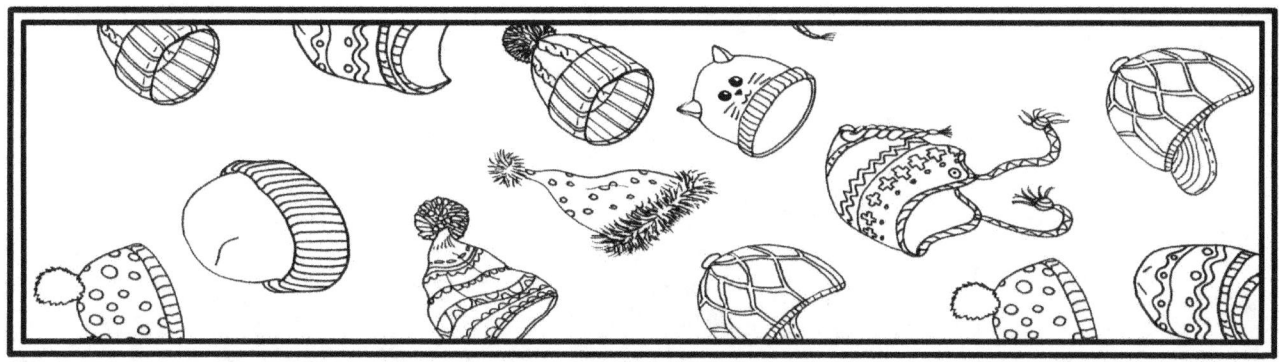

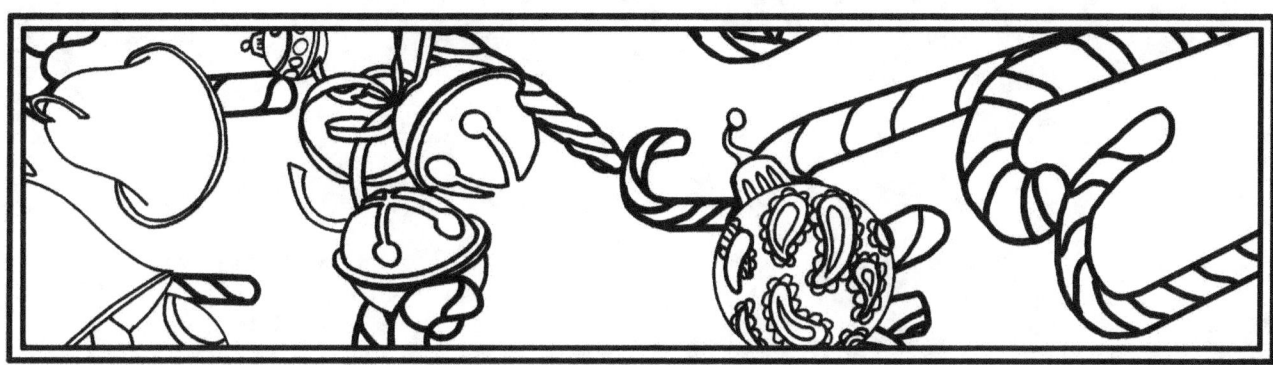

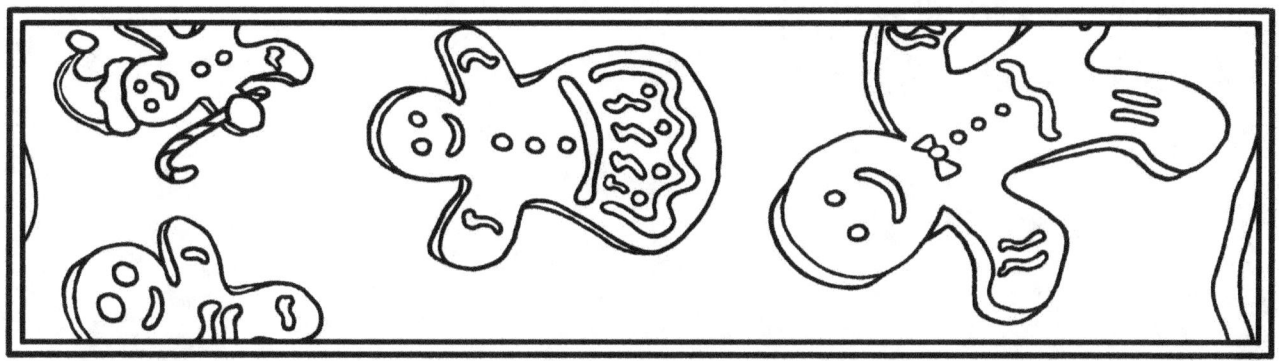

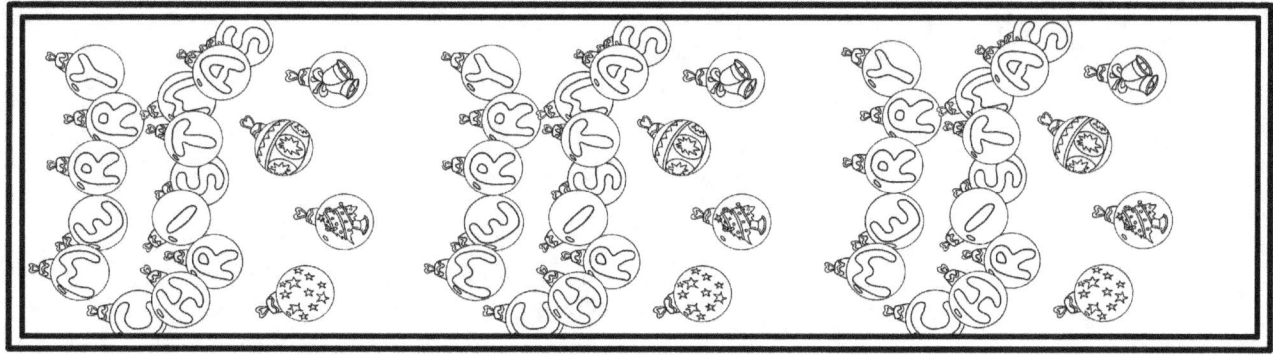

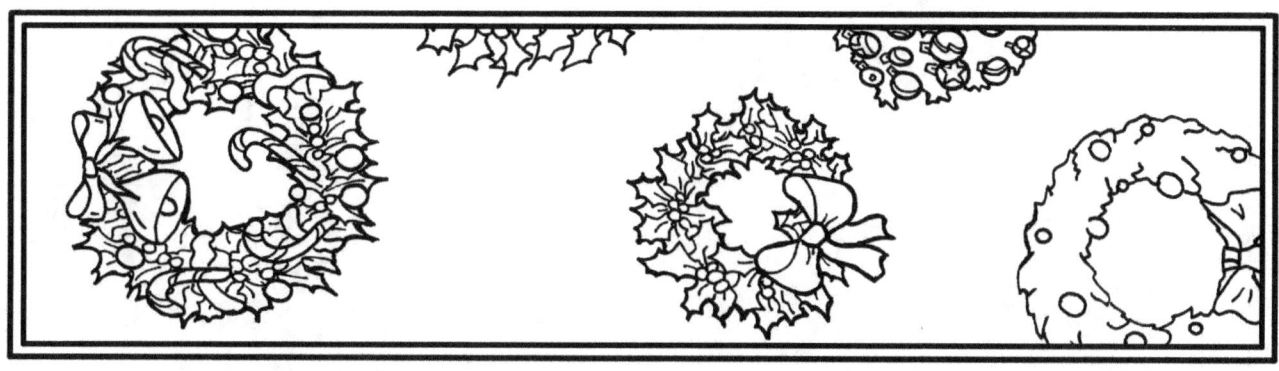

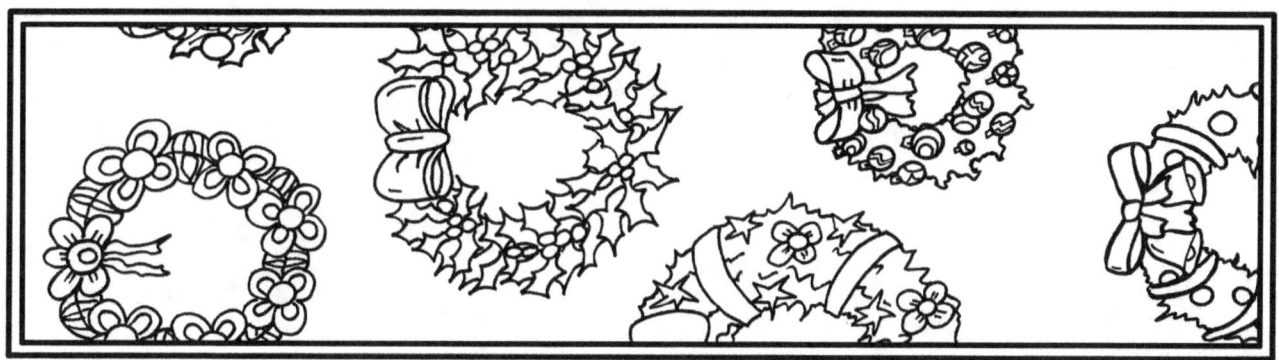

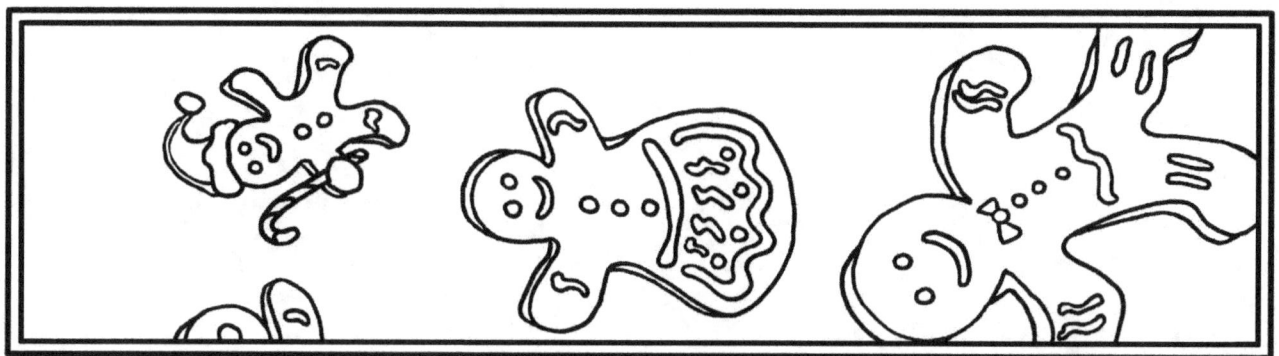

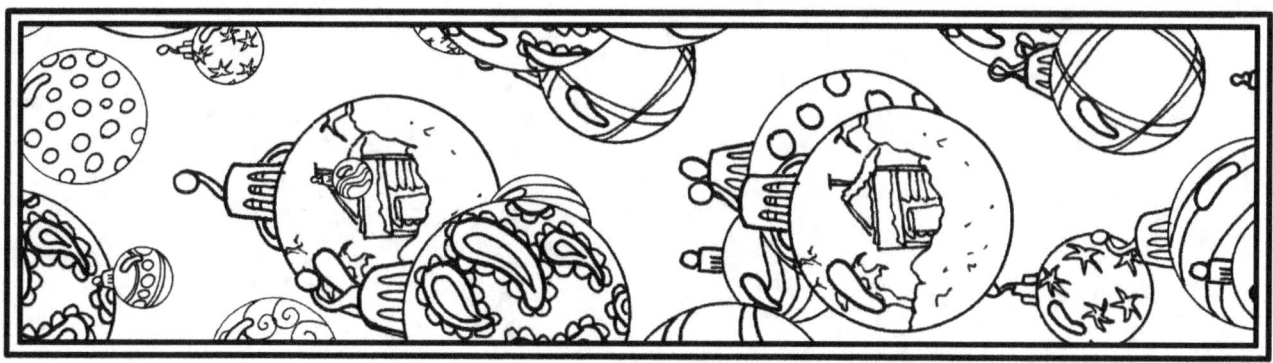

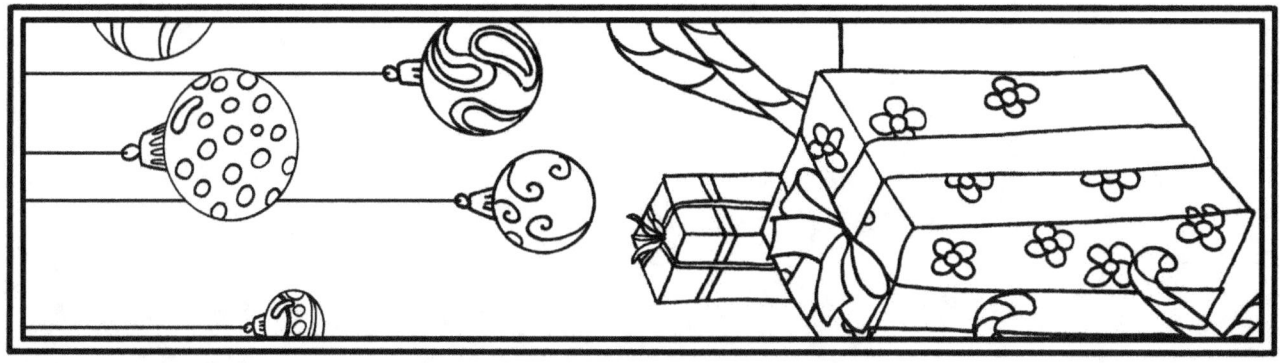

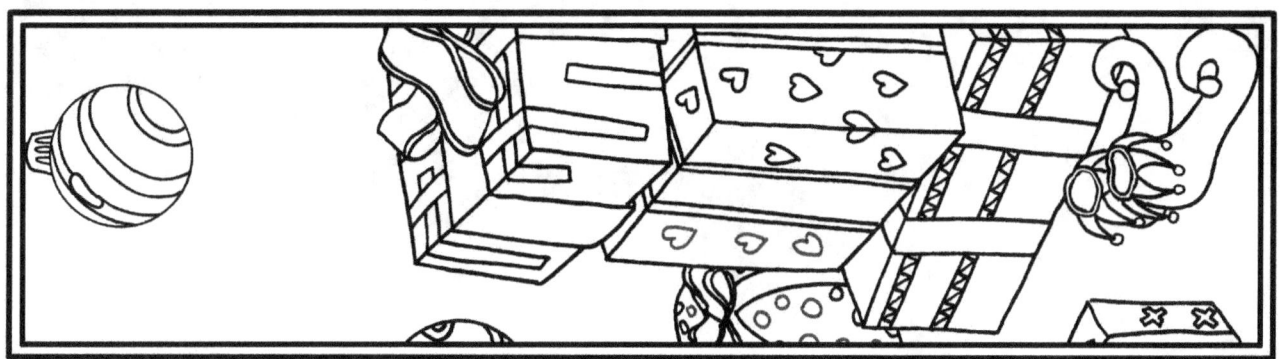

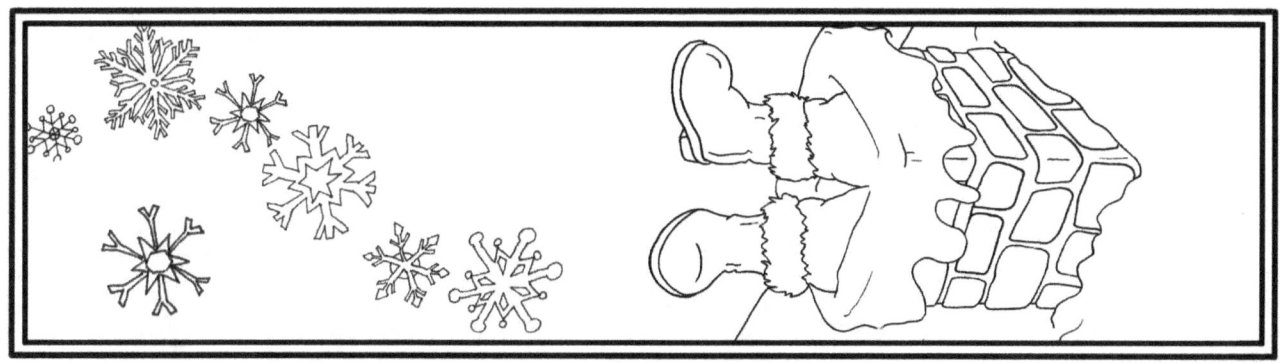

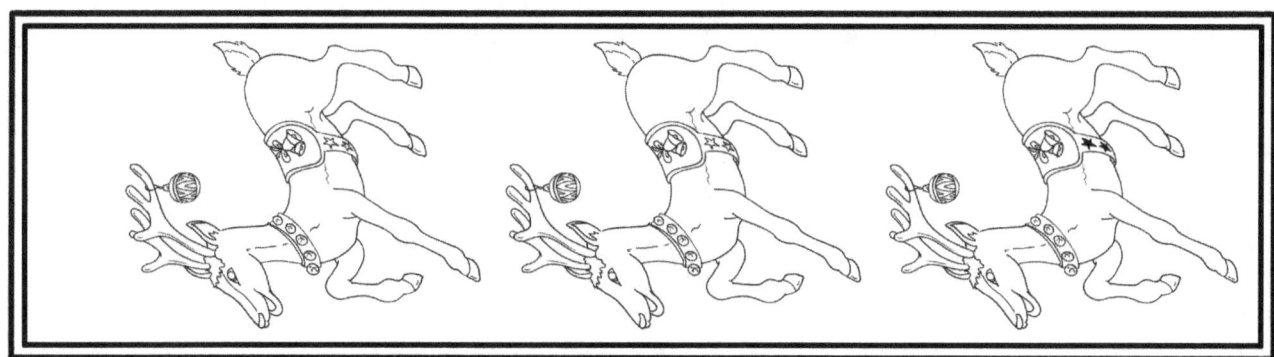

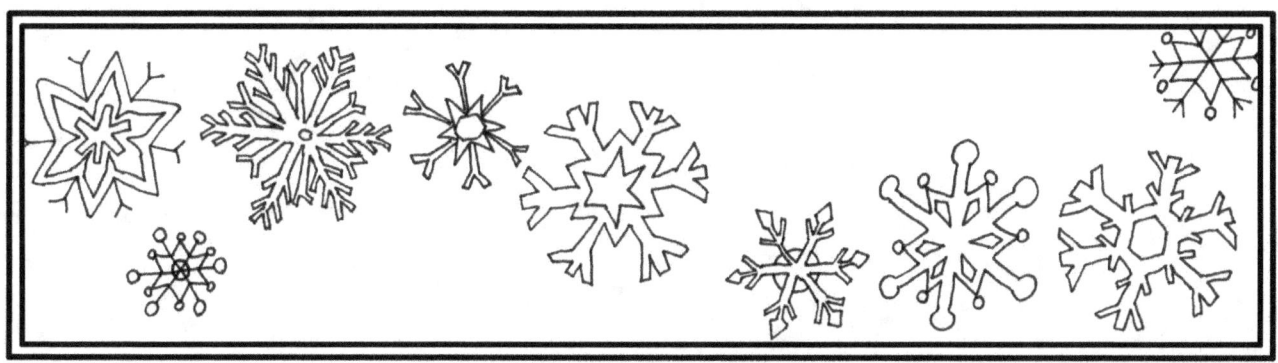

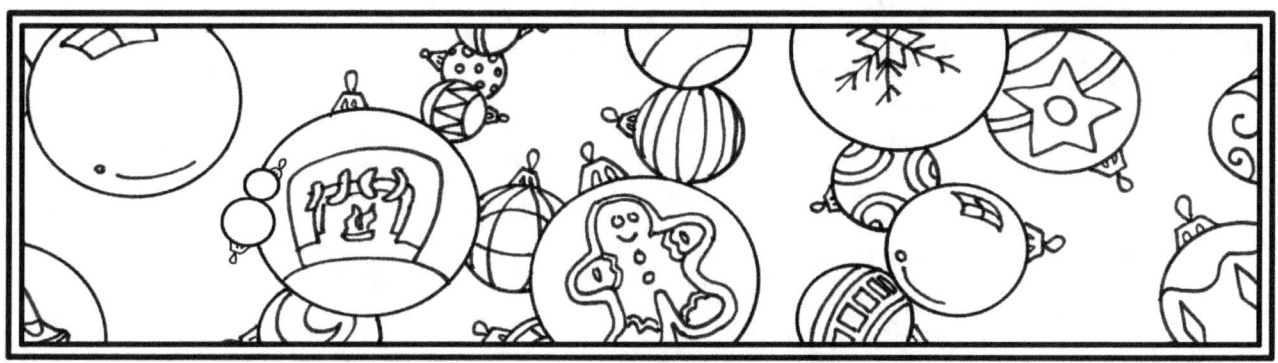

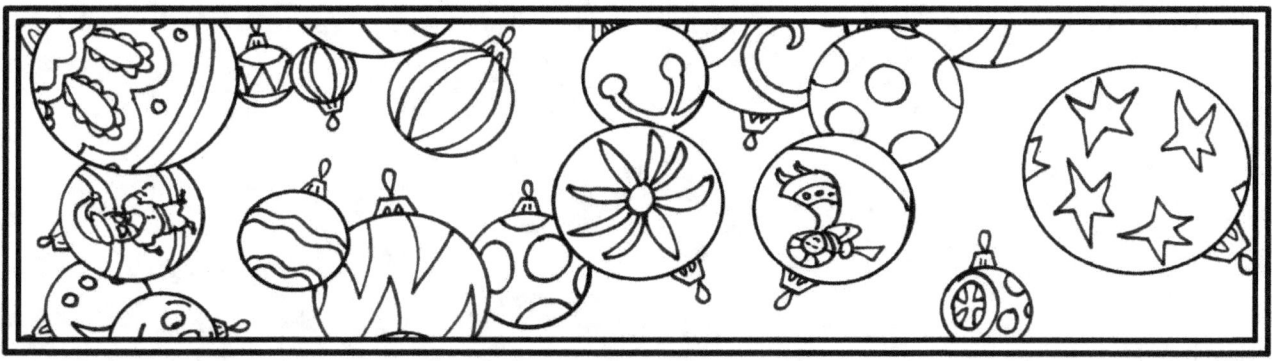

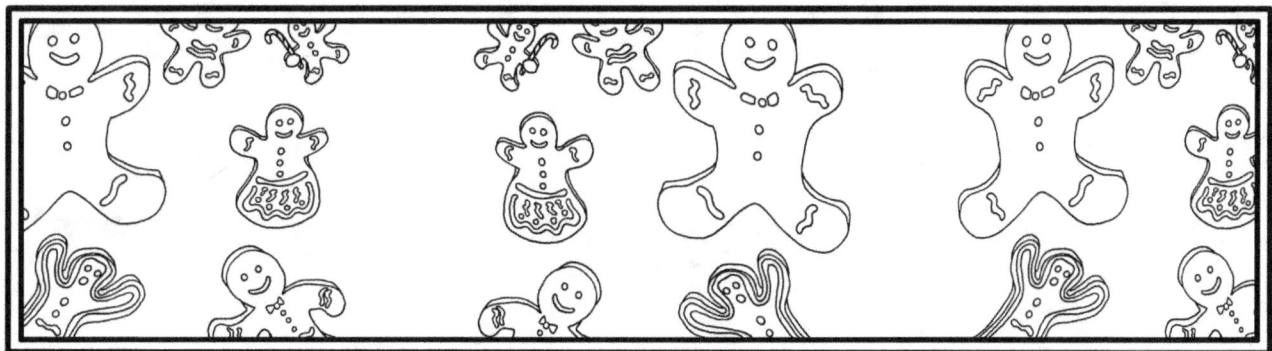

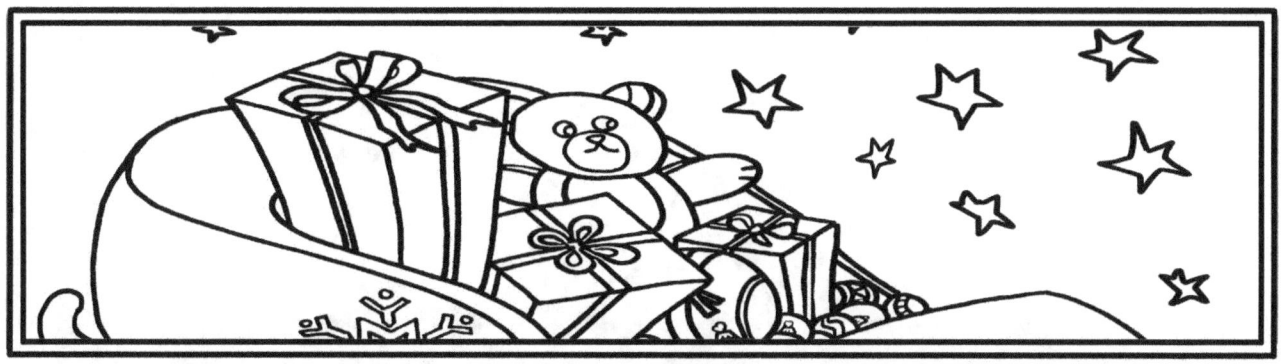
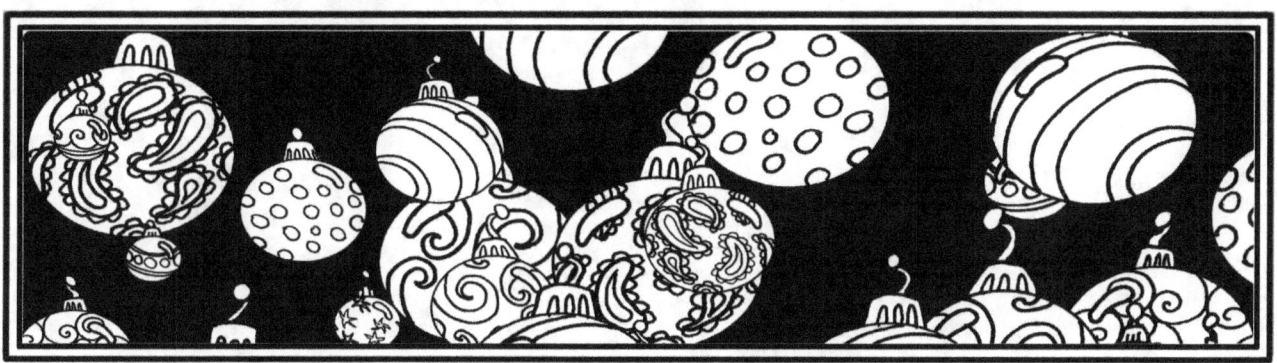
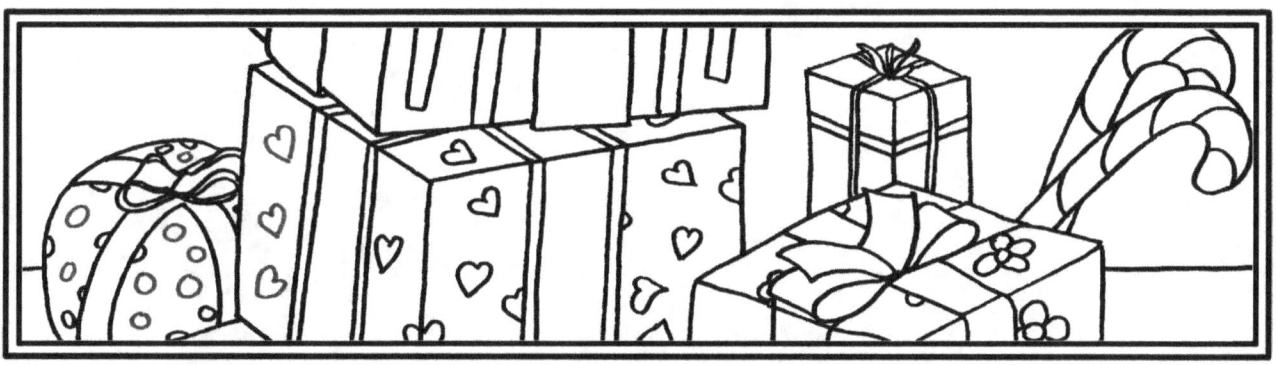
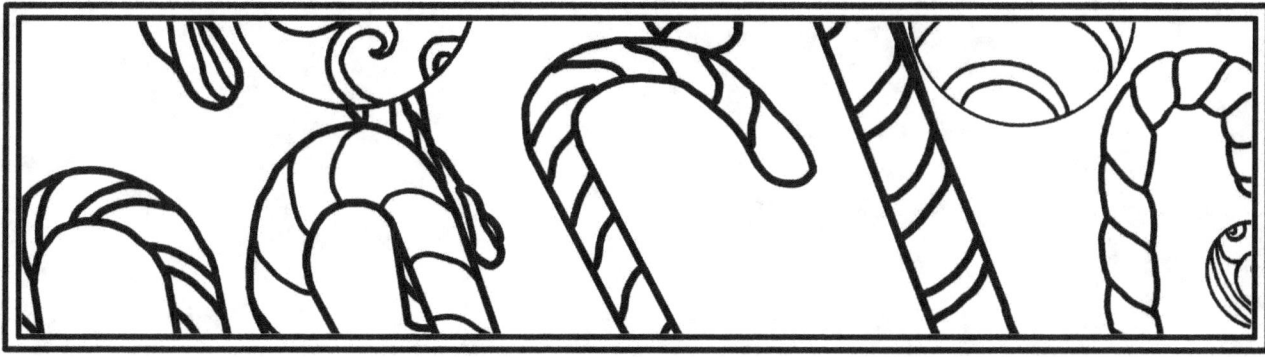

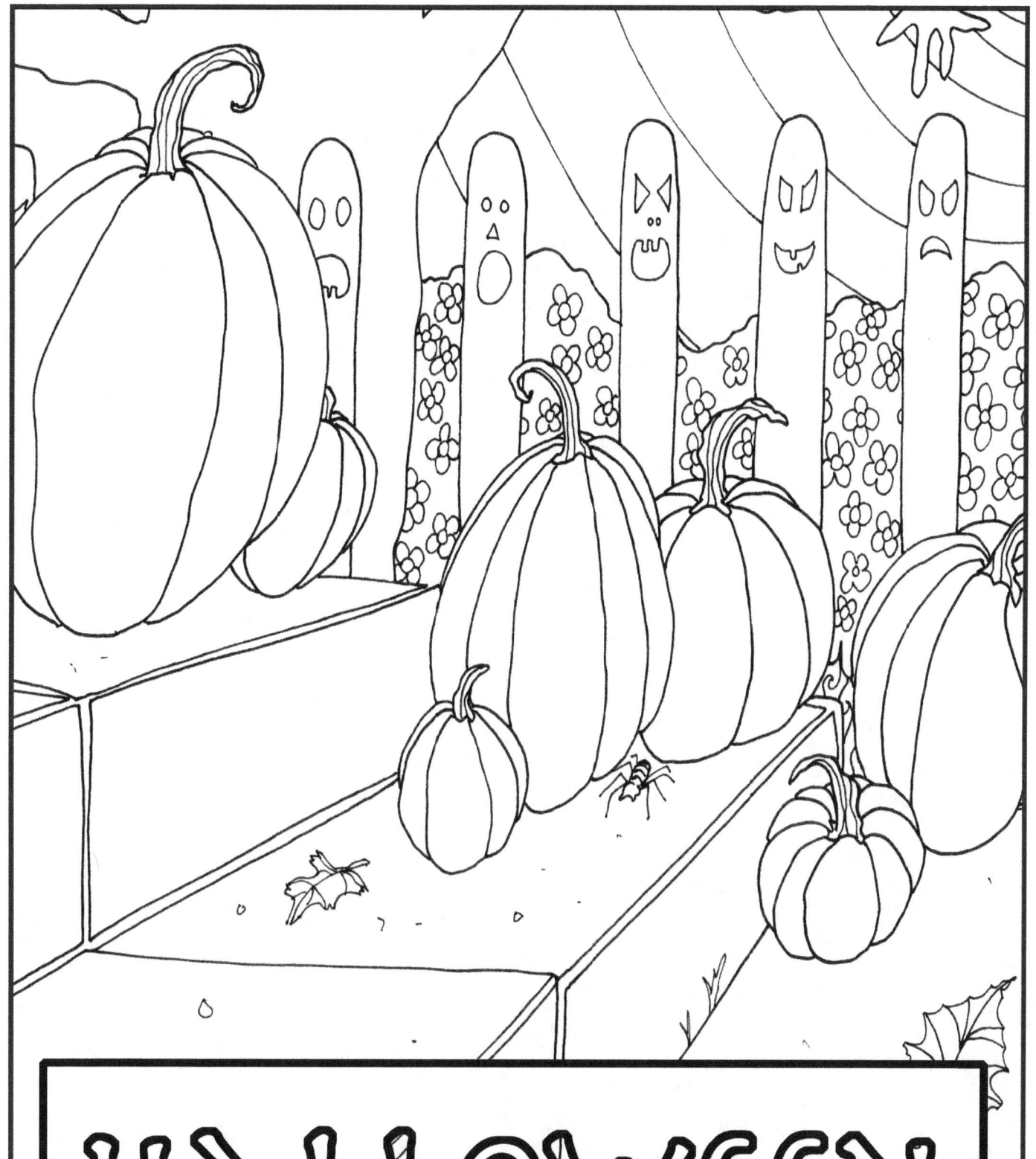

HALLOWEEN

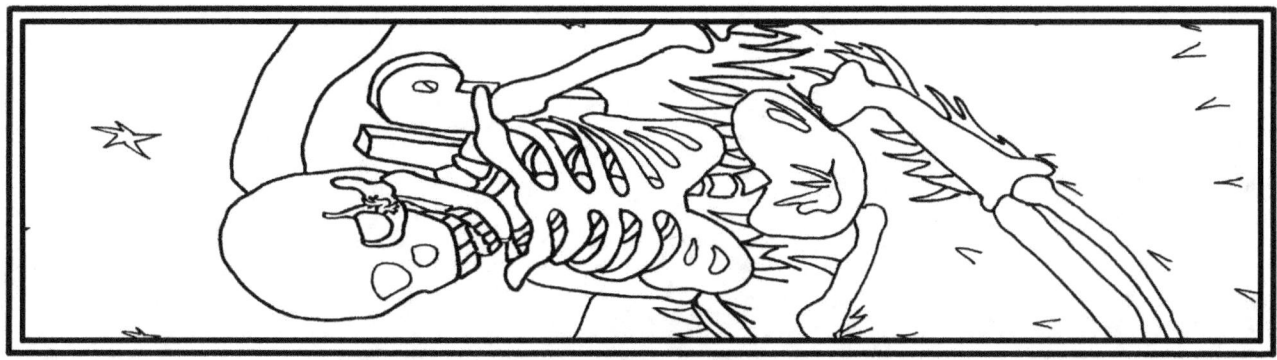
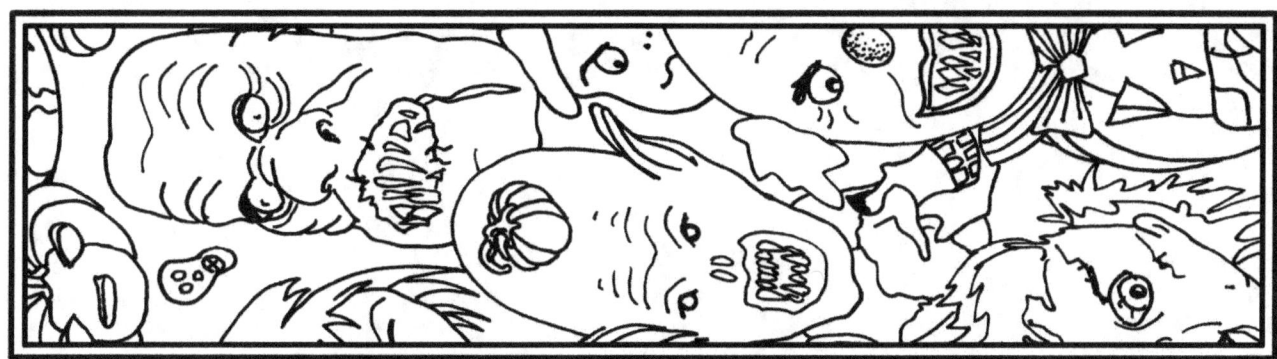
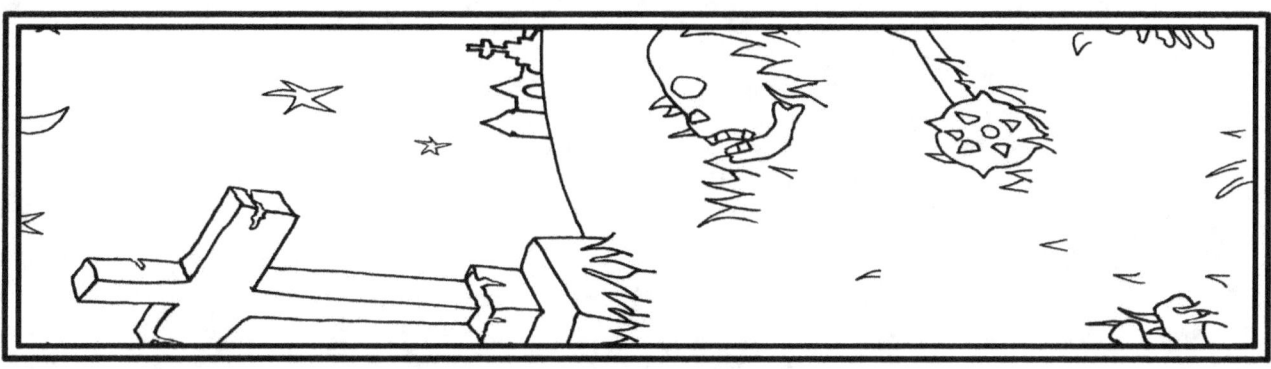
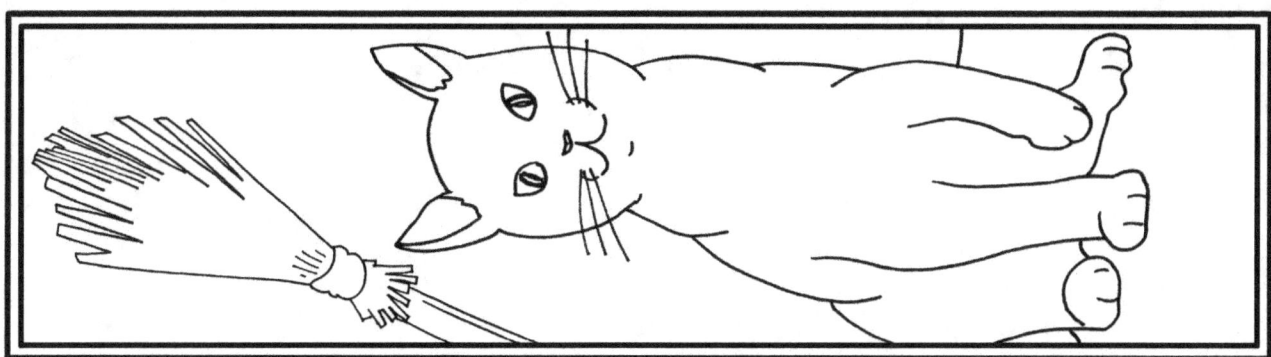

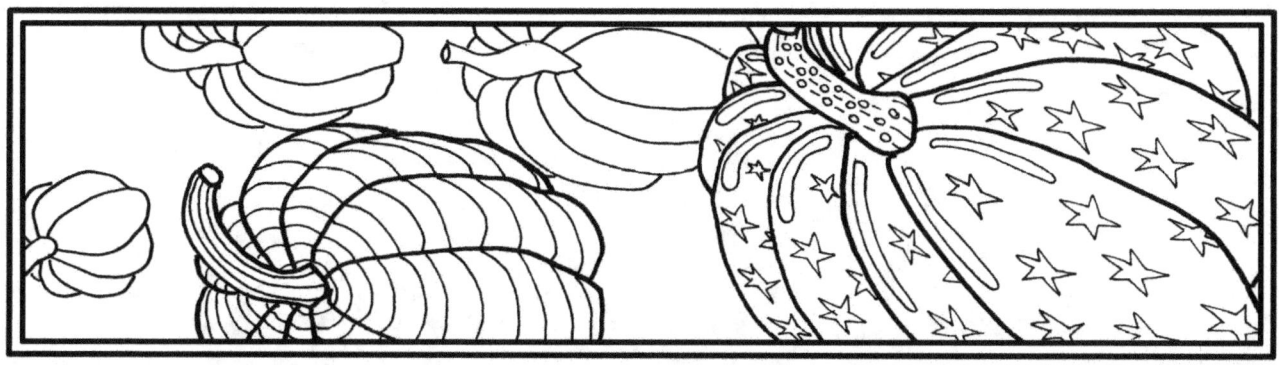
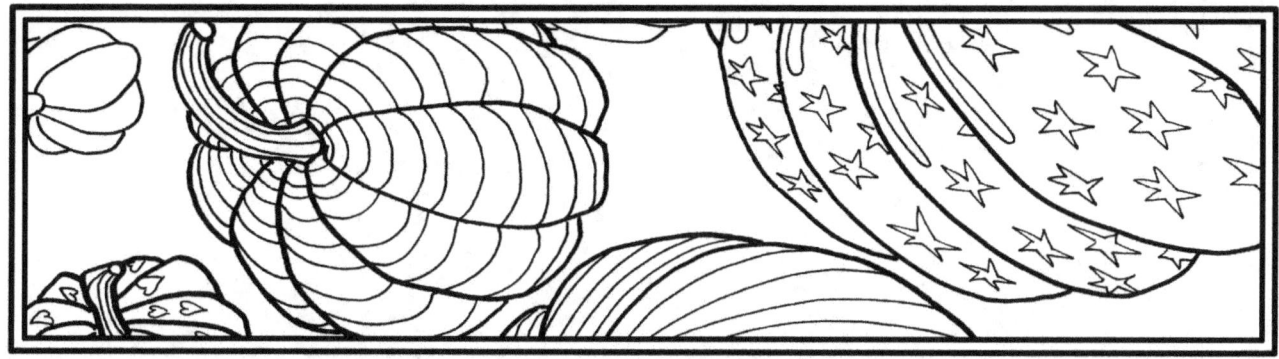
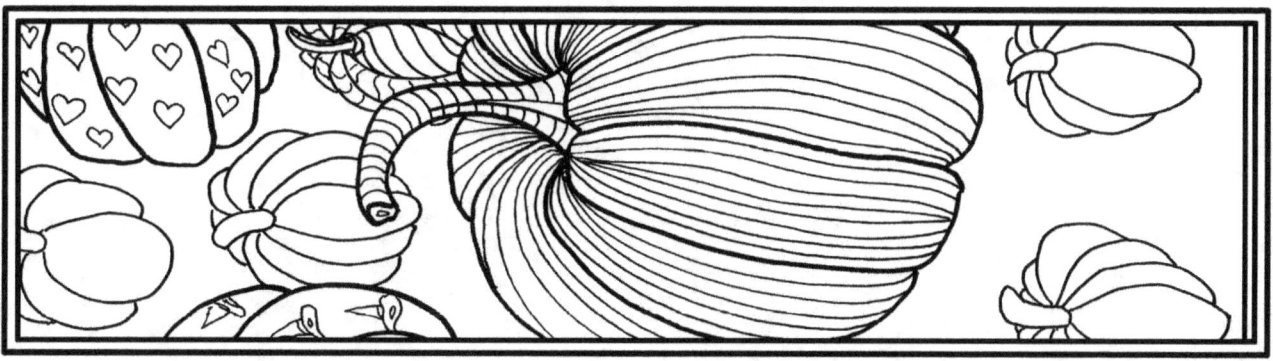
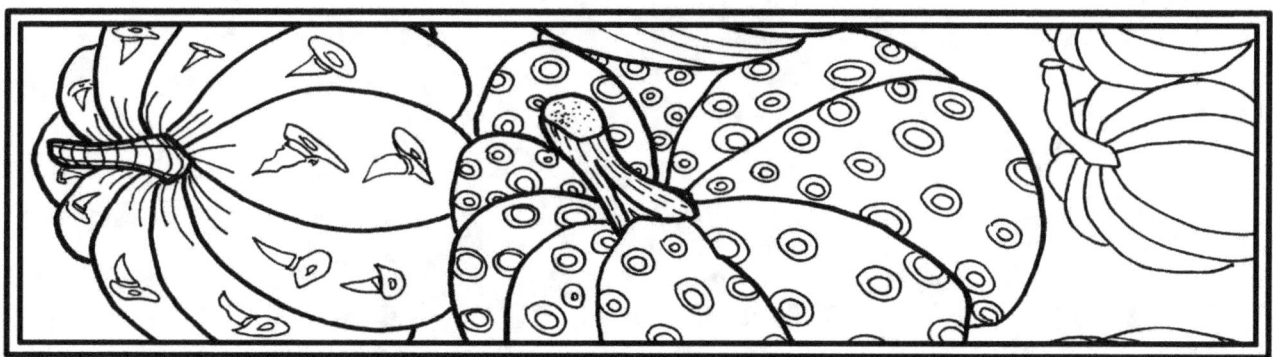

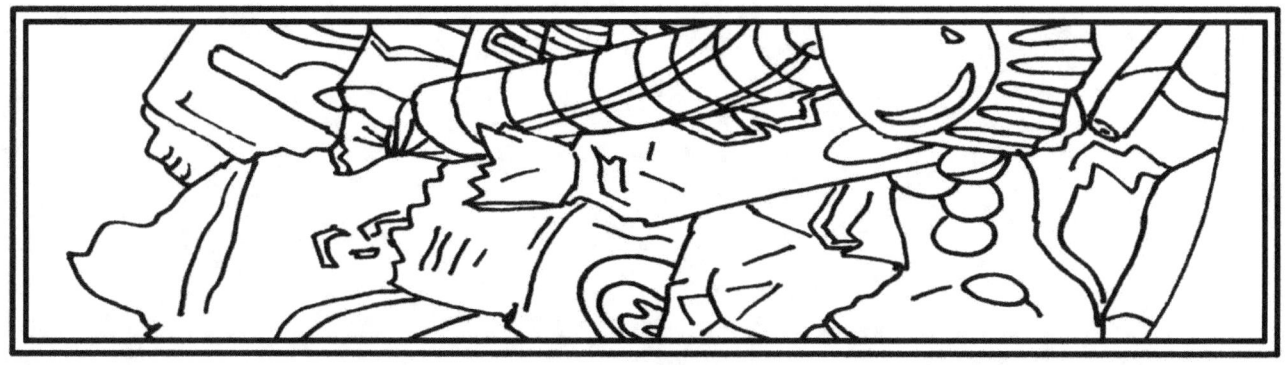

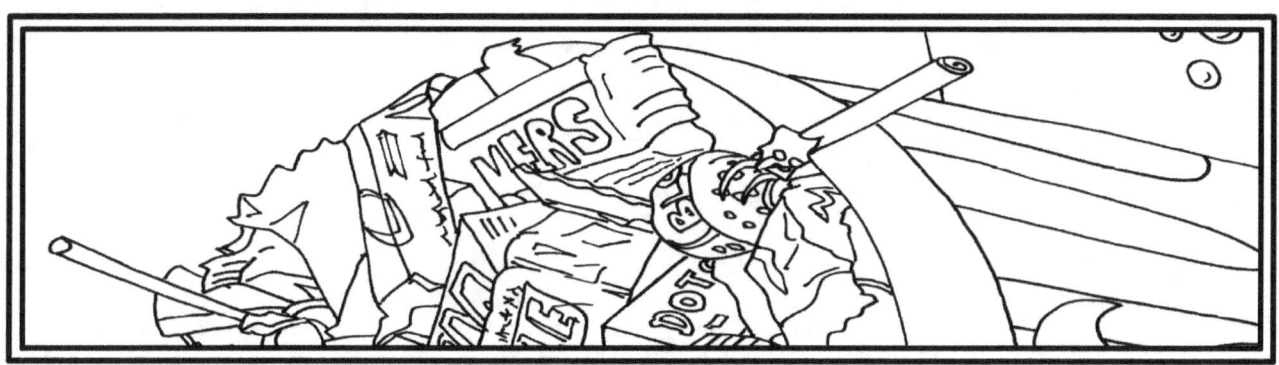

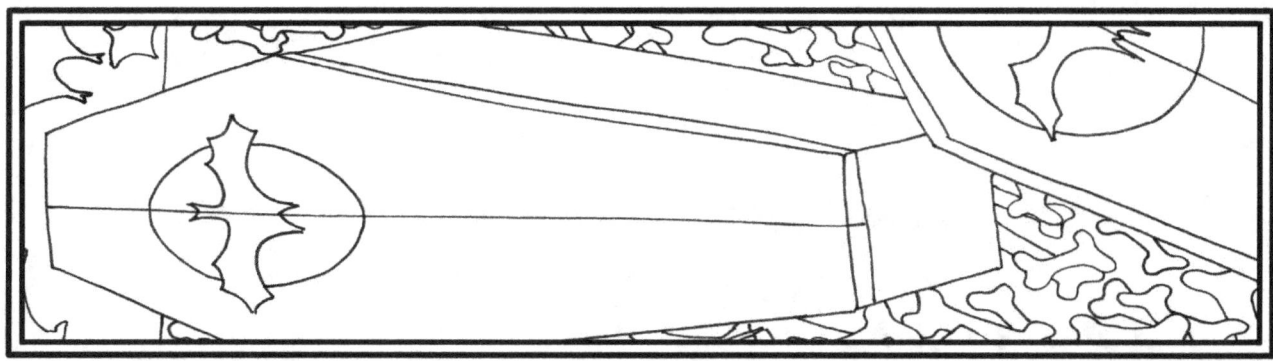

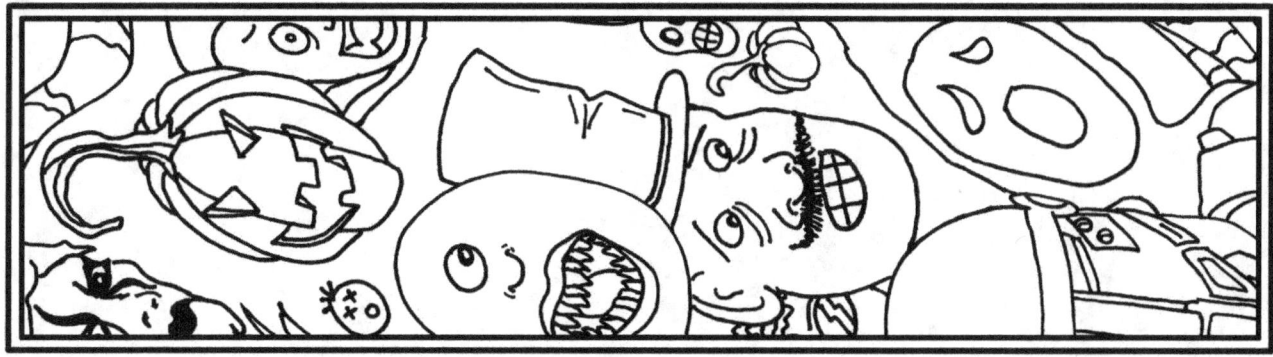

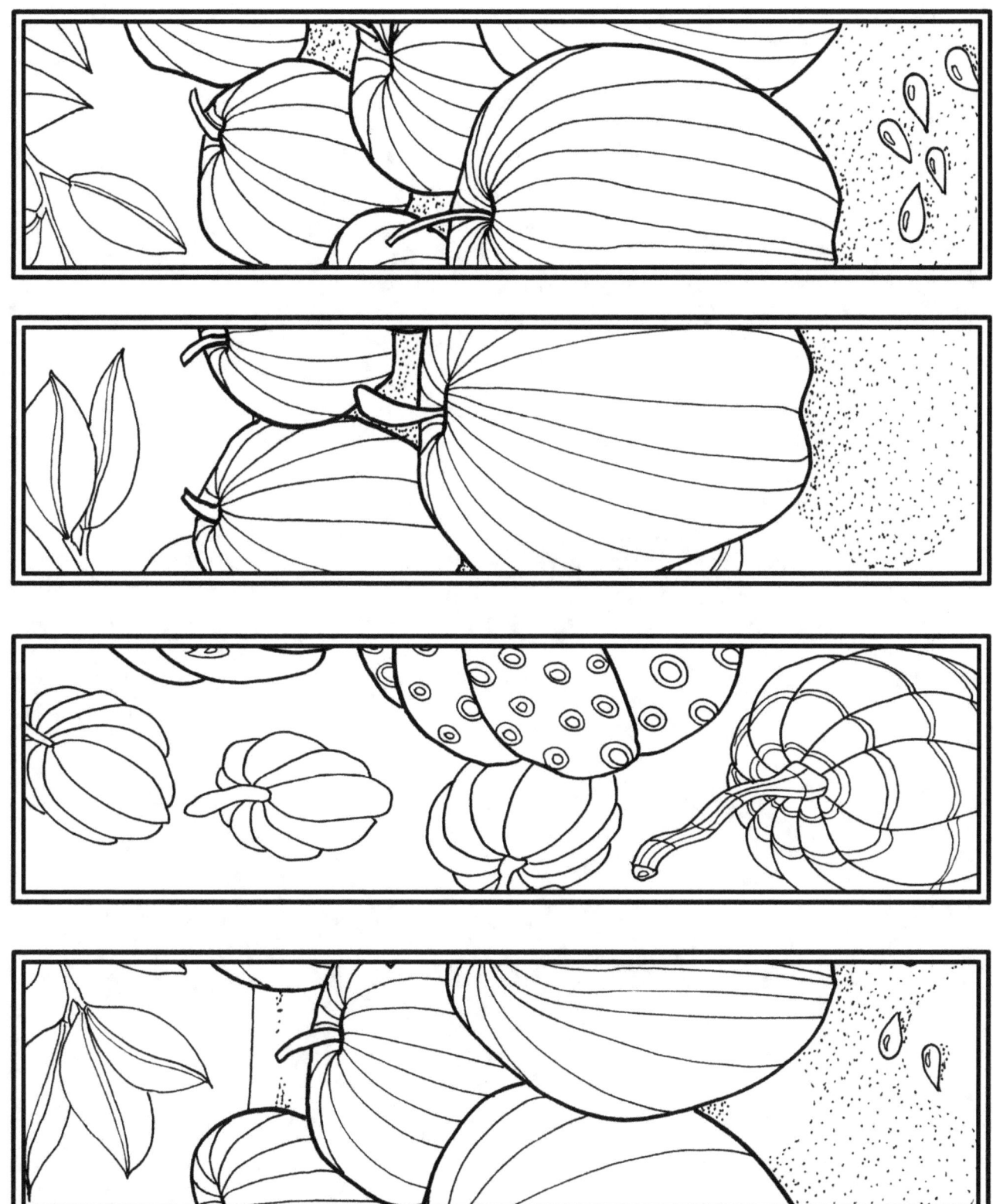

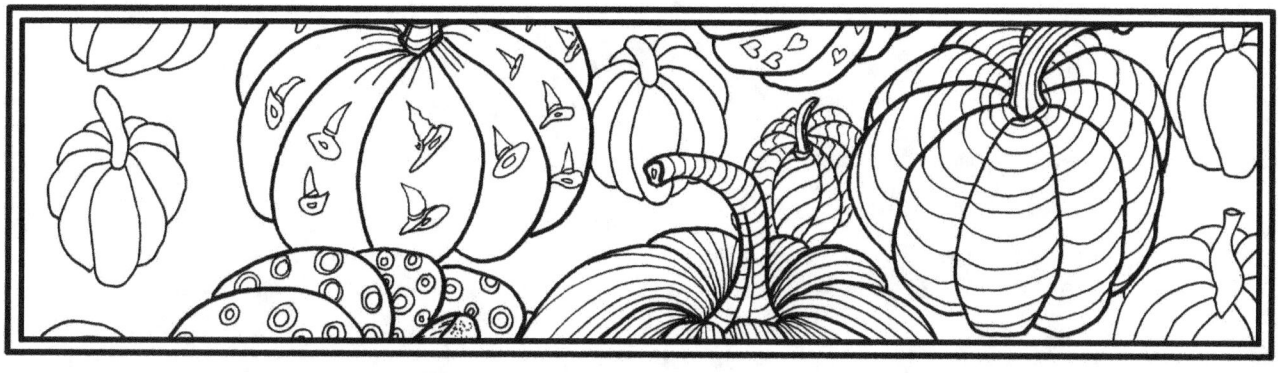

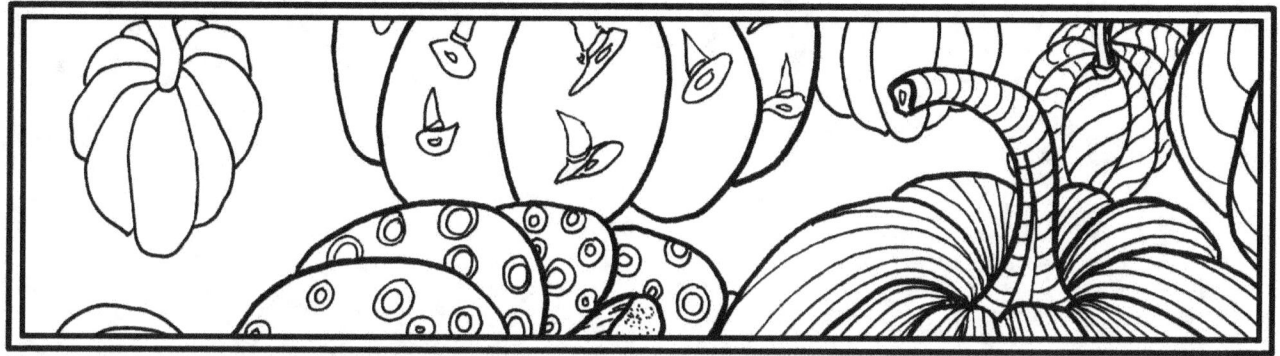

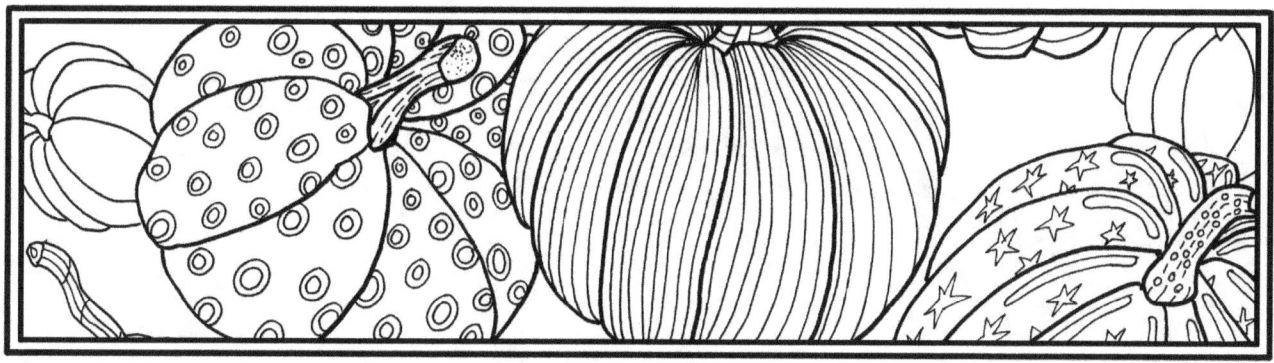

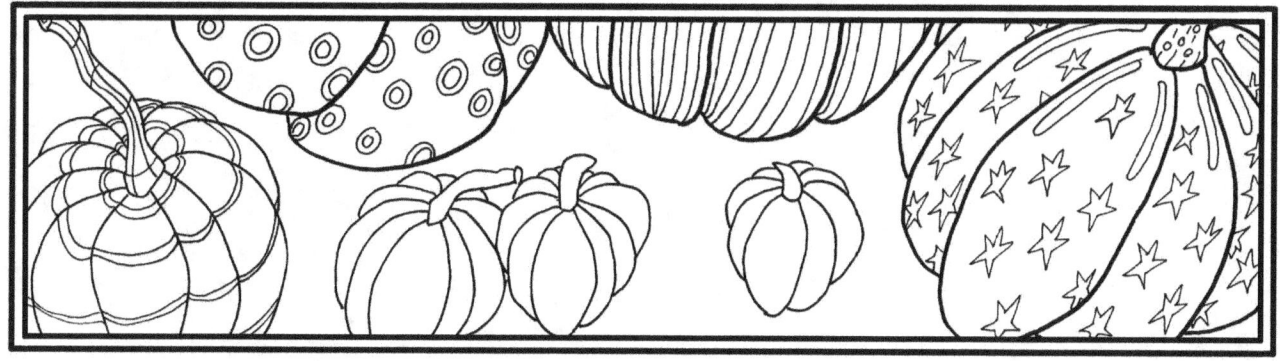

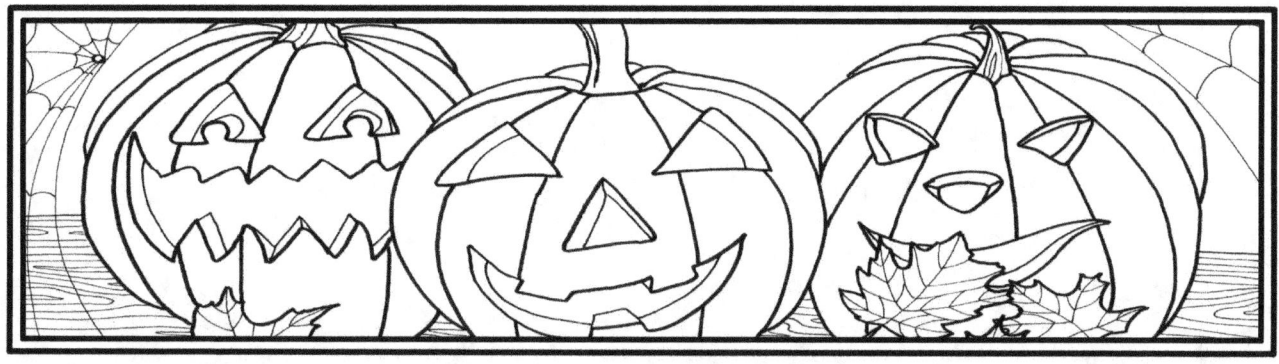
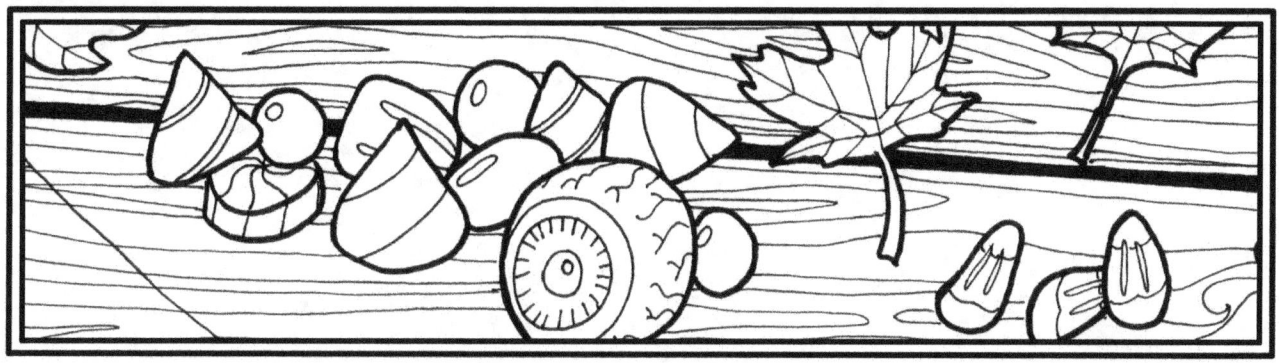
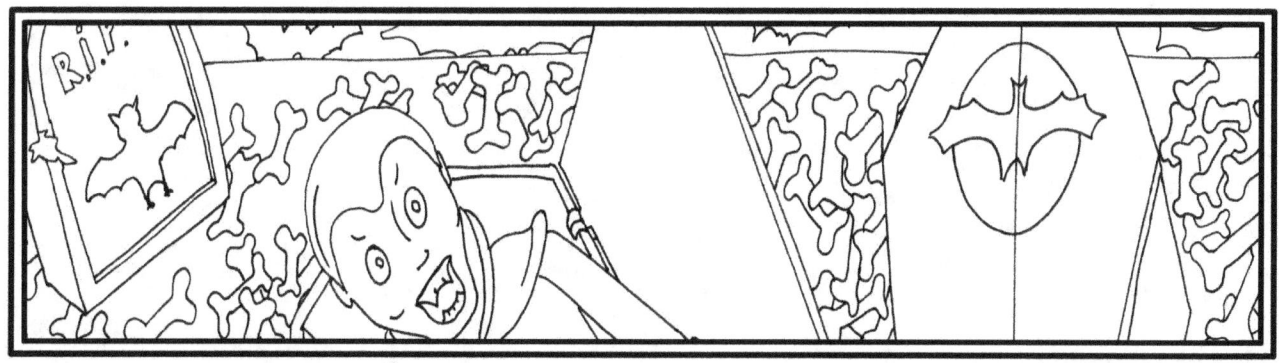
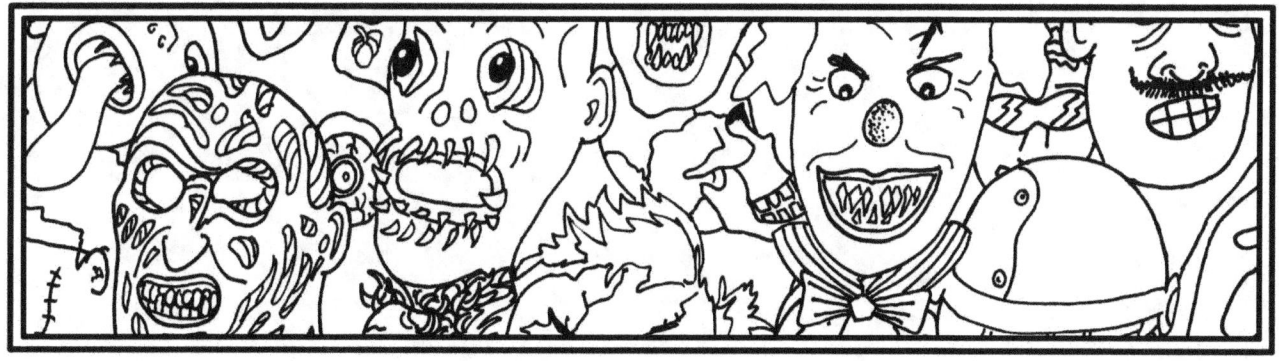

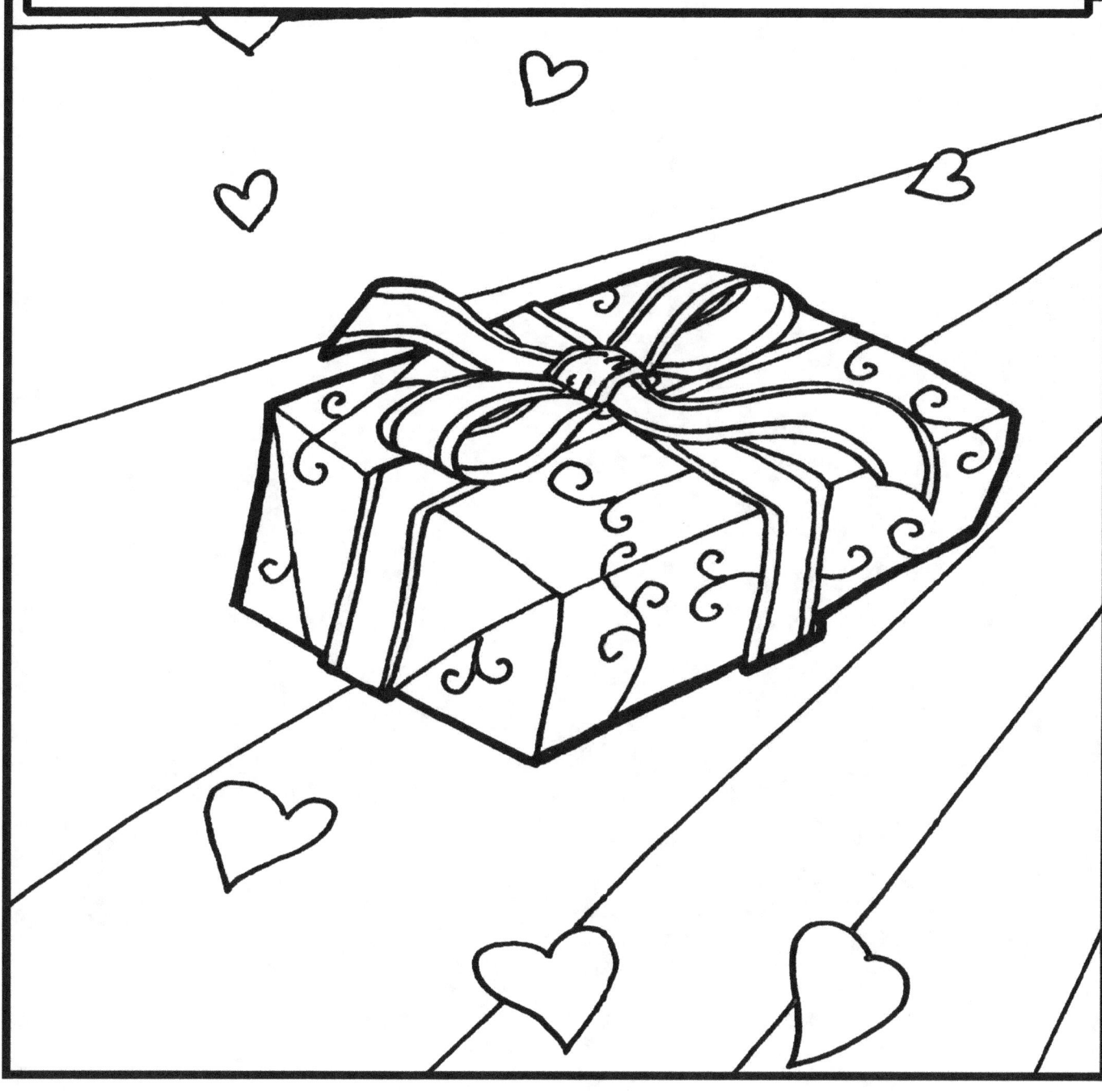

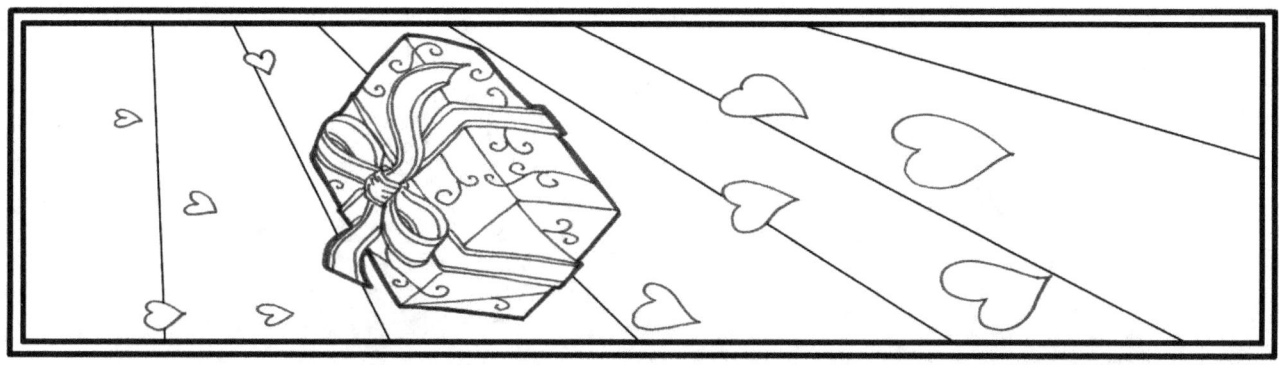
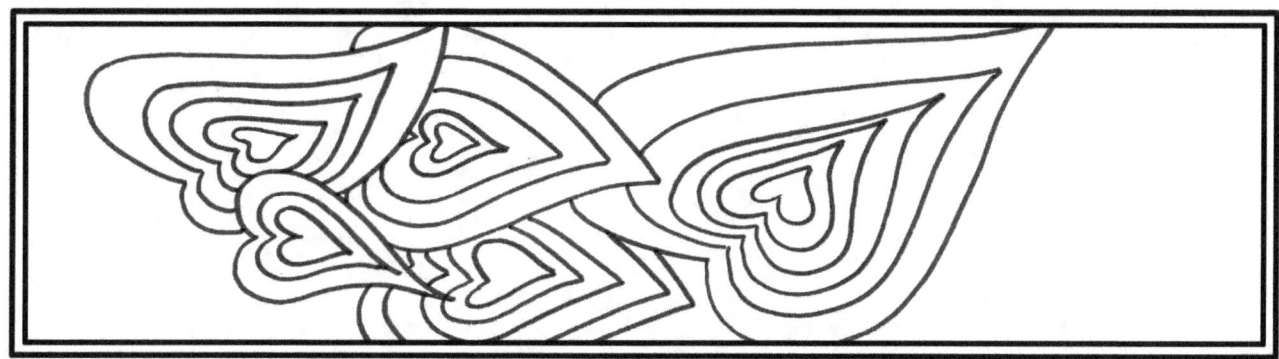
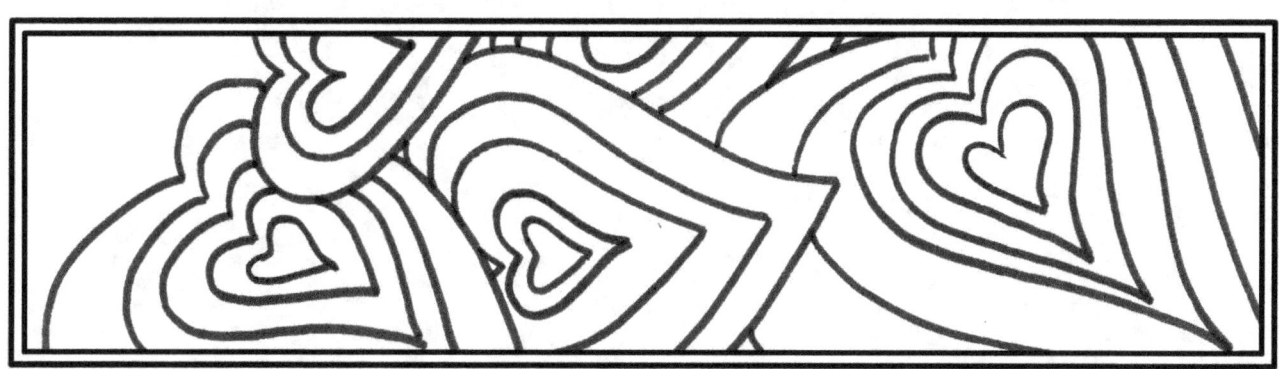
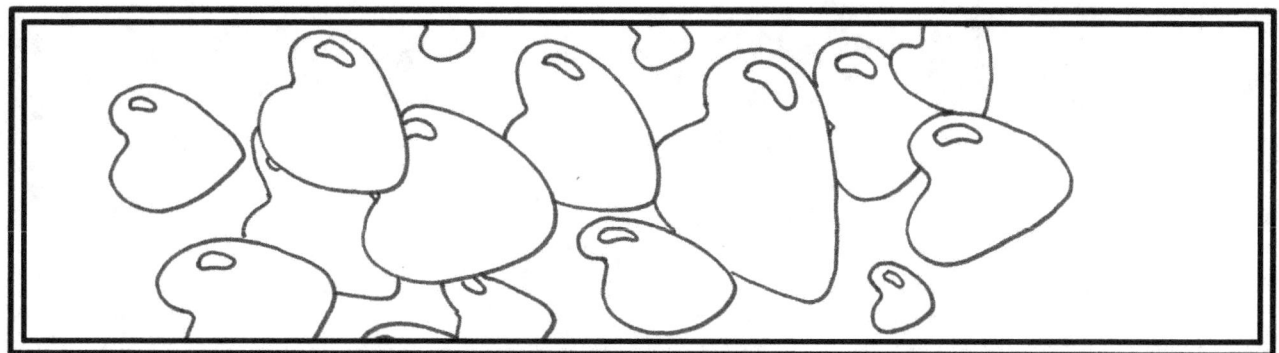

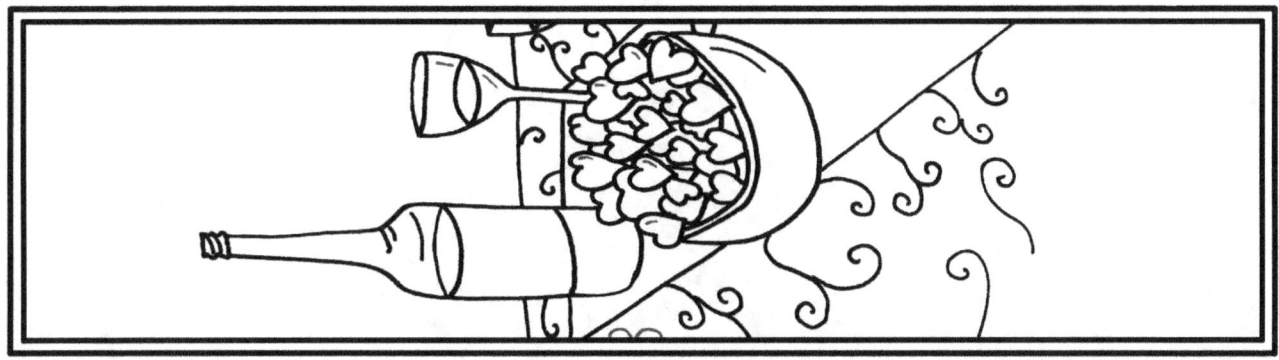

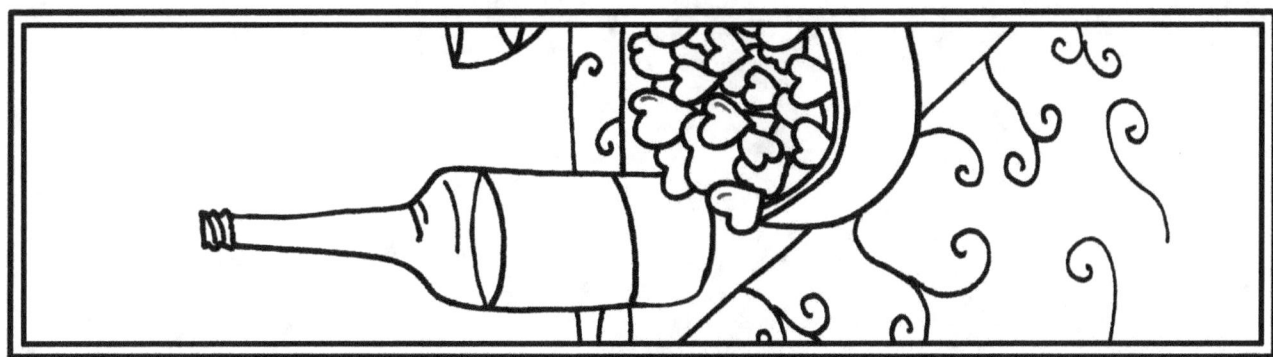

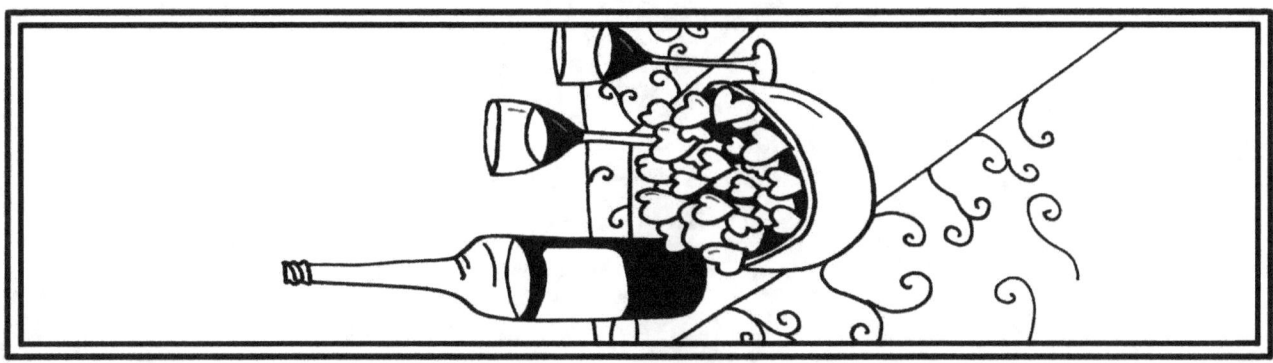

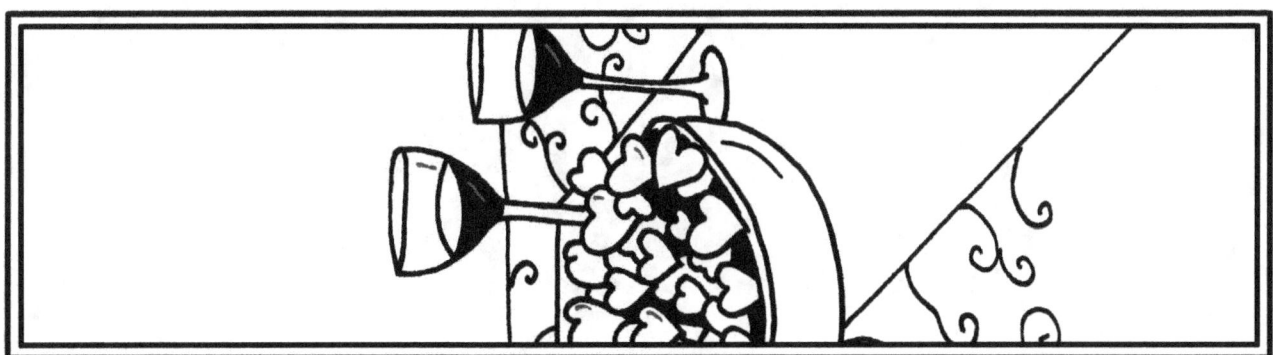

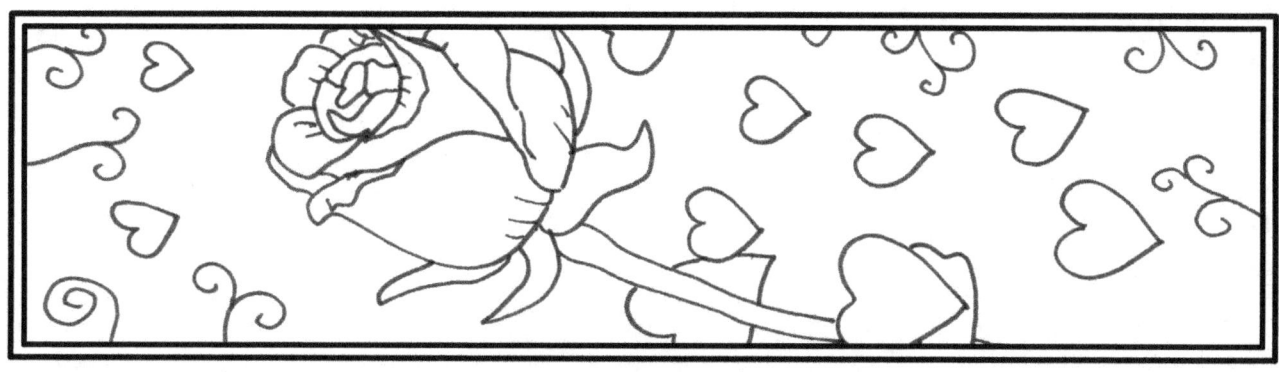

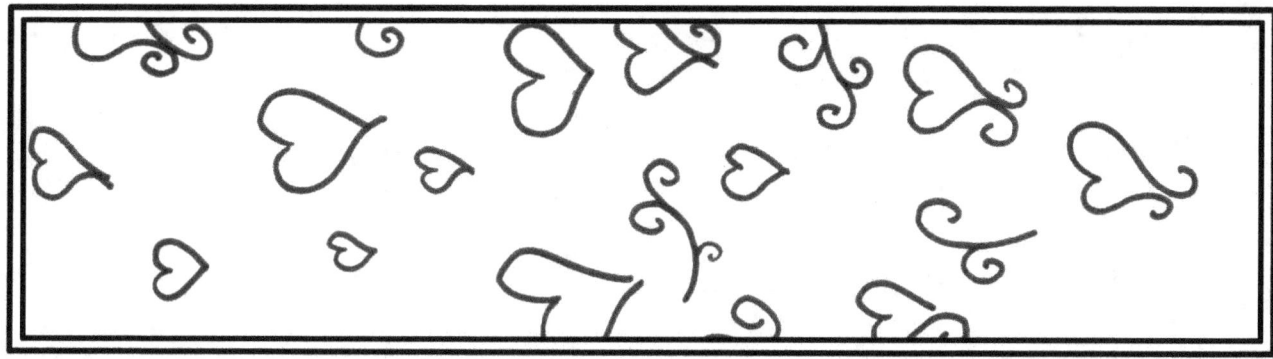

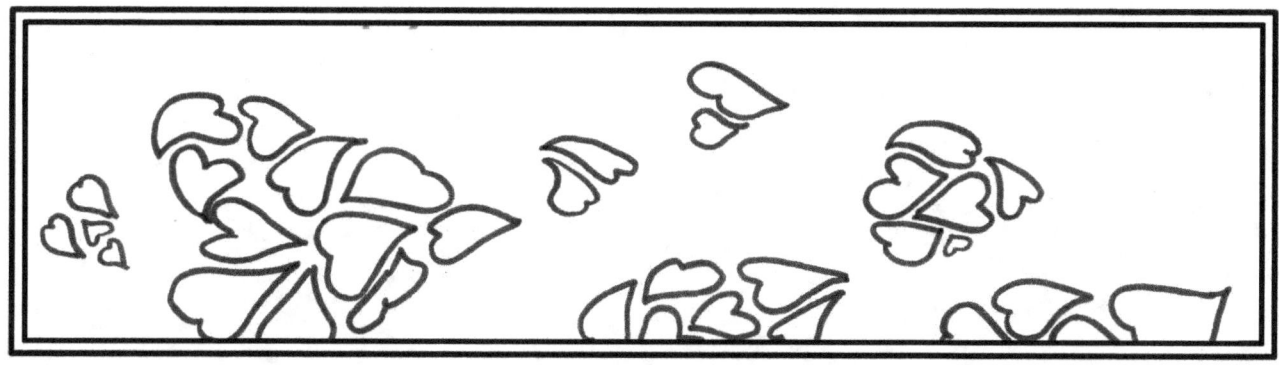

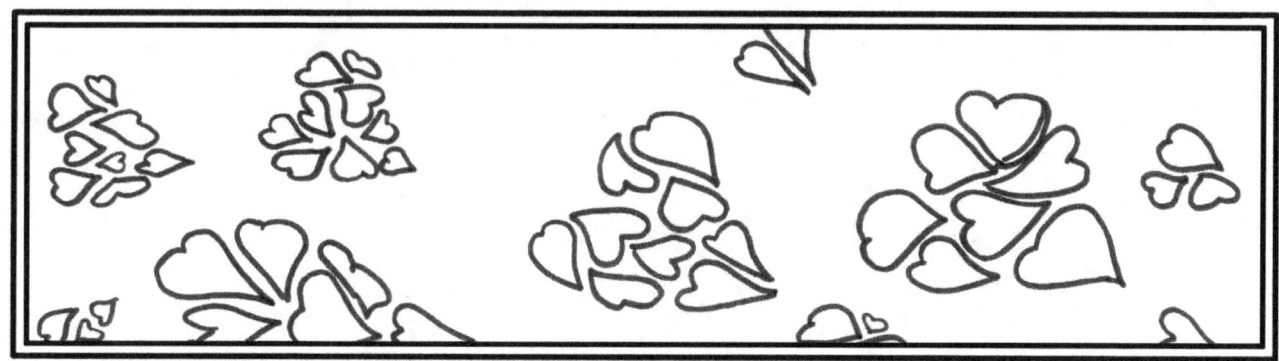

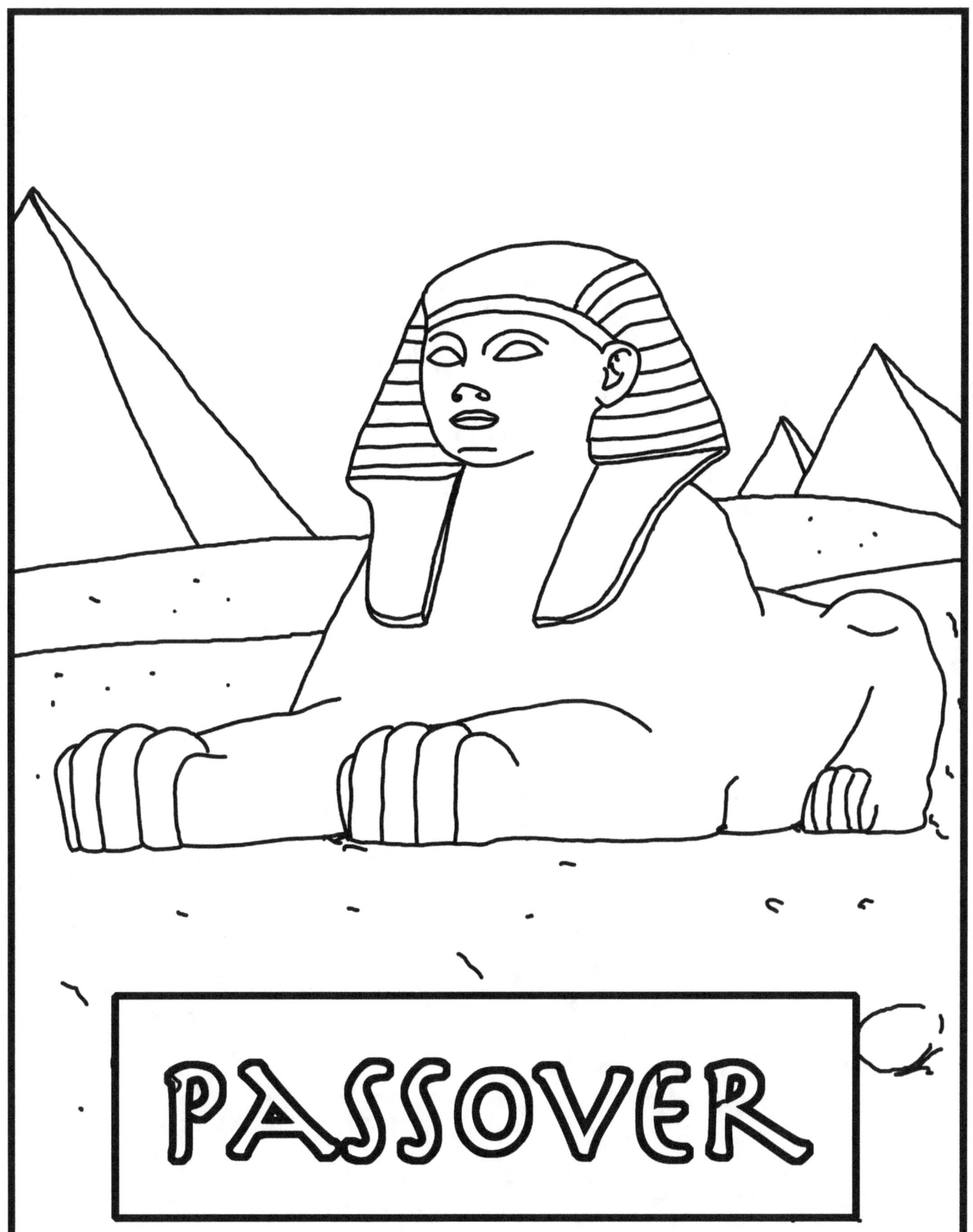

Happy Passover

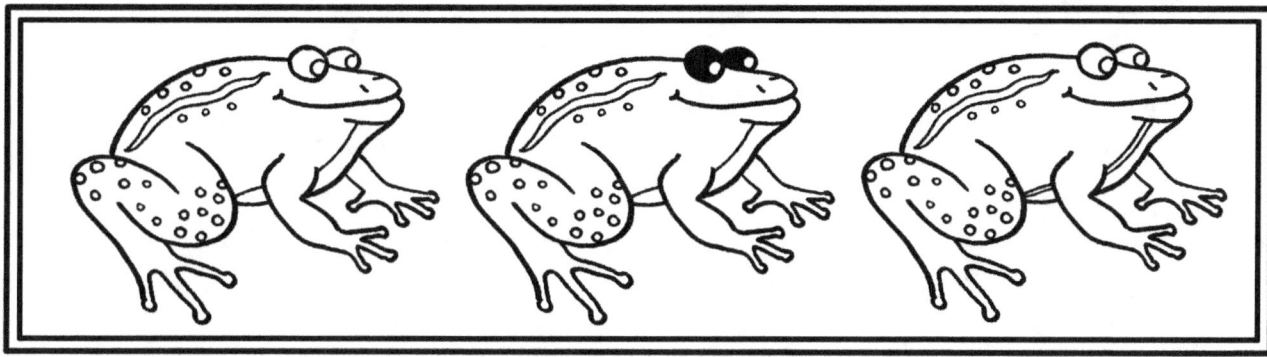

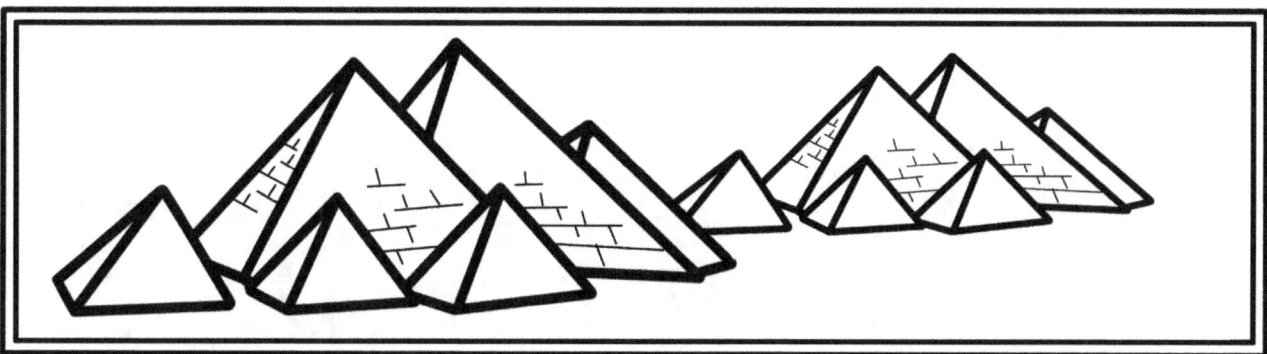

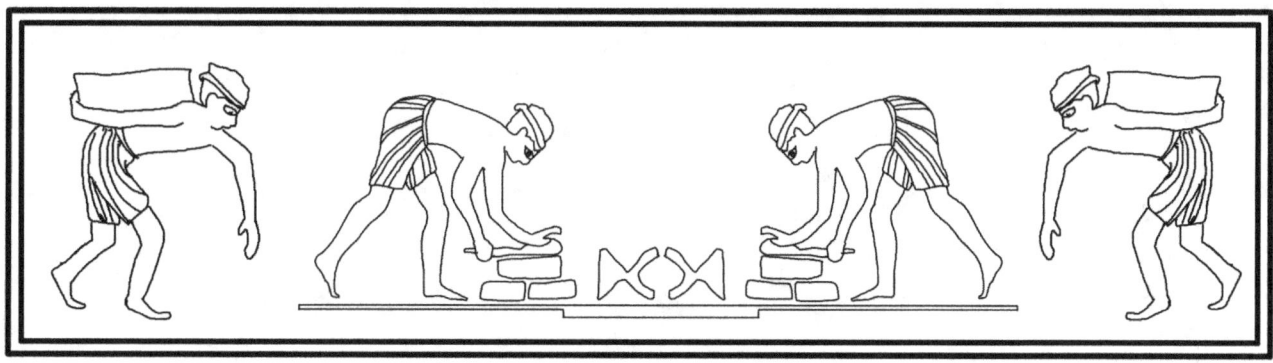

Happy פ Passover!

Happy Passover!

Happy פ passover!

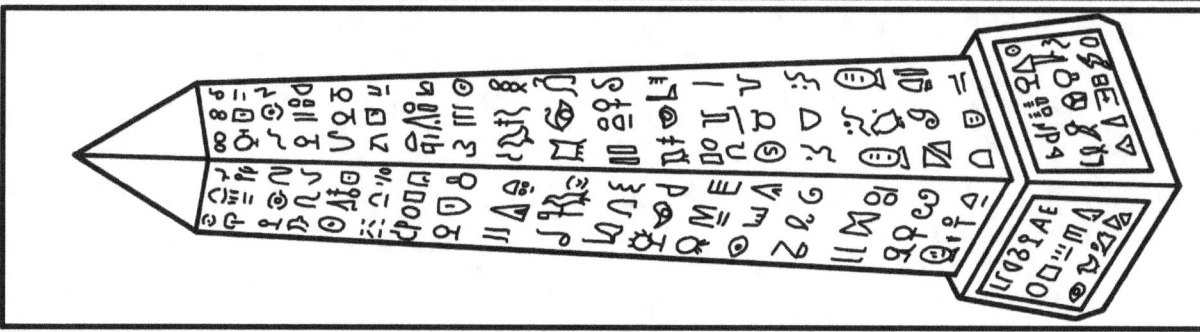

HANUKKAH

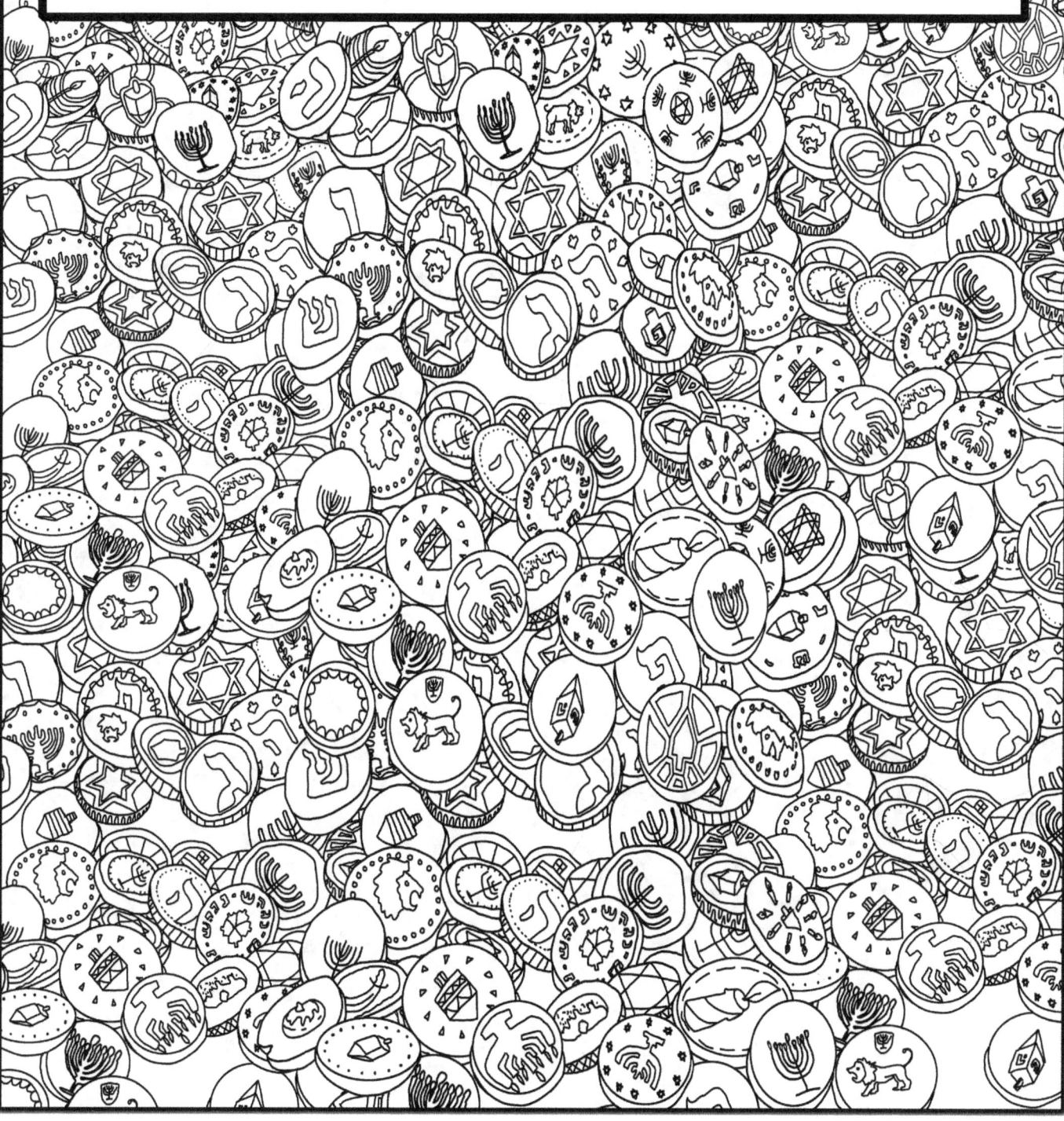

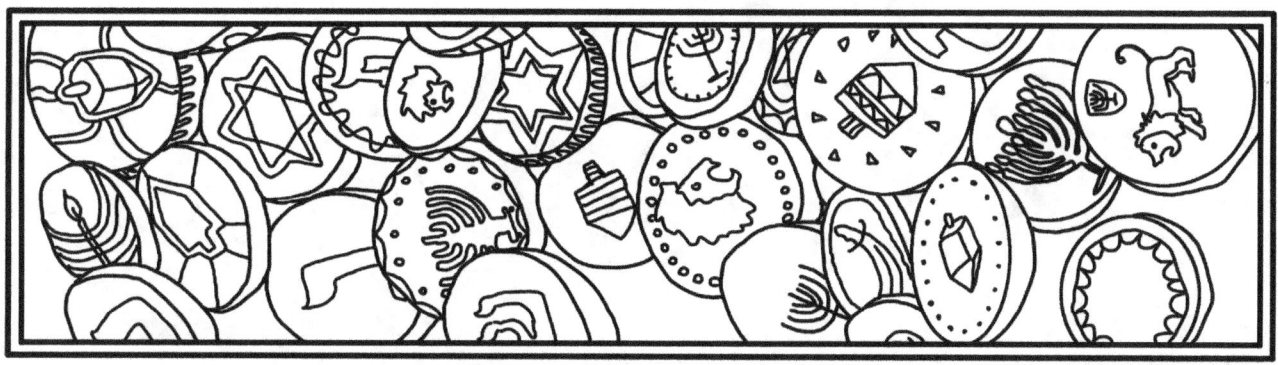

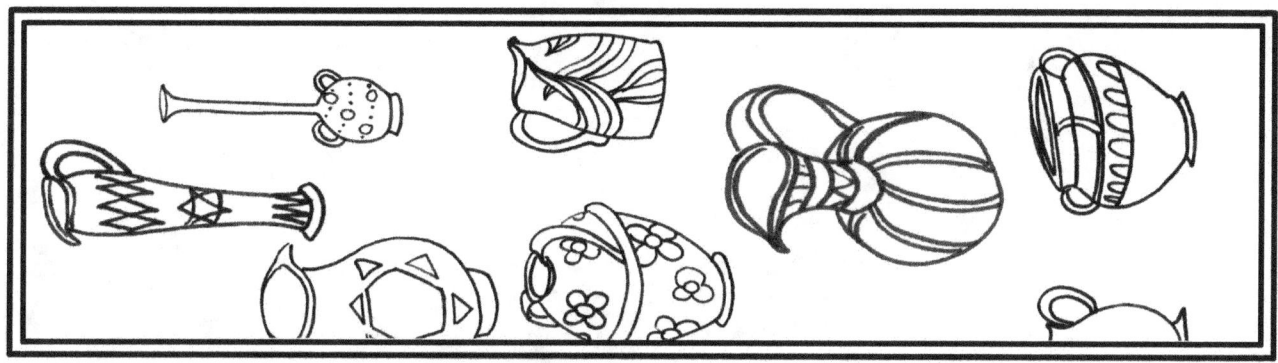

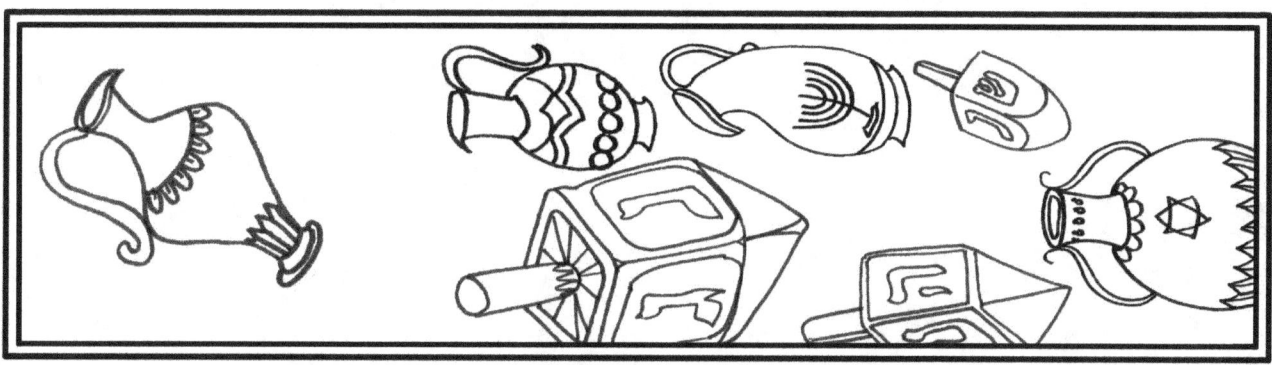

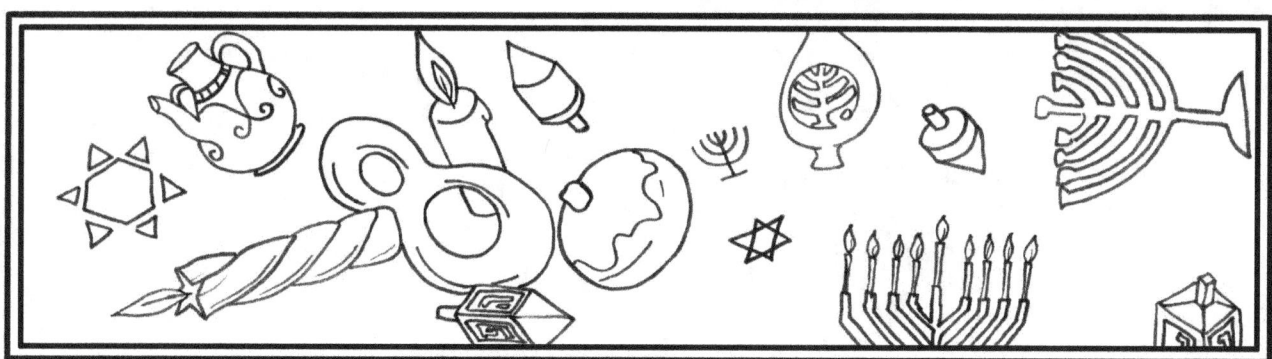

חג חנוכה שמח!

Happy Hanukkah!

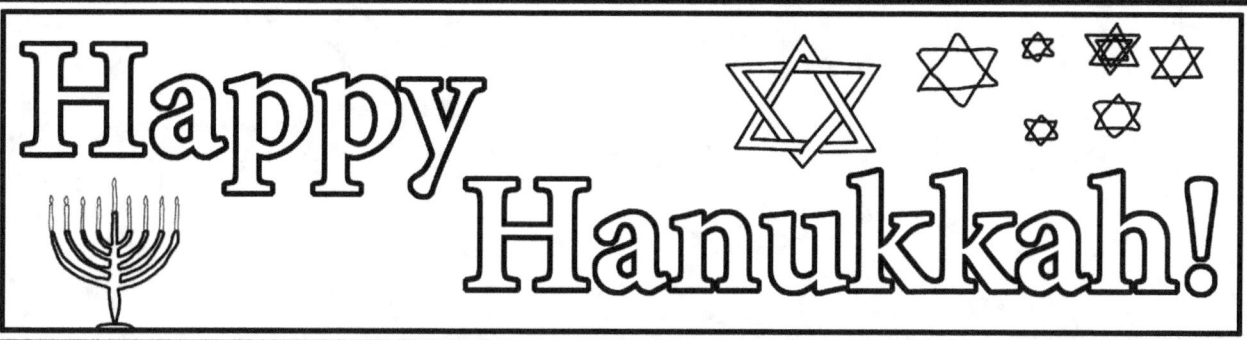

May Your *Hanukkah* Be Bright

Happy Hanukkah!
חג חנוכה שמח!

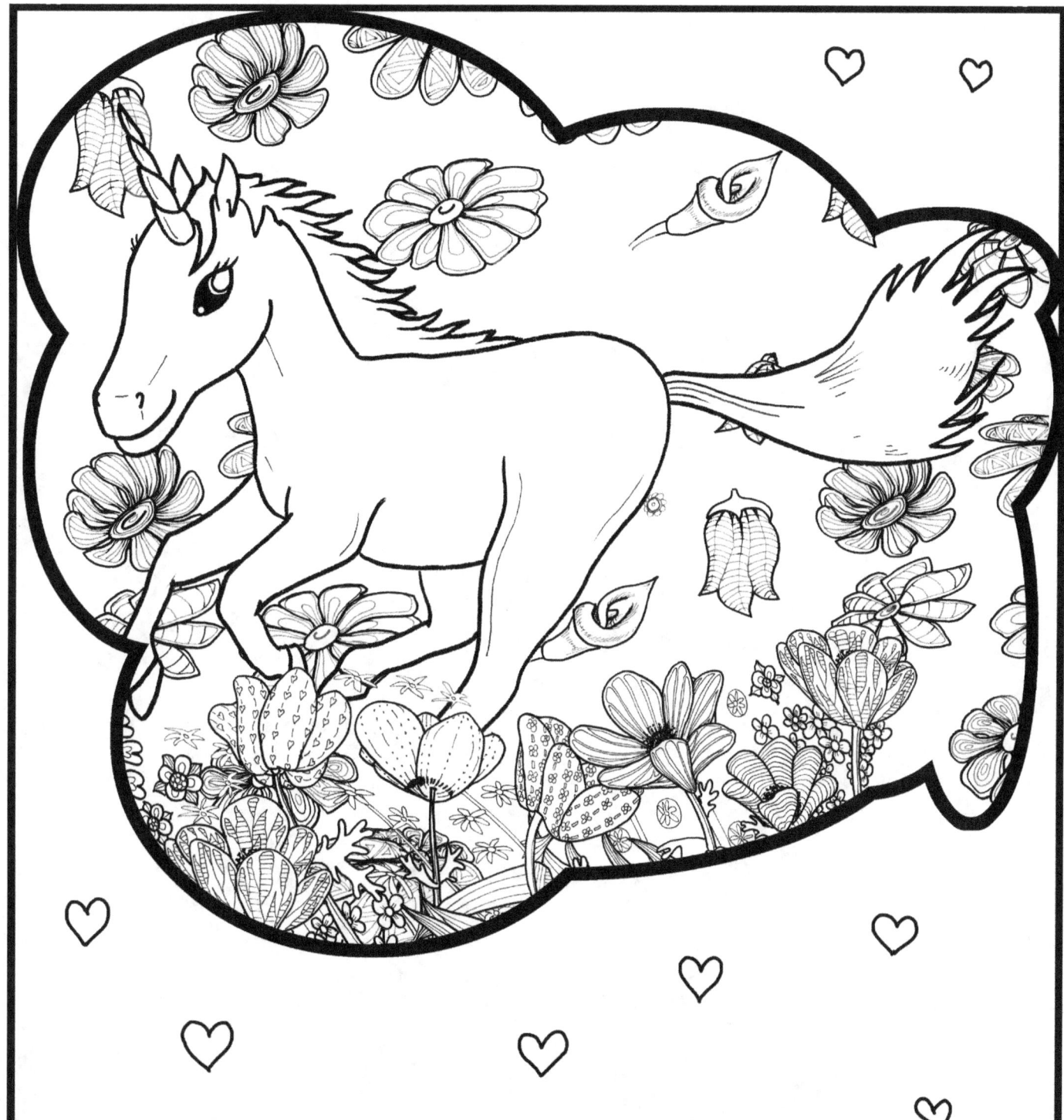

UNICORN

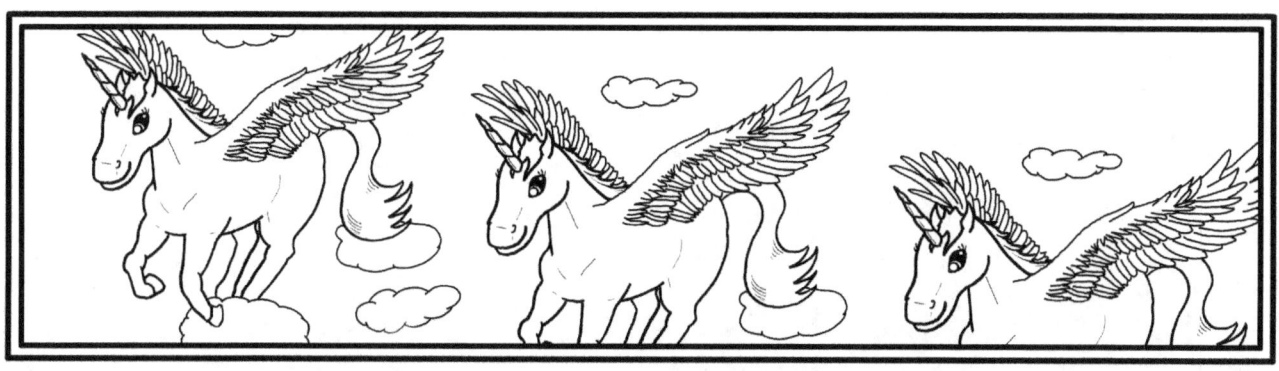

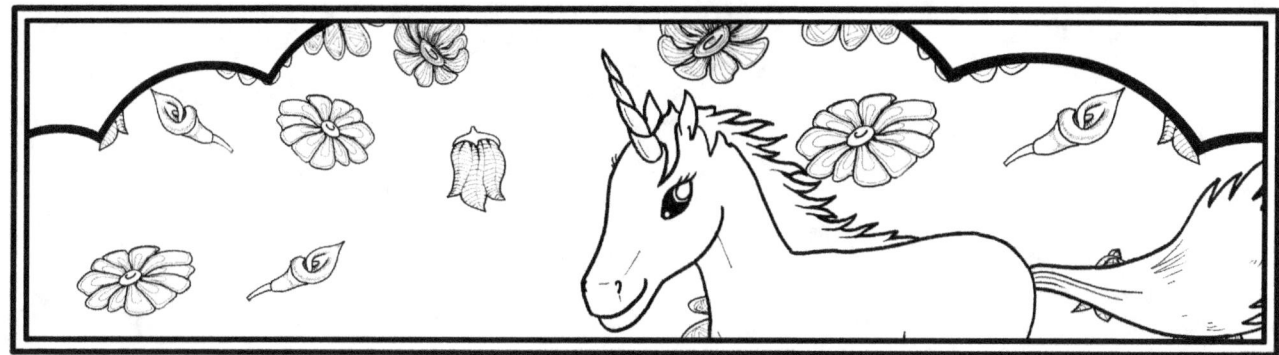

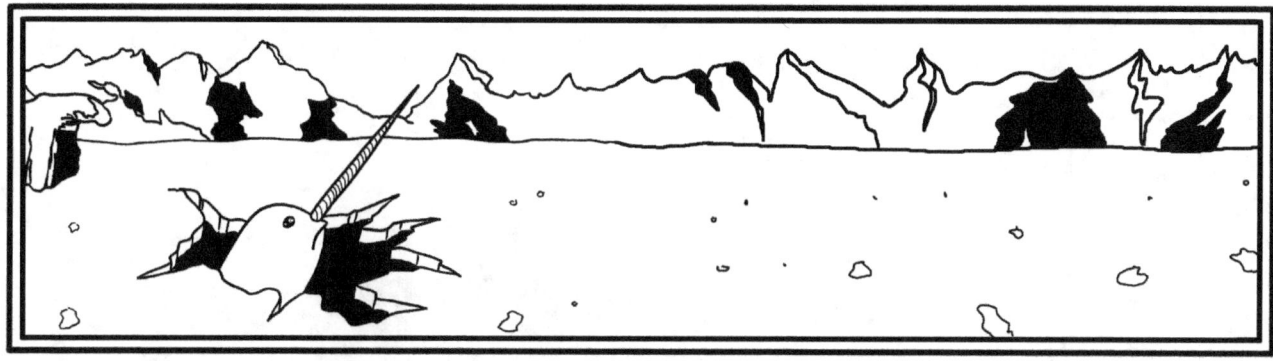

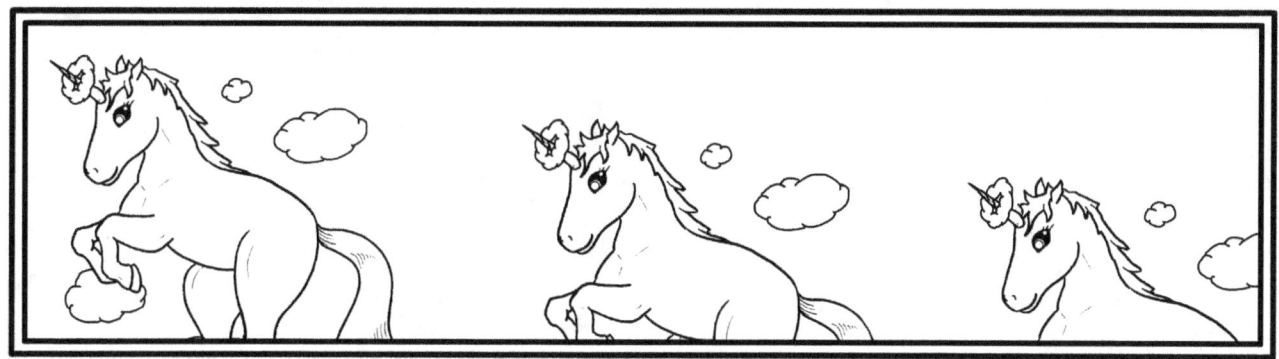

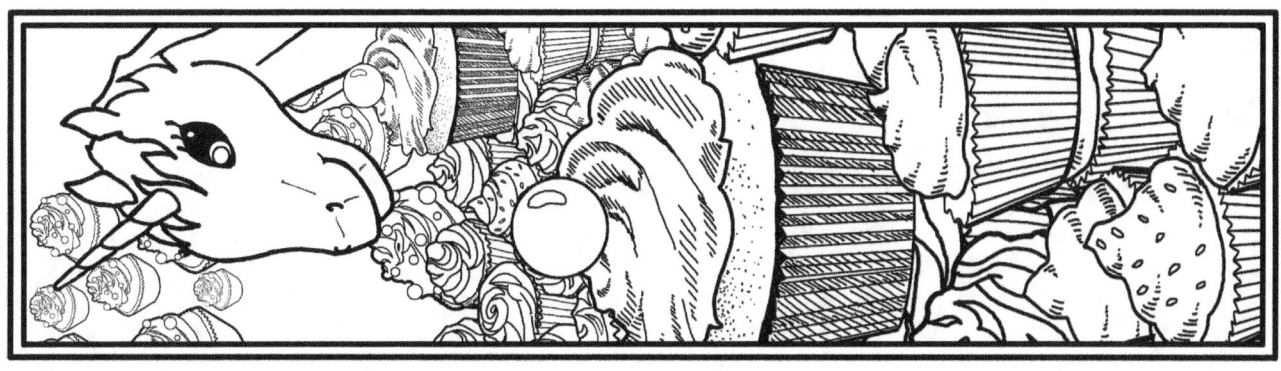
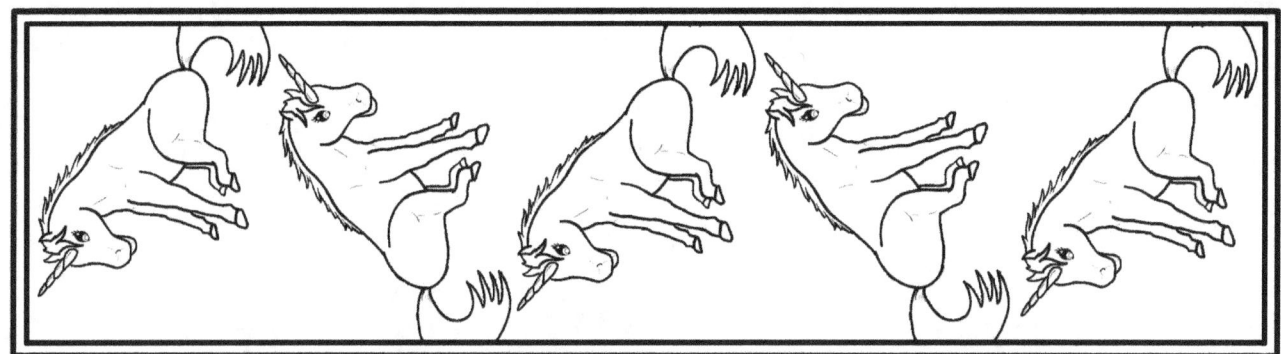
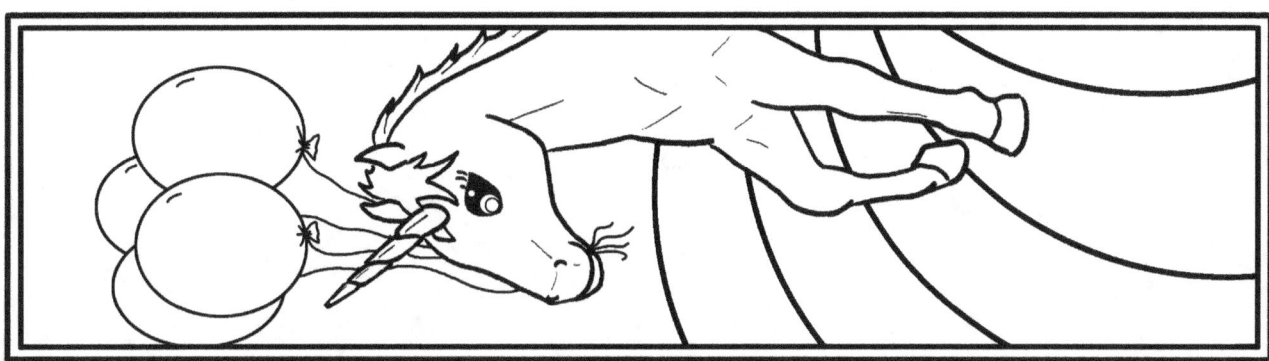
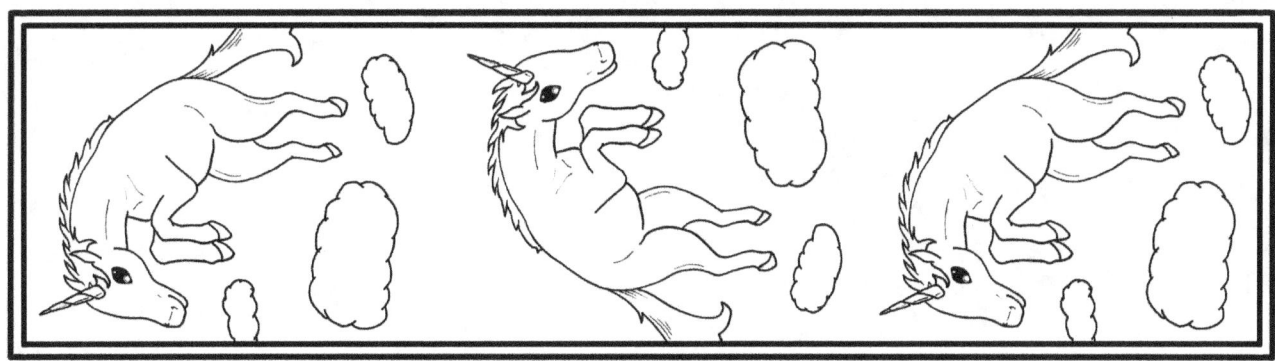

IN THIS PAGE YOU WILL FIND EMPTY BOOKMARKS -
DRAW AND COLOR YOUR OWN UNIQUE BOOKMARKS.

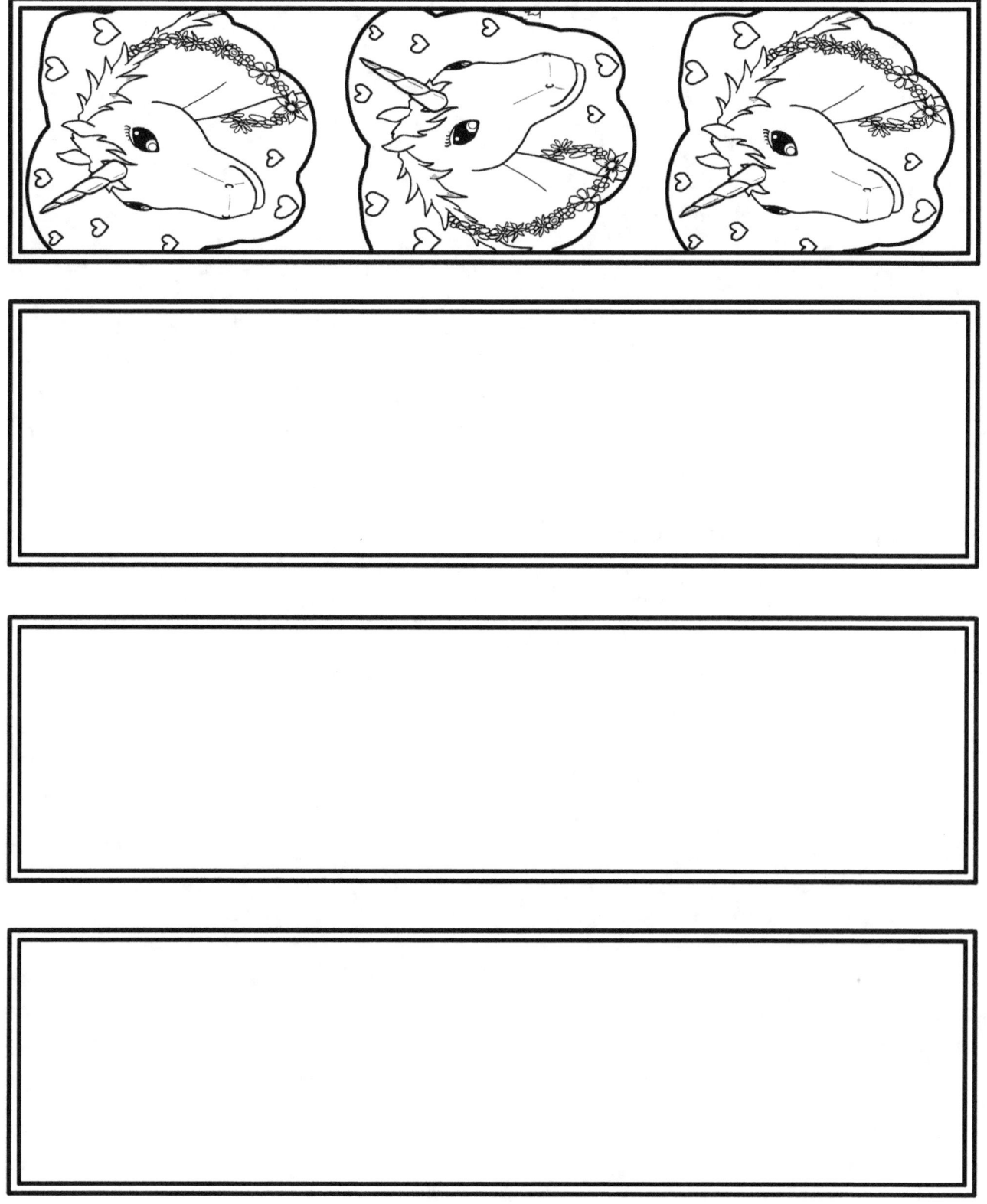

Dear reader,
Thank you so much for purchasing my book,
I hope you enjoyed it.
I will appreciate if you can leave a review on AMAZON.
Hope to see you soon.
ENJOY READING!
Alex

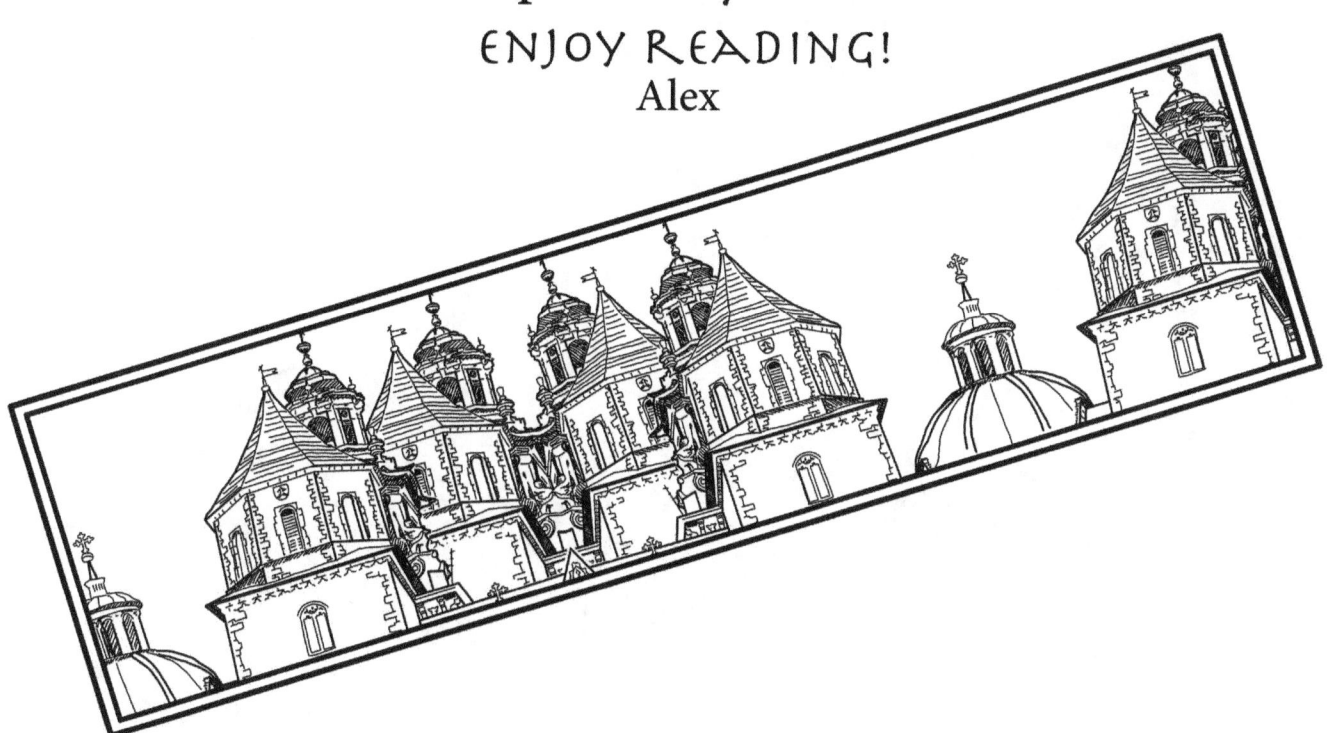

Find me at:
http://alexillustrationsart.wixsite.com/home